Advance Praise for *Saving Point Reyes*

"Gerald Warburg's *Saving Point Reyes* is an astonishing environmental history of how California's great national seashore was saved. The spate of legislation that grew out of the preservation victory is remarkable. And Warburg provides a vivid cultural history of Point Reyes to boot. While this book is full of heroes, it's the local save-the-seashore activists who shine brightest. The amount of research Warburg undertook is impressive. This is one of the finest books ever written about a treasured national park unit. Highly recommend!"—**Douglas Brinkley**, author of *Silent Spring Revolution: John F. Kennedy, Rachel Carson, Lyndon Johnson, Richard Nixon, and the Great Environmental Awakening*

"A fascinating account of the personalities and politics that managed to come together, over a long period of time, to protect the magnificent seashore at Point Reyes. This well-researched and inspiring study makes a major contribution to the history of both California and national environmental policymaking and offers important insights into how to better protect our natural environment."—**David J. Vogel**, professor emeritus of political science, Haas School of Business, University of California, Berkeley, and author of *California Greenin': How the Golden State Became an Environmental Leader*

"Gerald Warburg has written the definitive history of the titanic, and ultimately successful, struggle to preserve an irreplaceable seashore. *Saving Point Reyes* is a valuable account of the rise of the modern environmental movement as a formidable political force. Warburg captures the battle by which a determined coalition of preservationists prevails over the developers who viewed Point Reyes as a resource to be exploited rather than a national treasure to be safeguarded for future generations. A first-rate history of one of the most important public lands battles in the American experience that provides an accessible road map for how elected officials and community activists can collaborate to win lasting political victories."
—**John A. Lawrence**, author of *Arc of Power: Inside Nancy Pelosi's Speakership, 2005–2010*

"As a political science graduate student at Berkeley back in the 1990s, I visited Point Reyes countless times, never pausing to ask how this extraordinarily beautiful national treasure was conserved and protected from development. In *Saving Point Reyes*, Gerald Warburg not only offers a rich historical account of this remarkable victory, he also provides potent insights into how diffuse environmental interests are served in a political system that often discounts them. Warburg's deeply researched, sophisticated account shows that no single factor is responsible for environmental progress. Instead, meaningful change occurs when grassroots coalitions, entrepreneurial leadership, issue framing, insider lobbying, political timing, and the evolving economic and electoral context converge to open new possibilities for governance. This is an insightful analysis of democracy in action that will captivate and engage students of politics and public policy for years to come."—**Eric M. Patashnik**, Julis-Rabinowitz Professor of Public Policy and chair of the Department of Political Science at Brown University, and author of *Reforms at Risk: What Happens after Major Policy Changes Are Enacted*

"In *Saving Point Reyes*, Gerald Felix Warburg traces the absorbing, decade-long story of how relentless local organizing, careful coalition building, and shrewd DC lobbying created a sweeping, spectacular protected area next door to a major American metropolis. The strategies, themes, and many of the leaders of the campaign for Point Reyes National Seashore set a pattern for preservation efforts across the country and far-reaching changes in California politics. Warburg tells a story of cherished shoreline, wildlife conservation, and practical political lessons."—**David Sarasohn**, author of *The Party of Reform: Democrats in the Progressive Era*, and coauthor of *The Green Years, 1964–1976: When Democrats and Republicans United to Repair the Earth*

"You don't have to be from California or have visited the beautiful Point Reyes Seashore to appreciate the breadth and mastery of Gerry Warburg's history of the struggle to preserve this environmental jewel. It is a compelling story of politics, conflicting interests, and remarkable people who fought major odds, in a struggle that took many twists. This is a story about California, but also about the modern history of the environmental movement, and a lesson in how public policy is made."—**Norman Ornstein**, emeritus scholar, American Enterprise Institute

"The Point Reyes National Seashore is one of my favorite places on earth. This is a fascinating book for anyone who loves our great outdoors and wants to see it preserved for future generations, and it's also a superb road map for how environmental policy gets made. *Saving Point Reyes* is a story of how stakeholders big and small can influence politics and policy for the better."—**Tim Kaine**, US Senator, Virginia

SAVING POINT REYES

ENVIRONMENT AND SOCIETY
KIMBERLY K. SMITH, EDITOR

Saving
Point Reyes

How an Epic Conservation Victory
Became a Tipping Point for
Environmental Policy Action

Gerald Felix Warburg

 UNIVERSITY PRESS OF KANSAS

Published by the University Press of Kansas (Lawrence, Kansas 66045), which was organized by the Kansas Board of Regents and is operated and funded by Emporia State University, Fort Hays State University, Kansas State University, Pittsburg State University, the University of Kansas, and Wichita State University.

Library of Congress Cataloging-in-Publication Data

Names: Warburg, Gerald Felix, author.
Title: Saving Point Reyes : how an epic conservation victory became a
   tipping point for environmental policy action / Gerald Felix Warburg.
Description: Lawrence, Kansas : University Press of Kansas, 2023. | Series:
   Environment and society | Includes bibliographical references and index.
Identifiers: LCCN 2022061335 (print) | LCCN 2022061336 (ebook)
   ISBN 9780700635436 (cloth)
   ISBN 9780700635443 (paperback)
   ISBN 9780700635450 (ebook)
Subjects: LCSH: Point Reyes National Seashore (Calif.)—History. | Point
   Reyes Peninsula (Calif.)—History. | Environmental
   protection—California—Marin County—History. |
   Environmentalism—California—History. | Nature conservation—Political
   aspects—United States—History—20th century. | Environmental
   policy—United States—Citizen participation—History—20th century.
Classification: LCC F868.P9 W37 2023 (print) | LCC F868.P9 (ebook) | DDC
   979.4/62—dc23/eng/20221229
LC record available at https://lccn.loc.gov/2022061335.
LC ebook record available at https://lccn.loc.gov/2022061336.
British Library Cataloguing-in-Publication Data is available.

Printed in the United States of America
10 9 8 7 6 5 4 3 2 1

The paper used in this publication is acid free and meets the minimum requirements of the American National Standard for Permanence of Paper for Printed Library Materials Z39.48–1992.

This work is dedicated to the students, faculty, staff, and graduates of the University of Virginia's Frank Batten School of Leadership and Public Policy

and

to all the young leaders who will guide us to a brighter future.

I believe that this series of events constitutes a classic case of effective
bipartisan citizen action.
—*Katharine Miller Johnson to Chairman Peter Behr,*
Save Our Seashore, November 21, 1969

I don't know whether to liken the whole affair to a jigsaw puzzle or a
madcap Italian road race.
—*Congressman Clem Miller to George Collins,*
regional chief, Division of Recreational Resources and Planning,
National Park Service, May 14, 1959

One wonders who to thank of the heroes and heroines in the struggle to
set the region aside as wilderness—individuals and organizations. Their
success speaks not only of their own sensitivity, vision, and persistence.
It reflects on the rest of us. In spite of our preoccupation with material
things, in spite of consumerism and our mad race to accomplish and
succeed, we are still just enough in touch with wilderness as to constitute
a constituency for those who fought for wilderness in the halls of
Congress . . . there is still hope for ourselves and the world.
—*Phil Arnot,* Point Reyes: Secret Places and Magic Moments, *2001*

Contents

List of Illustrations ix

List of Tables xi

Acknowledgments xiii

List of Abbreviations xvii

Introduction: Saving the "Island in Time" 1

1. The Land and People of Point Reyes 9

2. Point Reyes and the Origins of the California
Conservation Movement 29

3. Mr. Miller Goes to Washington: The Fight in Congress for
Point Reyes 49

4. The Battle That Had to Be Won Twice 83

5. Who Saved Point Reyes? 105

6. What Happened Next: Point Reyes and Environmental Politics 123

7. Lessons Learned: Point Reyes and Future Policy Challenges 161

Timeline 187

List of Key Participants 189

Appendix: Key Documents Related to the Creation of PRNS 191

Notes 207

Bibliography 225

Index 235

About the Author 239

List of Illustrations

PHOTOGRAPHS

Photo 1. Point Reyes as seen from space xviii

Photo 2. President Kennedy signs the Point Reyes bill xx

Photo 3. Point Reyes Station after the 1906 Earthquake 12

Photo 4. Point Reyes Road after the 1906 Earthquake 13

Photo 5. Mount Tamalpais, looking south from San Anselmo 30

Photo 6. *San Francisco Chronicle* cartoon about Point Reyes 44

Photo 7. Clem and Katy Miller and family, 1956 49

Photo 8. Barbara Eastman, PRNS Foundation, 1960 60

Photo 9. Zena Mendoza Cabral preparing to testify, 1961 63

Photo 10. Limantour subdivision development plans 66

Photo 11. Clem Miller in his congressional office, 1962 78

Photo 12. Secretary Udall, Mrs. Johnson, and Governor Brown, 1966 81

Photo 13. Clem and Katy Miller and family, 1962 104

Photo 14. President Nixon at Golden Gate, October 1972 122

Photo 15. Limantour Beach and Drakes Bay 160

Photo 16. Drake's Bay Estates For Sale sign 163

MAPS

Map 1. Marin County, California xix

Map 2. Geology of Point Reyes Peninsula 11

Map 3. Historic A–Z Ranches of Point Reyes, c. 1900 26

Map 4. Point Reyes National Seashore 28

Map 5. Owners of Point Reyes lands, 1960 75

Map 6. Point Reyes National Seashore and Golden Gate National Recreation Area today 167

List of Tables

Table 2.1 California Population Trends, 1850–2020 43

Table 4.1 National Polling Data on Environmental Issues: Most Important Domestic Problems 91

Table 4.2 Polls on Environmental Issues: Increase in Public Concern about Pollution, 1965–1970 91

Table 6.1 Annual National Park and Seashore Visits, 1916–2021 130

Table 6.2 Land and Water Conservation Fund Spending, 1965–2020 131

Table 6.3 Trends in California Congressional Delegation Composition 135

Table 6.4 Membership Trends in Selected Environmental NGOs, 1970–2000 136

Table 6.5 New National Seashores and Lakeshores Created, 1961–1975 140

Acknowledgments

This work builds on the efforts of historians who interpreted a rich archival record. It is a documentary record scattered, however, in dozens of places. There are many dots still to be connected. These sources range from the transcripts of interviews with California political leaders conducted in the early 1990s by University of California scholars to oral histories that Berkeley anthropologists developed in the 1930s with surviving Coast Miwok elders to the files of grassroots organizations donated to the Point Reyes Archives preserved in the National Park Service's red barn in Bear Valley. The National Archives and Records Administration (NARA) now houses some pieces of the story in the NARA-run Richard M. Nixon Library in Yorba Linda, California. Others are in the John F. Kennedy Library in Boston, the Anne T. Kent California Room at the Marin County Free Library, and the Jack Mason Museum of West Marin History in Inverness, California.

To archivists at the libraries of Marin County and the University of California and to those working at the Point Reyes National Seashore and at presidential libraries: a very big thank-you. You help us see the past more clearly. This work especially benefited from the labors of Marin County historians John Hart and Dewey Livingston as well as longtime Point Reyes archivist Carola DeRooy Davis. Each was extraordinarily generous with insights. It is enriched by the transcripts of the interviews conducted by the University of California oral history project, led by Ann Lage. The research and first-person testimonies gathered by Lage and Bill Duddleson in the early 1990s are invaluable sources that capture what the participants believed to have occurred in these campaigns. Many thanks also to numerous sources in Marin County who helped detail differing perspectives, including the thoughtful insights of family members Clare Miller Watsky, Abby Miller, and Denny Duddleson.

Special thanks to the Miller family for sharing the rich correspondence of Katy Miller Johnson with grassroots leaders and elected officials, including the recently rediscovered files of the 1969–1970 Save Our Seashore campaign, which had been stored in a family library for the past half century. I am indebted to *Marin Independent Journal* editor Brad Breithaupt, who went above and beyond to help a fellow Redwood High alum with many Marin details, and to reporter Will Houston, who ably shed light on numerous points of view advanced by Marin County activists and ranchers.

To first readers of the initial case study—and subsequent drafts—from our extended Marin family, I am especially grateful for your encouragement and suggestions. My heartfelt thanks for sharing this journey from the outset—and for reviewing numerous drafts—go to Judy, Andy, Jason, Zack, and Pete Warburg; to Tom Guerin and Hillary Phillips; and to the late California state senator Gary Hart. Special appreciation goes also to my longtime friend and mentor Gordon Kerr and to the two pioneers who brought our family West and modeled an abiding love for the land, our late father, the architect Felix Warburg and our late mother, the author Sandol Stoddard. It has been a great joy learning from and engaging with each of these readers.

To early contributors at the University of California, Berkeley, UC's Haas School of Business and Goldman School of Public Policy, and the Institut Barcelona d'Estudis Internacionals—Professors David Vogel, John Lawrence, and Michele deNevers—I am especially grateful for new sources identified and new angles suggested. Thanks to Professors Pete Andrews and Matthew Lindstrom for outstanding and insightful critiques. This research also received extraordinary assistance from the staff of the University of California's Bancroft Library in Berkeley, including Theresa Salazar, Susan McElrath, Lee Ann Titangos, Fedora Gwertzman, and Dean Smith. I also want to express my gratitude to the numerous employees of the National Park Service who made extra efforts to provide archival access to research this book amidst a pandemic and to help me understand the backstory of the administrative challenges of creating and administering the park at Point Reyes. This study offers both praise and criticism for the work of career civil servants; it does so with great respect for their dedication to the public interest and in the hope that this research can further inform their worthy public service.

To colleagues at the University of Virginia's Frank Batten School of Leadership and Public Policy, special thanks for enduring support of scholarship by former practitioners. Early drafts of this work were workshopped in Charlottesville graduate school seminars on legislative strategy and NGO leadership as well as in the Batten School's faculty research seminar series. Thanks to alums from two seminars—Congress 101: Leadership Strategies and NGO Leadership Best Practices—for all your ideas, optimism, and engagement in challenging times. Colleagues at Batten's Center for Effective Lawmaking, led by friend, co-teacher, and fellow student of *badugi* Professor Craig Volden, were wonderfully supportive. Our leaders Dean Ian Solomon and Associate Dean Jay Shimshack assisted and encouraged the project in myriad ways, as did the infinitely patient director of our IT operations, Ben Hartless, and Assistant Dean Amanda Crombie. Big thanks to each of you. To my excellent graduate research assistants at the Batten School, Hannah Gavin, Savannah Rogers, and Owen Hart, thank you for your sustained commitment to improving this work, for your many contributions and months of patient labors with a technically challenged baby boomer. We are counting on your cohort to help guide the next generation of enlightened policymakers.

Of the publications team at University Press of Kansas, I am especially grateful to editors David Congdon, Kelly Chrisman Jacques, Derek Helms, and Connie Oehring for targeted suggestions on how best to tell this story and the persistent encouragement to do so. Thanks to Karl Janssen and Ali Abbas for their collaborative work on cover design, Cartographer Erin Greb worked cheerfully with me—guided by master Marin mapmaker Dewey Livingston—to create several of the excellent maps that help readers visually understand the park's challenges. Thanks to all those in Marin County and on the University Press team who helped bring this volume together and to make it accessible to a broad audience. Any sins of omission or commission remain my own.

List of Abbreviations

BCDC   San Francisco Bay Conservation and Development Commission
CCC   Civilian Conservation Corps
EPA   Environmental Protection Agency
GGNRA Golden Gate National Recreation Area
LCV   League of Conservation Voters
LWCF   Land and Water Conservation Fund
MMWD Marin Municipal Water District
NEPA   National Environmental Policy Act
NRDC   Natural Resources Defense Council
PRNS   Point Reyes National Seashore
PRNSA Point Reyes National Seashore Association
SOS   Save Our Seashore

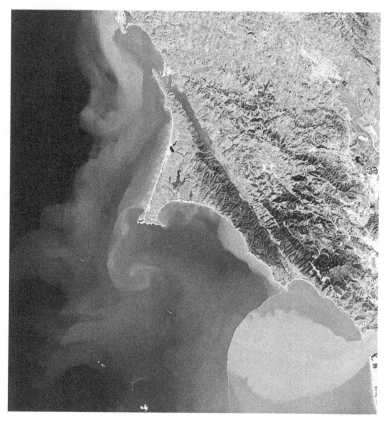

Point Reyes as seen from space. Courtesy of NASA.

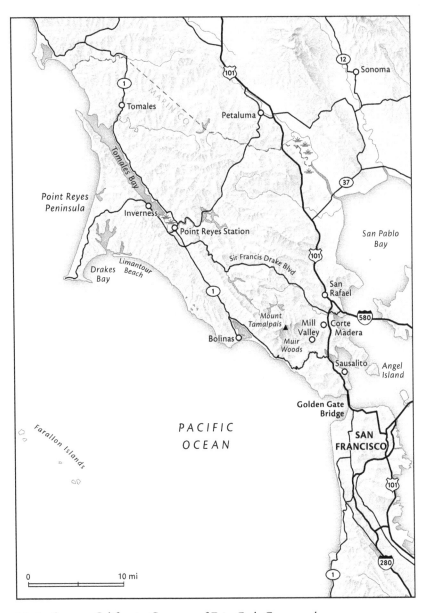

Marin County, California. Courtesy of Erin Greb Cartography.

President Kennedy signs the Point Reyes bill. Courtesy of the Point Reyes National Seashore Archives.

INTRODUCTION

Saving the "Island in Time"

On a bright morning in the waning days of the Washington summer of 1962, a group of federal legislators assembled in the Oval Office to witness what promised to be a momentous bill-signing ceremony. The proof sheets of photos taken at the White House of this exclusively White male group seem frozen in a particular moment in time. It is a moment full of hope.[1] Most of the legislators and cabinet members are grinning. Several clutch a lavishly illustrated book titled *An Island in Time*, shared with all members of Congress by its producers from San Francisco's Sierra Club. Their faces are unmistakably future-focused.[2]

There is second-term Democratic congressman Clement Miller of California, beaming alongside freshman senator Clair Engle behind the young John Kennedy. The president reaches over with a warm smile to hand each man a pen that he has just used to sign the legislation authorizing creation of a Point Reyes National Seashore (PRNS) on 53,000 acres of private lands just north of San Francisco. On the *Resolute* desk lies the Point Reyes measure. It is a bill that each man has publicly maintained will secure for future generations the pastures, lush wetlands, and long, arcing cliffs and beaches of the Point Reyes Peninsula.[3] The optimism is palpable.

From this moment of triumph on September 13, 1962, tragedy followed swiftly. All three of the young champions of the new California park would die within months of this bill-signing ceremony.[4] Absent their coordinated leadership, the prospects for completing the challenge of buying valuable private holdings to create a large new national park within 20 miles of San Francisco foundered. Over the course of the rest of the 1960s, the dream of securing these seashore lands appeared at times to have died with them.[5] An epic struggle ensued.

The results of this political fight proved to be profound, part of a wave of environmental policy battles that together came to a tipping point from which major changes in national politics flowed. This is the story of that fight, the political history of a battle over a unique piece of land that helped change how Americans think about their parks and open spaces.

A Story Rich in Lessons Learned

The politics of public lands policies in the United States offer few case studies richer in consequence than the decades-long fight to create PRNS just north of San Francisco's Golden Gate. It was one of the first two large national parks created almost entirely through the purchase of private lands. It remains the only American park that hosts such substantial private ranching operations, making it a public-private land management challenge unlike any in the National Park Service system. The original preserve at Point Reyes was one of the first two US national parks secured near a major metropolitan center. It remains the only national seashore on the Pacific Coast, larger than any on the Atlantic seaboard. Its conservation, beginning with a proposed 28,000-acre set-aside, involved overcoming the imminent threat of housing developments and subdivisions that were under construction as the 1962 federal legislation authorizing creation of the seashore passed.

David rarely bests Goliath in such confrontations. For decades after World War II, the contest between commercial developers and conservationists was hardly a fair fight. Smart money was on victory for those determined to build roads, bridges, and dams while extracting timber, minerals, and oil. Freeway builders and housing developers prospered in this era, a natural response to surging population demands, which were especially intense in California. Growth was a religion embraced with equal fervor by leaders of both major political parties.

Despite the odds, the local grassroots lobbying organizations created to advance the cause of the Point Reyes seashore and related Northern California environmental campaigns won. These victories helped lay the foundations for some of the powerful national environmental groups that continue to shape policies on the climate action challenges of the United States today. After the bipartisan success of 1970 in freeing funds for Point Reyes and a dozen other parks throughout the country, the grassroots environmental movement would make great progress on public lands fights in almost every subsequent decade. Small ad hoc local organizations grew into national powerhouses with soaring membership rolls. These included the Sierra Club, Friends of the Earth, the League of Conservation Voters, the Sierra Club Legal Defense Fund (later Earth Justice), and a national collaborator with origins in New England, the Natural Resources Defense Council. (Note that the Sierra Club still had modest membership numbers when it was involved in canyon and river preservation battles in Colorado, Utah, and Arizona prior to the Point Reyes fight.) These groups aggressively pushed environmental regulation in Washington through subsequent decades. Their annual budgets grew from a few thousand dollars in 1972 to, in some cases, more than $100 million in 2022.

Political compromises made to conserve Point Reyes in the turbulent 1960s sparked major policy changes. These included the doubling of federal funding for the acquisition of parklands. The federal response to the San Francisco Bay Area environmental groups of the 1960s helped fuel a golden era for federal environmental protection. Legislation curbing pollution and protecting public lands poured forth from Washington and Sacramento in the "Green Years" from the late 1960s through 1980.

This momentum for green activists also led to the expansion of PRNS lands under National Park Service control from the original plan of 28,000 to more than 71,000 acres. PRNS was soon joined by the creation of a contiguous greenbelt through the Marin County Headlands and south along the Pacific Coast through the addition of what has become the now 80,000-acre Golden Gate National Recreation Area (GGNRA). These two Golden Gate parks, built upon the original Point Reyes initiative, now enjoy the second-highest number of annual visitors—peaking at fifteen million in 2020—of any run by the US National Park Service. The scope of this greensward created in the San Francisco Bay Area is unique. As geographer Richard Walker notes, 3.75 million of the 4.5 million acres in the nine San Francisco Bay Area counties are now greenbelt or open water, home to more than two hundred publicly owned parks. Consequently, "every inch of (this) greenbelt, even the air we breathe and the water we drink, vibrates with history and politics."[6]

Solving a Mystery

Why did this happen? How? What can be learned from analyzing this experience? The following story of environmental activism addresses these questions, drawing from archival materials, oral histories, and new interviews with veteran federal policymakers. It seeks to analyze a key precedent from a specific place and time, Point Reyes in the 1960s, and then to connect this history to the broader national narrative of these times, working to identify trends that have animated US policymaking since 1960. It asks the following questions:

- How could coalitions and legislative bargaining secure such valuable land for the public?
- What lessons can be applied from the fight for Point Reyes to inform future policymaking on issues from public lands to climate change?
- Who saved Point Reyes?

The narrative is driven by an effort to resolve a mystery: *How did the remarkably beautiful and diverse lands of Point Reyes—so close to a major city and so tempting to housing developers—survive in a relatively pristine state?* In solving this mystery, this case study examines the political maneuvering and unusual coalitions that protected these lands.

There are many surprises to be found in the careful reexamination of this political history. For example, environmental activism in the United States today is associated with activists in the Democratic Party. Early local champions of San Francisco Bay Area parks measures, however, were mostly Republicans. The unlikely heroes in Washington for Point Reyes included such Republican leaders as Richard Nixon, presidential counselor John Ehrlichman, and California congressman Pete McCloskey. Nixon's and Ehrlichman's association with conservation gains may cause cognitive dissonance for some progressive activists; it is therefore especially important to examine the full record to understand their distinct and disparate motives for selectively embracing environmental protection efforts between February 1969 and November 1972.

Environmental Politics Drive National Change

The environmental politics manifested in the Point Reyes fight also helped drive the political transformation of the state of California. In just one generation, the Golden State political landscape was profoundly altered from that of a state that sent predominantly Republicans to the House and Senate well into the 1950s to that of an electorate whose congressional delegations and state leadership have been dominated, with a few exceptions, by Democrats since the 1980s.

California's conservation campaigns were led at the grassroots level primarily by women, a fact often overlooked by historians. The legislative outcomes ultimately empowered groups that helped fuel the meteoric rise of a series of Northern California political leaders into the highest reaches of the Democratic Party. These included the four most powerful women in state history: Nancy Pelosi, Barbara Boxer, Dianne Feinstein, and Kamala Harris.

Boxer's story is emblematic of the outsized impact of Bay Area environmental activists on national politics. She advanced from her work as a local reporter for an alternative weekly news magazine, the *Pacific Sun*—where she covered the Marin County public lands controversies explored in this book—to local and then federal office. Boxer ultimately rose to chair the US Senate Environment and Public Works Committee, where she helped shape progressive climate and public lands policies for two decades.

This work focuses on the political consequences of the fight to preserve a unique series of fragile ecosystems on the Point Reyes Peninsula—parts of which are within sight of San Francisco and the metropolitan region of seven million people. It explores the series of compromises made by policymakers in 1962 and 1969 while assessing the legislative effectiveness of different tactical approaches to shaping local, state, and federal environmental policy. It explains how this decades-long policy contest impacted American environmental politics. It offers evidence that the legislative bargaining and grassroots politics featured in the Point Reyes fight helped create a tipping point, by April 1970, when the first nationwide celebration of Earth Day marked an enduring change in voter behavior and environmental interest group tactics in the United States. This study seeks to more fully evaluate the tactical decisions made by these activists while closely examining the roles played by the citizens and lawmakers who shaped these consequential outcomes.

The final victory for Point Reyes coincided with a new national environmental consciousness. This grew into an environmental movement that opened the door to the creation and funding of dozens of national parks and seashore preserves across the country. The body of environmental protection laws and generous parkland acquisition funding passed in the wake of the first Point Reyes fight in 1962 changed the nation. The legislative legacy of these battles in the 1960s and 1970s includes the Wilderness Act, the Land and Water Conservation Act, the National Environmental Policy Act, the Endangered Species Act, the Clean Water Act, the Marine Mammal Protection Act, and numerous other federal laws and parallel state efforts, especially in California. In the decade after PRNS was authorized, another eleven shoreline parks were created to be run by the National Park Service, from the Gulf of Mexico and the Great Lakes to the Atlantic seaboard.

The Point Reyes story also offers a cultural history that is a rich blend of the best and worst of the American West. From Englishman Francis Drake to the early Spanish missionaries led to the region by Father Junípero Serra, from violent disputes over Gold Rush–era land claims to the tragic destruction of the Coast Miwoks' way of life, there is no shortage of drama. The fact that the seashore's three most visible legislative champions all died within months of passing the first Point Reyes authorization measure threatened the effort to complete the park. Their deaths lend poignancy to the long struggle to conserve the lands at Point Reyes.

The narrative provides solid examples of how grassroots politics created models for grass*tops* advocacy, here defined as the deliberate recruitment by activists of local business and government leaders to, in turn, lobby senior federal decisionmakers. The record reveals that local campaigns were manipulated at key junctures by federal legislators who took the initiative to create the appearance of broad local public support well before it was, in fact, developed. In the concluding chapter, this study will weigh the lessons learned and explore how they might be applied to current challenges, such as energy and climate change policy. Readers are encouraged to observe how three themes play out: first, that legislative victories are difficult to sustain; second, that the timing of launching new public policy initiatives is crucial; and third, that building creative coalitions and securing opposition converts is often essential.

The study offers promising models for collaborative progress and, in the end, some cause for hope. Here is a case where tough bargaining in tumultuous political times produced, through the efforts of local activists and a changing bipartisan cast of national lawmakers, both a park and a key precedent. Each proved to be a turning point for American environmental politics.

Viewed as political history, the story of the park at Point Reyes has its own sharp trajectory. Placing these events in context helps us to understand much of what has happened since the 1960s in national environmental policymaking. It brings into stark relief the subsequent political transformation of California and its impact on both national politics and US environmental policy. It also sheds a different light on some of the social inequities, including lack of affordable housing, that still bedevil one of the most desired locales on the planet, the San Francisco Bay Area.

A Land of Myths

The story of Point Reyes has been told in parts by biologists, geologists, historians, journalists, and local activists. Generations of promoters have colored this narrative. California, after all, is a land named for a mythical figure: Queen Califia. The state's history is replete with fables, driven by dreams of getting rich in the sunshine. Romantics have spun tales about the Point Reyes lands since the days of Drake's 1579 visit. Lawyers, ranchers, and environmentalists have embellished parts of the park's origin story with mythmaking, often as part of an effort to secure an advantage in litigious disputes over land use policies.

This work seeks to dispel many of these myths by providing a more precise legislative history. It is the first study of Point Reyes to take as its singular point of focus the *politics* of conserving these parklands. A careful reading of the full record can generate an accurate synthesis and provide clear conclusions. Such a reading can bring into focus the extraordinary efforts of ordinary citizens to preserve places of great beauty and biological diversity.

Each time the vision of a national park on the Point Reyes Peninsula faltered, it somehow survived to rise phoenix-like from the ashes of defeat. It is therefore especially useful for political scientists to try to determine *why.* As John Hart, the California historian, concludes, "Logical explanations do not satisfy. The achievement required something less easily accounted for: consistent and unreasonable luck."[7] When the first legislative proposals for a national seashore park at Point Reyes were debated in Congress more than half a century ago, several political leaders warned explicitly that future generations would enjoy—or suffer—the consequences of the momentous decisions to follow. Many of these warnings proved accurate. As the California population pressures pushed housing subdivisions beyond the suburbs and deep into exurbs formerly in agricultural use, stark public policy choices were presented.

Those who have cared for the verdant lands and pristine beaches of the

Point Reyes Peninsula and those who have fought for their preservation can help us understand our past. They can help us prepare together to chart policy courses—on public land use and climate action challenges—toward a brighter future for all.

Readers are encouraged to visit the Point Reyes Peninsula and reflect upon the work of these citizen activists. While there, take a moment to recall the tribute offered in marble at St. Paul's in London to the church's architect, Sir Christopher Wren: "If you seek [their] monument, look around you."

CHAPTER ONE

The Land and People of Point Reyes

Why such a big fight—with national implications—over the Point Reyes Peninsula, a relatively small, isolated, often fog-shrouded land?

The Point Reyes Peninsula is a freak of nature, a geological unicorn. The parklands are still home to just a few hundred people and a few thousand cows. The green hillsides of the Marin County Headlands, seen in dozens of TV ads and aerial bumper shots—captured in camera angles looking south through the towers of the Golden Gate Bridge to the San Francisco waterfront—remain public open spaces.

The fights over the best uses for these lands are linked to others in the American West. As the frontiers of the nation pressed ever westward to the Pacific Coast and Native American communities were decimated, tensions between city-dwelling voters and rural landholders, between favorites of one regime and favorites of its successor, resulted in frequent fights over land titles. Many political battles in California were resolved by lawyers and litigation over land use.

The struggle to create Point Reyes National Seashore (PRNS) and its partner, the Golden Gate National Recreation Area (GGNRA), involved a series of public-private partnerships negotiated through years of highly contentious bargaining. These deals, like those contesting the early Point Reyes Peninsula land grants in the 1800s, were subject to decades of lawsuits. It was two Vermont brothers named Shafter, partners in the San Francisco law firm that handled the mid-nineteenth-century litigation, who ended up owning most of the Point Reyes Peninsula. The brothers then bequeathed it to generations of Shafter and Howard family successors from the 1860s into the 1920s. They worked the lands aggressively, looking for oil and gold, proposing subdivision, and creating the small resort town of Inverness on Tomales Bay. Yet the dairies run by tenant farmers buffered the peninsula from much of nineteenth- and twentieth-century American life. It remained frozen in another era, a rural redoubt quite separate from the bustling ports, refineries, shipyards, airfields, and high-rise-filled cities along San Francisco Bay to the south and east.

A Unique Land Form

The Point Reyes Peninsula is a world apart. One needs to go back in geological time to understand why. It appears on maps as a chicken wing, an appendage floating on the open sea. The peninsula catches fierce Pacific Ocean storms that roll in from the north and west; it is one the windiest and foggiest places in the United States. This triangle-shaped preserve is virtually stapled to the vast North American Plate. The western boundary of this continental plate runs thousands of miles in a relatively straight line from the northwest and the Gulf of Alaska south by southeast all the way to Central America. Consequently, the geology of Point Reyes is unlike that of the land immediately to the east and south.

The Point Reyes Peninsula covers less than 100,000 acres, yet it leaves most visitors feeling as if they have journeyed to another place and time. (For a sense of scale, Manhattan Island is 14,000 acres and the City and County of San Francisco measures 30,000 acres.) The parklands combine several distinct climate zones, providing habitats for an astonishingly diverse series of ecosystems: coastal, wetland, chaparral, and woodland forest. The peninsula is home to more than 450 bird species and over 800 different plant types. These include several fragile life forms, from tule elk to sea otters. Northern elephant seals nurture their pups annually at Drakes Estero (see cover photo). Just offshore from the towering 600-foot cliffs at the Point Reyes headlands, whales migrate twice annually, frolicking in the open Pacific waters as they pass from the Gulf of California to Alaskan waters and back.

Famously dubbed "an island in time" by *San Francisco Chronicle* conservation reporter turned environmental advocate Harold Gilliam, Point Reyes was shaped by plate tectonics. Shifting continental plates tore the granite and chert core of this land from its twin in the Tehachapi Mountains, which today remain some 350 miles to the south near Bakersfield, on the North American Plate, while the Point Reyes Peninsula drifts relentlessly north on the Pacific Plate.

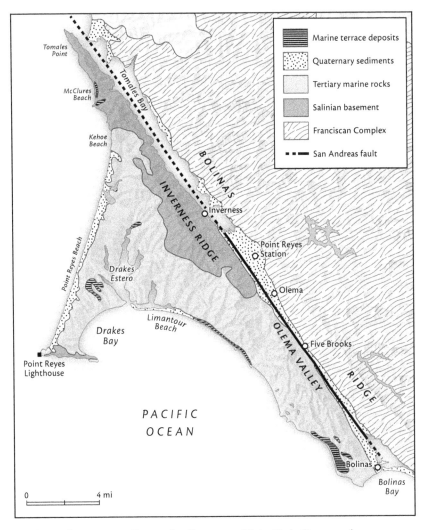

Geology of Point Reyes Peninsula. Courtesy of Erin Greb Cartography.

The peninsula is separated from the rest of Marin County and North America by the San Andreas Fault. This fault cuts unmistakably like a knife scar up the park's eastern boundary through the Olema Valley from the coastal town of Bolinas and the Bolinas Lagoon to Point Reyes Station, then continues along shallow Tomales Bay. Point Reyes remains an active seismic zone. The violent 1906 earthquake that devastated San Francisco moved some sections of land and fence posts in Point Reyes as far as twenty-four feet. The tremors originating offshore to the south flipped the

Point Reyes Station after the 1906 Earthquake. Courtesy of the Point Reyes National Seashore Archives.

morning train just about to depart from Point Reyes Station, tossing the locomotive sideways like a rag doll.

Here, the San Andreas Fault creates remarkable biodiversity. More than one hundred years after the devastating earthquake that Californians still refer to as "the Big One," different types of trees grow in the different soils on opposite sides of the fault line. Bishop pines favor the granite of the peninsula, while the surviving redwoods prefer the softer mainland soil along the creeks east of the fault.

The Ubiquitous Fog

Steep underwater canyons west of the Point Reyes Peninsula are home to abundant sea life. The ocean depths yield an upwelling of frigid north Pacific waters. These currents clash daily with spring and summer heat rising from interior valleys to create marine layers that locals just call "fog." These are the very same omnipresent "nipping cold and stinking fogges" that Drake's chaplain, Francis Fletcher, lamented in his detailed journal from the summer of 1579, when the English ship *Golden Hind*, overladen with plundered Spanish silver, was repaired in the vicinity over the course of six weeks. These heavy fogs often obscure to mariners the nearby entrance to San Francisco Bay. For centuries, shipwrecks have haunted the narrow entrance to the vast bay and Sacramento River delta to the north and east.

Point Reyes Road after the 1906 Earthquake. Courtesy of the Point Reyes National Seashore Archives.

The fog plays its own role as one of many buffers that protected Point Reyes lands long enough for legislation and funding to be cobbled together to preserve the peninsula. For centuries, in voyage after voyage, mariners from Portugal, France, Spain, England, and Russia missed finding the passage into the fabled bay. Advance scouts leading Catholic priests finally sighted the vast expanse of San Francisco Bay and its inviting harbor in 1769. Only then was the vast bay's location fixed on the maps of European leaders and colonists on North America's Atlantic seaboard.

Offshore of Point Reyes, the frigid north Pacific tides sweep into Drakes Estero, a shallow saltwater bay within a bay that is rich in migratory birds and sea life, a favored resting ground for seals. Puffins, red-tailed hawks, pelicans, kites, cormorants, and hummingbirds ply the air. Marsh rosemary and salt grass are abundant. Indian paintbrush and California poppies dot the hillsides. Fields are filled with wild lilac, lupine, aster, sage, goldenrod, monkey flower, bluebells, buttercups, milkmaid, daisies, and blackberry vines. Foxes, skunks, and an occasional bobcat inhabit the woods. Forests moistened by winter rains and summer fogs are thick with the pungent aromas of California bay, oak, and madrone under the canopy of Douglas firs. Burbling creeks roll through deep woods where sword ferns unfurl among alders and buckeyes. The air blowing in from the thousands of miles of open Pacific to the west is as fresh as any on the North American continent. Willets and sandpipers scamper along the nearly deserted white sand beaches that extend for more than a dozen miles below steep cliffs and sand dunes. These tawny cliffs bear a striking resemblance to those off Dover, England, one of many reasons most historians agree Drake anchored along this same Point Reyes shoreline when he gave the territory the name Nova Albion (New Britain) in the summer of 1579.

Biodiversity at the Crossroads

San Francisco and Point Reyes share many characteristics with the great crossroads of the planet. Crossroads from Mesopotamia to Paris, from Istanbul to New Orleans demonstrate how a confluence of cultures often creates synergy. In turn, the intersection of cultures features great biological diversity; these cities often were sited at the confluence of multiple ecosystems. It is at such crossroads, where different climate conditions and social traditions converge, that many of the world's most dynamic trading communities arise. The intermingling of influences enriches commerce while fueling intellectual creativity and advancing human knowledge. These characteristics of crossroads are especially apparent in the biological and human history of Point Reyes; they also helped to shape the political fight to create a national seashore.

California was a remote outpost for many centuries, on the edge of the North American continent. Before the coming of the Europeans, Northern California was home to hundreds of Native American communities. The Coast Miwok at Point Reyes commuted seasonally from the coastline in spring, summer, and fall to inland villages along the Olema Valley in the rainy winter months. Contemporary accounts indicate that they inhabited more than one hundred seasonal sites in the Point Reyes Peninsula area.

With the arrival of the Europeans, this region constituted the westernmost outpost of the overextended Spanish empire, which faced decline throughout the eighteenth and nineteenth centuries. The northernmost of the dozens of original California missions was first located in San Francisco. Subsequently, Marin County's San Rafael mission and another mission 30 miles to the north in Sonoma were established. On the coast, Russian merchants established a trading post at Fort Ross as a resupply base for their distant Alaska holdings. Into the 1830s, the San Francisco Peninsula was still the northernmost reach of Alta California, a remote territory managed loosely by a series of beleaguered regimes in Mexico City. After rebellious Yankees sought in 1846 to establish the Bear Flag Republic in northern

California, the region remained a backwater on the westernmost edge of the North American continent.

The Point Reyes Peninsula grew at the intersection of diverse cultures. Drakes Bay and, later, the San Francisco harbor served as havens for European explorers eager to find sanctuary halfway around the world. (Note that local custom has eliminated the possessive apostrophe on all Drake landmarks, although a few developers—for example, "Drake's Bay Estates"—did not adopt the practice.) The prospect of a safe harbor was especially important for the Spanish Manila galleons. Loaded with the luxury goods of the day secured in the Far East—spices, porcelain, silk, and beeswax—these ships would stagger onto the Pacific Coast with scurvy-afflicted crews after riding trade winds for some two hundred days at sea.

In the last half of the nineteenth century, the Bay Area would again become *the* American gateway to Asia. San Francisco was the primary port of entry for migrants looking to make their fortune in the California gold rush and the economic boom years that followed. San Francisco remained the most important city in the American West for its first one hundred years. It would continue to be the port of choice for immigrants headed into the interior farmland of California's Central Valley after the gold rush fever abated.

Point Reyes was largely spared the relentless growth experienced by its metropolitan neighbors to the south and east. Geography and topography were initially key factors. The rugged, often fog-shrouded coastline near the San Francisco headlands and Marin's Mount Tamalpais protected the Point Reyes seashore from filling in with suburban tract homes. Policy choices mattered too. There would be no PRNS if certain actions had not been taken in San Francisco, Sacramento, and Washington to protect these open spaces. While this case study of how the park at Point Reyes was created is grounded in political science, it is better understood when grasping key points from geology and natural history.

Northern California has many parallels to the African Great Rift Valley and its fault lines that became migratory routes for multiple species, including *Homo sapiens*. The Bay Area follows a similar pattern as a meeting of different cultures. For centuries, its vast delta was thick with waterfowl, tule elk, and grizzly bears. The first white explorers to traverse the region were astonished by the abundance of wildlife at this confluence of rivers, rich marshlands, fertile valleys, bays, and an ocean teeming with otters, whales, and seals. The herds of elk "must have existed in the millions," one of Marin's first American citizens, Stephen Richardson, later reported; "the largest herd in the world roamed over the deep grasslands of Point Reyes. . . . On an ordinary jaunt from Sausalito to San Rafael, I would see enough elk, deer, bear, and antelope to fill a good sized railroad car."[1] Marin's hillsides were thick with rich stands of oak, madrone, and old-growth redwoods.

Prior to first contact with European explorers, Native American communities thrived on the abundant shellfish, salmon, and game. In the San Francisco Bay delta, multiple ecosystems merged where exceptionally strong tidal forces mixed the salty waters of the Pacific Ocean with the massive flows of meltwater carried annually from the Sierra Nevada mountain snowpack by the Sacramento, San Joaquin, and American Rivers. The San Andreas and Hayward Faults have reshaped the land for eons; plate tectonics continue to edge the Point Reyes Peninsula north toward Canada at a geologically swift rate of about two feet per decade.

Point Reyes is heavily influenced by the Pacific Ocean. The peninsula catches the strongest full-frontal ocean storms, winds, and tides from the open sea. The San Andreas Fault also helps to render the peninsula quite remote. Some of the first government contractors resident on the Point Reyes Peninsula were sent from Washington after Marin County's first federal appropriation in 1857; more funds were allocated in the following years to build a lighthouse above the rocky headlands, a notorious graveyard for shipwrecks.

There can be limited access in West Marin through seasons of drought, flood, and fire. To this day, the principal access is via Sir Francis Drake Boulevard, a two-lane road from the eastern half of Marin, where 95 percent of the county's population lives. The route winds over hilltops and down gullies, a poorly maintained road with deliberately limited signage.

The Point Reyes Ecosystems

Point Reyes features multiple different ecosystems within a walk of just a few miles. For many generations, these special factors have attracted hunters, biologists, and hikers eager to view the spectacular scenery. Parts of Point Reyes look like the brooding English moors, others like the pastoral scenes above the cliffs of Dover, others still like the fern- and pine-filled forests of the San Juan Islands north and west of Seattle.

It was this diversity and proximity to the awe-inspiring power of the Pacific and the coastal mountains that helped shape the politics of the region for generations. The striking closeness of majestic natural landforms to its new cities—and the omnipresent threat of fire, floods, and earth tremors—has always been at the core of California's appeal. As pre-eminent California historian the late Kevin Starr observes, "A streak of nature worship . . . runs through the imaginative, intellectual, and moral history of California as a fixed reference point of social identity. A society that had consumed nature so wantonly, so ferociously, was, paradoxically, nature's most ardent advocate."[2]

California political culture has always been shaped by the relationship of residents to the land and water. This has been especially true in the region deemed most desirable for commerce and transportation, the San Francisco Bay Area. Almost every nation that sent emissaries and explorers to the west coast of the American continent was looking for natural resources to extract as well as shelter and fresh water. Francis Drake, laden with twenty-six tons of Spanish silver, sought a place to repair and restock the last of his five ships as well as a shortcut water passage home to Europe. The Spanish needed a port to load fresh water and repair the Manila galleons that rode the prevailing ocean currents from Asia to offshore the coast of present-day Oregon before turning south for Mexico. The Russians came to the California coast for seal pelts and the supplies needed to provision their Alaskan forts, establishing a base just up the coast from Point Reyes at Fort Ross, the outermost limit of Russian imperial expansion. Then, the Americans came for whale oil, hunting in the north Pacific and wintering in Sausalito and Richardson Bay.

The so-called forty-niners who flooded through San Francisco in 1849 on their way east to the gold fields in the Sierra foothills rarely cast a glance north. Those who fed the miners did, however, as did the loggers who would build and heat the homes of the growing city of San Francisco. Soon the Marin County hillsides were stripped of their stands of oak, and the creeksides and canyons where redwoods thrived were heavily logged. Bolinas Lagoon, Corte Madera Creek, and Richardson Bay were clogged with logging detritus. Sharp business interests selling to the flood of humanity, investors who knew the crowds would ultimately return from the mining camps, then looked farther north and west over the gum-drop triple peaks of Mount Tamalpais to Point Reyes for meat, hides, lumber, butter, and cheese. The returning miners also recalled the verdant shores and ample harbors of Marin that they had passed as they sailed upriver to Sacramento en route to the gold country.

The Contracting Bay

The waters of the San Francisco Bay flowed, as recently as ten thousand years ago, as a deep river down a lush valley through the narrows of the Golden Gate. The river flowed west another 40 miles to the edge of the North American continent, which was then near where the rocky Farallon Islands sit today. The Marin Headlands north of the Golden Gate once stood over a narrow opening to a wide valley in what is now the San Francisco Bay. The peaks of the mountains in this flooded valley became today's most recognizable Bay Area features: Angel Island, Alcatraz, Mount Tamalpais, and Mount Diablo.

With the passage of the most recent ice age, the sea level rose by several hundred feet. The Point Reyes Peninsula became a virtual island; today it is surrounded on three sides by water. Only the creek-lined Olema Valley, bordered on the south by Bolinas Lagoon and on the north by Tomales Bay, connects the Point Reyes Peninsula to the rest of the continent. The creek flows have been altered over the centuries by fractures in the San Andreas Fault.

San Francisco and San Pablo Bays and the vast Sacramento River delta were clogged with silt for decades as gold mining became an industrial enterprise in the years following the initial 1849 rush. The Sierra foothills were dynamited and carved by water cannons. The millions of tons of silt left as residue flowed down the canyons, filling up the rivers and marshlands east of San Francisco and west of Sacramento, exacerbating flooding. One of the first conservation movements in California history was created in response. It is especially noteworthy for the purposes of our study that this early environmental effort was led not by wilderness proponents but by *commercial* interests—farmers, hoteliers, and landowners disturbed by the plugging and alteration of the rivers of the Central Valley and the San Francisco Bay caused by industrial mining. Railroad, hotel, and tourism interests finally succeeded in obtaining a federal court ban on hydraulic mining in 1884.[3] This Northern California precedent was one of the first major legal victories embraced by American conservation advocates.

European Colonization of Marin and Point Reyes

For nearly two hundred years, the harbor in Drakes Bay was essentially a consolation prize for explorers. Most voyagers were on their way elsewhere, intent upon finding a shortcut Northwest Passage back to Europe or discovering the location of a first-class California harbor protected from the open Pacific.

For many centuries, California remained a land of myths. The state's very name comes from a novel penned by Garci Rodríguez de Montalvo in 1510. This popular thriller told of Queen Califia, who ruled the land and went into battle with weapons fashioned of gold: "Know that on the right hand of the Indes there is an island called California, very close to the side of the Terrestrial Paradise."[4] Thus, long before Hollywood became a dream factory, stories such as that of Queen Califia generated images of a golden paradise by the sea.

The few European merchants who visited were navigating for nearly two centuries after Drake's voyage with maps that showed a blank space Drake had named "Nova Albion." Explorers cautiously probed the Northern California coastline near Point Reyes, noting the abundant wildlife on land and sea even as they dodged the bedrock outcroppings and offshore stacks of rocks. Shipwrecks in the area were common, beginning with the spectacular breakup of the Portuguese trader Sebastián Rodrígues Cermeño's *San Agustín* at Drakes Estero in 1595. It was the nineteenth-century shipwreck of French trader Joseph Yves Limantour, who conducted an extensive trade in luxury goods from a Mexico base, that gave an enduring name to the most prominent of the arcing white sand beaches lining the western shore of Point Reyes. Records indicate that at least fifty-five large ships have sunk near the cliffs towering above the Point Reyes headlands since the fate first befell Cermeño.

The safest route for mariners was west of both Point Reyes and the Farallon Islands, where some ships would stop to collect birds' eggs. They had to penetrate pervasive fogs and make a straight shot 30 miles due east from the Farallon Islands to find the Golden Gate narrows that yield to the vast inland San Francisco Bay and Sacramento River delta.

The Coast Miwok population that Drake first encountered in West Marin is believed to have numbered around three thousand. They were a small group among the estimated 350,000 Native Americans then living in what is now California.[5] The Coast Miwok were hunter-gatherers who enjoyed relatively peaceful relations with neighboring tribes and the ecosystems they inhabited. The Coast Miwok lived on the abundant sea life from the Pacific and rich game and venison from inland, aided always by their steady dietary supplement: acorns from the numerous oak trees native to the coastal hills. They used clamshells as a local currency and are believed to have used controlled burns to clear and renew areas where the abundant game foraged. Their way of life would not survive the coming of the Spanish missionaries at the end of the eighteenth century, who brought disease, labor, and land use practices that devastated native communities. By 1880, census counters found fewer than one hundred Coast Miwok people living in Marin County. For several subsequent generations, even the fact that the region bore the name of a Miwok leader, Chief Marin, was obscured. As scholar Betty Goerke notes, "The popular press and textbooks . . . failed to describe the complexity, variety, and creativity of California Indian culture from [Marin's] time and place. Until the 1990's, textbooks one-sidedly emphasized how the mission system had benefited Native Americans and avoided mentioning the mission experience had disrupted Indian culture and had hastened the deaths of many."[6]

The intriguing story of Drake's first encounter with the Coast Miwok was featured by Sierra Club advocates David Brower and Harold Gilliam when they shaped the first edition of *An Island in Time*. As the two activists crafted the book with which to lobby members of Congress, they led their 1962 narrative not with a treatise on biodiversity or a paean to parklands but rather by teasing out the lingering mystery about the precise location of Drake's six-week stay in the region.[7]

Myths about Drake persisted for four centuries. The author of the most popular pre–gold rush American work about the California coast, Richard Henry Dana, Jr., assumed that Drake had harbored not at Point Reyes but rather inside San Francisco Bay. Generations of historians searched for more clues, even forming competing treasure hunting clubs to solve the mystery. Their trail was muddied by an elaborate ruse in the 1930s; amateur sleuths believed they had found the brass plate that Drake reported he had left affixed to a prominent tree near his landing site to claim the lands for Queen Elizabeth of England. It was not until 1977 that the plate found in the 1930s was determined to be a fake made of nineteenth-century materials.[8] Today, both the local government and federal authorities, supported by a strong majority of scholars, deem Point Reyes to be Drake's landing site.[9]

Because of their military value, Drake's ship logs were closely held as an English state secret; these have been lost to history. However, given the combination of details provided by the journals of Drake's chaplain, Francis Fletcher—replete with vivid descriptions of windswept shorelines, the protected south-facing harbor, the dialect used by the native Coast Miwok, and detailed reports of verdant pastures just over the steep coastal ridgetops—the preponderance of evidence shows that Drake was at Drakes Estero at Point Reyes from the middle of June to late July 1579. His crew were the first Englishmen to set foot on the North American continent.

The Search for a Safe Harbor

The goal of successive European mariners from 1579 until 1769 was the search for a harbor along the northern coast that would be safe from the strong Pacific storms. The first recorded return visit to the region by a European ship captain was that of Cermeño in 1595. Laden with precious cargo from Manila, his ship was wrecked in Drakes Estero in a freak southerly windstorm. His surviving men made it all the way back to Acapulco, Mexico, by launch. Eight years later, Don Sebastián Vizcaíno revisited the region, searching for a sound harbor and hoping to find some of the goods from Cermeño's wreck. The date was January 6, 1603, the day of the Three Holy Kings. Vizcaíno named the site Punta de los Reyes.

Vizcaíno also failed to find the San Francisco Bay, and for many subsequent generations, none of the European ships found the Golden Gate and the inland delta with multiple protected anchorages. When European explorers finally did find the San Francisco Bay in 1769—nearly two centuries after Drake made landfall—it was a party that arrived not by sea but over *land*. The governor of Baja California, Gaspar de Portolá, accompanied by a modest military escort and Franciscan priests, then established the Presidio just inside the bay on the southern end of the Golden Gate headlands.

For another seventy years after Portolá, the great San Francisco Bay drew only occasional foreign visitors. In the early nineteenth century, these might have included a Russian supply ship from the Alaska colony or a British whaler seeking provisions on an eastward leg back from the "Sandwich Islands," as Hawaii was then called. However, with the settlement at Yerba Buena, renamed San Francisco in 1845, the location of the best harbor was established. It was assumed by Americans for decades thereafter that this was where Drake had landed.

The San Francisco Bay was still considered a sleepy backwater in the decade before the gold rush. Its beauty and commercial promise were first popularized to a mass audience in the eastern United States by the young author Richard Dana, a Harvard College student taking a gap year. He was troubled by weak eyesight, and doctors suggested that he take time away from his books and try to restore his health, so he joined the crew of a ship bound for the Pacific. In *Two Years Before the Mast*, Dana wrote of the San Francisco Bay's promise from his first visit in 1835:

> We sailed down this magnificent bay with a light wind, the tide, which was running out, carrying us at a rate of four or five knots. We passed directly under the high cliff on which the Presidio is built, and stood in the middle of the bay, from whence we could see small bays, making up into the interior, on every side; large and beautiful islands; and the mouths of several small rivers. If California ever becomes a prosperous country, this bay will be the center of its prosperity.[10]

Dana's prophecy and his call in the 1830s for more Americans to colonize California shaped popular opinion on the East Coast. By the time Dana revisited the city in 1859, San Francisco's population had exploded from a few hundred at the time of his first visit to over 100,000. By the time Dana's son visited in 1911, the city's population had soared to 400,000. This is the type of exponential growth that repeatedly threatened the isolation of Point Reyes.

Spanish Missions Devastate Native American Communities

The Spanish colonization of Alta California was led by soldiers in 1769 and then Franciscan priests through the turn of the nineteenth century. The system of missions and lightly defended presidios that they created lasted less than fifty years.

The day Sergeant Ortega sighted the San Francisco Bay with an advance party of the Portolá mission, November 1, 1769, spelled doom for the Coast Miwok. The Spanish mission system decimated the Native Americans, reducing their population by some 90 percent in just two generations. European imports of smallpox, measles, and pneumonia, as well as venereal diseases and forced labor by the Catholic priests, proved disastrous. The Spaniards' push to convert the Coast Miwok and tie them to the yoke of subsistence farming and town dwelling proved to be a virtual death sentence.

Mission San Rafael had as its primary source of cash the sale of cowhides used by Eastern shoemakers. The padres ran some three thousand open-range cattle in the region. Indigenous peoples who fled the mission confines were dealt with harshly. The consequences of mission rule were recounted unquestioningly by most historians of previous generations, whose prejudice permeated the retelling. "Most of the Indians were withdrawn to San Rafael," an oft-quoted 1970 history of Point Reyes reports, "leaving these lands vacant. Under mission supervision the Indians thrived [*sic*]."[11] The narrative continues in the same vein: "After secularization of the mission in 1834, the Indians were assigned great herds of cattle and spacious lands at Nicasio, but the white man ended up owning all of it. The Indian was no rancher. He learned to drink aguardiente, acquired the white man's diseases, and soon had a reputation for shiftlessness and impotence."[12]

Lands long inhabited by the Coast Miwok were taken by grants made first by the Spanish and then, after the Mexican Revolution, by the Californios, Mexican citizens of Alta California. Their *vaqueros* (cowboys) used the Point Reyes Peninsula for cattle grazing and hunting, but there was very little farming in the area, as summer fogs could not be relied upon to provide enough moisture to grow many crops in abundance.[13] By the gold rush era, Stephen Richardson, the son of the founder of Sausalito, reports, "the killing of an Indian was regarded as a sportsmanlike pastime."[14]

If the Spanish rule from 1770 to 1820 brought devastation, the brief Mexican interregnum from 1821 to 1846 brought administrative chaos. Both left a legacy of vague, disputed land claims that would bedevil Californians through much of the latter half of the nineteenth century. During the quarter century that Mexico held sovereignty over Alta California, what is today Marin County was governed by officials in distant Mexico City. Beset by unrest in the capital, Mexico experienced dozens of attempted coups.[15] Officials in Mexico City insisted that the colonies be self-sustaining, and the authorities afforded little military support. Corruption abounded. Choice lands in Marin were granted by local authorities to port officers from Sausalito and Tiburon, two of whom, William Richardson and John Reed, were married to daughters of the Presidio commandant. The rich lands from San Anselmo to Point San Quentin went to the brother-in-law of General Mariano Vallejo.

The maladministration of Alta California and Marin County by successive incompetent regimes, the Spanish and Mexican governments, allowed Point Reyes to continue to escape development. Marin County remained isolated by the exceptionally powerful tides that race through the often fogbound Golden Gate narrows. Marin was never connected to El Camino

Real, the main trail that connected Alta California, running south from San Francisco through San Jose and Monterey down to Los Angeles and San Diego.

In the 1840s, the Oregon Trail brought American settlers hungry for farmland west, with some who were originally headed to Oregon's Willamette Valley instead choosing to take a more southerly route into California. Time appeared to stand still in these years at Point Reyes. Then, in a period of just four years, from 1846 to 1850, sweeping change arrived. The Mexican-American War led to a declaration of a Bear Flag Republic in California, backed by Yankee merchants. In January 1848, California history was altered forever when gold was discovered along the south fork of the American River east of Sacramento.

Gold Rush Marin County

The discovery of gold in the Sierra Nevada foothills 120 miles east of Point Reyes brought thousands of miners and fortune hunters to the region. Hundreds of ships sailed from the Eastern Seaboard of the United States only to be abandoned in San Francisco harbor as passengers and crew headed for the hills. The rotting hulks were buried in shoreline mud to form platforms for the steady filling in of waterfront marshlands. The new city that evolved from this massive influx of population benefited from being at the crossroads between west and east, between the United States and Asia, between the verdant Pacific Northwest and the arid Southwest. The city grew at the terminus of the three large rivers irrigating California's Central Valley below the foothills overrun with miners. Its ravenous population fed on the region's abundant natural resources like locusts. Marin County's lands suffered "irreparable injuries" in the years following the 1848 gold discovery, as the county's first post-statehood historian, J. P. Munro-Fraser, ruefully observed in 1880: "Magnificent forests were swept away that can never be restored. Fine redwood groves stretched between San Rafael and San Anselmo. Even the stumps are gone. Great madrone trees grew on the ridges. Not a tree of them remains. . . . The devastation wrought through the Ross Valley and along the foothills and canyons down to Corte Madera was nothing short of sacrilege."[16]

At the time of the gold rush, a man named Rafael Garcia, favored by the local Mexican military leaders for his zeal in capturing and enslaving native laborers, was granted title to many lands at Point Reyes. Garcia ran longhorn cattle in Bear Valley while making his headquarters just footsteps from the San Andreas Fault on the site of the present-day NPS headquarters. After California statehood was hastily approved by the US Congress in 1850 and a series of poorly documented land deals took place in Marin, the corrupt county sheriff began to sell local lands to which he did not have clear title. One dispute over Point Reyes land sales led to a spectacular murder in a San Francisco hotel, followed two days later by a lynching of the gunman by local vigilantes who controlled the city in the wild years just after the gold rush.[17]

The resolution of competing claims over lands on the Point Reyes Peninsula led—as often occurred elsewhere in California—to control by the lawyers who adjudicated them.[18] As historian Dewey Livingston notes, in Garcia's case, "the uneducated former Mexican soldier was no match for sharp lawyers like the Shafters who handled land cases."[19] The problem was by no means unique to Point Reyes. A California State Land Grant Commission set up in 1851 spent years sorting through such claims. In the 1850s, as Lincoln Fairley notes, ninety-nine percent of Marin County's acreage was controlled by just two dozen cattle barons, and there were only 1,500 acres of publicly available lands.[20]

From 1857 to the 1920s, the Shafter family controlled the great majority of the Point Reyes land. They were not native Californians; they were transplants from a prestigious Vermont family of politicians and dairymen, brothers who had thrived in their reincarnation as first-generation San Francisco lawyers. After leading efforts to litigate competing claims, they took shares of West Marin land as payment and then bought the remaining parcels. The total cost for the Shafters to obtain most of the Point Reyes Peninsula has been calculated as $85,000 in 1870, though much of their payment was in the form of forgiven legal fees. The sum is less than $2 million in 2022 dollars.[21]

The San Francisco–based Shafters initially held their new Marin County lands close. They gouged the federal government for an exorbitant price for a small parcel of land at the point where a lighthouse would be constructed, delaying the project for several years. Evidence of centuries of Miwok habitation on their lands, including Native American village structures along Tomales Bay, vanished. The Shafters developed elaborate plans for Point Reyes, building a home ranch near its center. They then divided the peninsula into twenty-six ranch parcels they designated A to Z. They rented each parcel to carefully recruited tenant dairymen who were subjected to rigorous interviews prior to occupancy. Most of these tenant families were

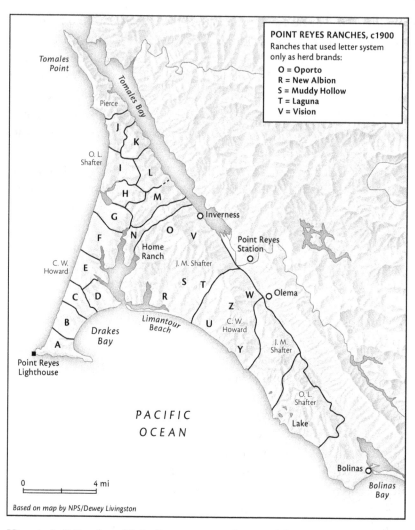

Tomales
Point

Tomales Bay

Pierce

J

K

O. L.
Shafter

I

L

H

M

G

Inverness

F

N

O

V

Home
Ranch

Point Reyes
Station

C. W.
Howard

E

J. M. Shafter

C

D

R

S

T

W

Olema

Z

B

Limantour
Beach

Drakes
Bay

U

C. W.
Howard

A

Y

J. M.
Shafter

Point Reyes
Lighthouse

O. L.
Shafter

PACIFIC
OCEAN

Lake

Bolinas

0   4 mi

Bolinas
Bay

Based on map by NPS/Dewey Livingston

Historic A–Z Ranches of Point Reyes, c. 1900. Courtesy of Erin Greb Cartography.

of European stock, with many being Portuguese from the Azores or Italian-speaking Swiss from the alpine region bordering Italy and Switzerland, along with a few Irish.

Marin soon became the butter and cheese capital of the young state. Point Reyes was dubbed "cow heaven" by a few local dairy farmers. Marin produced more butter than any county in California, and the Shafters ran the single largest dairy operation in the state (and one of the largest in the entire nation) at the height of their power in the 1870s. The Shafters alone owned more than 3,000 cows on 17 dairies producing 700,000 pounds of butter. They also feasted on some of the hundreds of thousands of ducks and geese transiting the Point Reyes wetlands, flocks so thick, Oscar Shafter wrote, that "there is little to do but load and fire."[22]

The Shafters were ambitious entrepreneurs, trying numerous ways to cash in on the growing value of their lands; "they were a little bit of everything," historian Dewey Livingston notes.[23] Before the turn of the century, the family also worked to create an elaborate summer resort inland on Point Reyes's Tomales Bay shoreline, which they named Inverness; they then floated plans in 1905 for subdivision of Inverness Ridge to accommodate several thousand homes. The 1906 earthquake and resulting financial hardships throughout the region crushed hopes for such an investment. By holding most of the remaining peninsula lands in tenant blocks and keeping them pastoral, however, the Shafters insulated Point Reyes from most development of roads and housing until after World War I.

In the aftermath of the Great War, the Shafter heirs accelerated their efforts to sell land, often to the tenant families. The Point Reyes Peninsula still housed the remaining dairies, but a significant source of income during the Prohibition years was a criminal enterprise: "rum-running." Smugglers offloading ships full of liquor from Canada favored remote Drakes Bay or the inlet at Tomales Bay. Bootleggers also worked stills in the West Marin backcountry, an illicit use of land that would be echoed a half century later when remote parts of Inverness Ridge were used by Mexican-based drug cartels for massive marijuana grows.

As the onset of the Depression in the early 1930s stalled economic growth, Point Reyes remained a somnolent backwater. Its dairies were in disrepair amidst plummeting sales, with titles to tracts spread among nearly five dozen families. San Francisco had been rebuilt after the devastating earthquake and fire. Neighboring Oakland and Berkeley had grown. Yet across the Golden Gate narrows, Marin County was still a chilly ferryboat ride away, a rural county with small towns, winding roads, and a lifestyle much slower than that of neighboring cities.

Three great events would soon transform the region, creating immense pressures on the Marin County lands of Point Reyes and the slopes of Mount Tamalpais. The completion of the Golden Gate Bridge in 1937, the Japanese attacks on the US Pacific fleet at Honolulu's Pearl Harbor in 1941, and the advent after World War II of a new Cold War in 1945 would forever change Marin County. These events threatened to bring dramatic

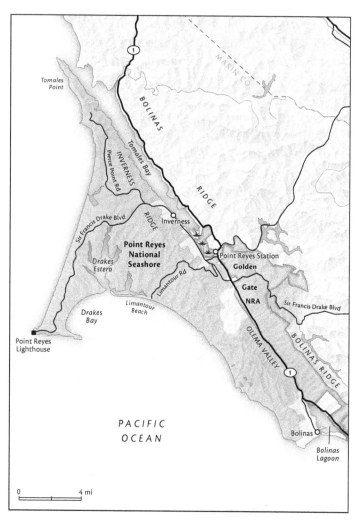

Point Reyes National Seashore. Courtesy of Erin Greb Cartography.

alterations to Point Reyes and the wild Marin Headlands. Amidst the existential threats of world war and the economic challenges of rapid military and industrial mobilization, fundamental land use decisions awaited. Conservation interests had the odds stacked against them. How they prevailed at Point Reyes is a story that sheds light on an era of sweeping legislative ambition.

CHAPTER TWO

Point Reyes and the Origins of the California Conservation Movement

The bridging of the Golden Gate narrows, completed on May 27, 1937, was celebrated as a modern engineering marvel. The 1.7-mile-long roadway connecting urban San Francisco with rural Marin County rode atop what was then the world's largest and longest suspension bridge. Completed for a total cost of $35 million, it was a full year ahead of schedule and several million dollars under budget.

The burnt-orange span connected the bustling commercial center and urban port of San Francisco with the Pacific Northwest via the iconic highways US 101 and California Highway 1. Whereas to the immediate south of the bridge along the San Francisco streets were block after block of dense housing and commercial buildings, Marin County and Point Reyes were still populated mostly by rural "cow towns," while the entire length of the Pacific coastline in Marin remained undeveloped. Yet in the years just before World War II, it was clear that change was coming fast. Fundamental public policy choices would have to be made by the political leaders of the day.

Californians' Love Affair with the Outdoors

The history of the lands of the Point Reyes Peninsula and the adjacent Marin Headlands underscores a key point: unique geographic circumstances—and the ubiquitous fog—served to protect Point Reyes from development. Another key guardian that protected Point Reyes from development between the Civil War and World War II was Mount Tamalpais. The majestic mountain's deep woods, steep slopes, and water supply reservoirs limited construction. In the late nineteenth and early twentieth

Mount Tamalpais, looking south from San Anselmo. Author's collection.

centuries, "Mount Tam" had become the favored site for hikers from San Francisco and Oakland. It was accessible not just to the wealthy families arriving by ferryboats from San Francisco's fashionable Pacific Heights but also to lower- and middle-income families throughout the region.

Hikers could board one of the jumbo ferryboats in San Francisco, arrive in the Marin port of Sausalito, and then take a railway clear to the Mount Tamalpais summit or take a train on to Point Reyes Station for day hikes at the seashore. Beyond the ranches, Marin had virtually no industry in those years except for some logging activity and a state prison at remote Point San Quentin. The first villages in Marin that were not built to support timber cutting or to serve as railheads were in fact summer homes for San Franciscans looking to escape the fog. City dwellers would use modest cabins in towns such as Larkspur and Fairfax as jumping-off points for weekend hikes. Soon they would encircle Mount Tamalpais with an astonishing array of trails for hikers.

Well before the coming of the Europeans, Mount Tamalpais was regarded with reverence by Native Americans. It bears a Coast Miwok name, translated variously as "western mountain" or "coastal mountain." Later still, writers from San Francisco began to refer to the 2,579-foot summit as "the sleeping maiden" or "the Indian princess." One did not have to be a lonely cowboy or miner in a population where males outnumbered females by more than ten to one to see the unmistakably female profile of its three peaks and the long, deep blue-green torso. Real estate developers would later seize the mythical image of a magic mountain for promotional materials, much as environmentalists such as David Brower peddled the mystery of Drake's landing site, to argue for its preservation. It wasn't just realtors who pushed the notion of an enchanted mountain; poets and even rock-concert impresarios ran with the theme: an epic Summer of Love concert in June 1967 featuring the local Jefferson Airplane and LA's The Doors attracted thirty-five thousand rock fans to Tamalpais' Magic Mountain Music Festival.

Tamalpais dominates and defines the human geography of the lands just north of San Francisco. Its story shapes every part of Marin County history. It is a story that proved key to what happened in subsequent generations at Point Reyes to protect the peninsula. The Tamalpais story and the effort to create Muir Woods, together with another California fight—over the flooding of the Hetch Hetchy Valley adjacent to Yosemite to serve as a water reserve for San Francisco—were major factors leading to the creation of the National Park Service (NPS) in 1916.

Origins of the California Conservation Movement

Mount Tamalpais and the ridgetops of Point Reyes were first exploited for timber. Marin County provided wood to support the tenfold growth of the new state of California in the 1850s. New towns in Marin County were essentially villages for the loggers; they bore names such as Mill Valley and Corte Madera, Spanish for "cut wood." These towns had a singular purpose: to harvest wood for new San Francisco homes and for the fireplaces to heat them. From 1850 to 1870, the woodlands throughout Marin County were subject to aggressive logging.

The next wave of Marin visitors, the hikers, was initially far more benign. American political histories often make this recreation movement synonymous with Theodore "Teddy" Roosevelt, the first great outdoors advocate in the White House, who served from 1901 to 1909. Roosevelt was an ardent conservationist, having spent years ranching in the South Dakota badlands. He proved instrumental in saving Muir Woods, just 10 miles south of Point Reyes. The story of the movement to save Point Reyes, however, reveals important antecedents to Roosevelt.

In fact, hiking clubs sprouted in San Francisco and Marin decades *before* the first Roosevelt presidency. The focus of many of these clubs was Mount Tamalpais. Their rambles were celebrated in the literature of that era, from 1870 to 1900, with men such as Bret Harte and Charles Warren Stoddard writing lyrical sonnets about the beauty of Point Reyes's Bear Valley and Mount Tamalpais with its extraordinary views. Later regional favorite Jack London wrote bestsellers set in California and the American West with similar themes exploring the impact of nature on humans and glorifying the call of the wilderness.

In May 1892, local naturalist John Muir and wealthy colleagues founded the Sierra Club at a meeting in a San Francisco law office. As David Vogel notes, the Sierra Club's location in the Bay Area with a relatively affluent, educated membership provided a key foundation: "The Club's formation marked the beginning of the San Francisco Bay Area's longstanding role as a center of local, regional, and national environmental activism."[1] Geographer Richard Walker expands on the point in his history of California environmental policy: "The green tendency has been a pillar of Bay Area life and politics for more than a century, and it inflects every other social movement to some degree. It has been as significant a marker of the place as the Gold Rush, Silicon Valley, or the Beat movement . . . we can call it, simply, a *green political culture.*"[2]

Conservation was not, from the outset, an issue with a diverse set of champions. Preservation of places such as Yosemite was often a cause advanced by the wealthy and well educated. Those with more leisure time and more land often had considerable self-interest in preservation as well. As Walker observes, "Conservation began as—and to some extent remains—a bourgeois conceit, to be sure. One cannot deny the upper-class sources of the open space ethic."[3] It was here in the San Francisco Bay Area that environmental activism would expand its reach and help drive a mass movement, impacting the nation's politics.

The upscale Olympic Club of San Francisco sponsored in Marin what is now the nation's oldest distance run, the Dipsea Race, which began in 1905. This rugged route has contestants climb up stairs cut by the hiking clubs. These mark the path that ascends more than 2,000 feet from Mill Valley to the shoulders of Mount Tamalpais before plunging down canyons to the Pacific at Stinson Beach just across the Bolinas Lagoon from the Point Reyes Peninsula.

Threats from logging companies eager to harvest the last old-growth redwoods and clear-cut Douglas firs raised alarm at the turn of the century. The collection of local hiking clubs devoted to Marin was instrumental in the effort to save the last big grove of ancient redwoods in the county.[4] The clubs bore such names as Alpine and Conservation and championed access to hiking trails and preservation of open spaces. Often these clubs had distinctly German American roots, a fact later systematically obscured during both world wars. Taken together, these local conservation efforts at the dawn of the twentieth century created the dynamic of some 49 percent of the land in Marin County being owned today by local, state, or federal government agencies and remaining off limits to housing development.

These Mount Tamalpais hiking clubs provided the grassroots foundation on which the Save Point Reyes efforts would grow decades later. Their commercial allies—the Bay Area rail and steamship companies that ran the jumbo passenger ferries, the narrow-gauge rail operators that shuttled tourists, and the hoteliers who catered to travelers—were also key allies for conservation as a best practice for their business interests. A similar phenomenon occurred when the Northern Pacific Railroad and other transport companies lobbied for national parks in remote places such as Yellowstone, Glacier, and Yosemite. Early conservationists routinely benefited from coalitions with business leaders.[5]

At the same time, James Shafter was a leading funder of the North Pacific Coast Railroad running from Sausalito to Tomales Bay and the redwood country up the north coast. This line would help bring dairy products and lumber south to markets and, later, bring tourists and potential home buyers to the new vacation resort planned at Inverness on the Point Reyes Peninsula by the cash-strapped Shafter heirs. The new rail links also served to bring lumber to market from Shafter investments in Sonoma and to hasten the journey of perishable products from Point Reyes to San Francisco.[6]

Republican Benefactors and the Push for a National Park in Marin

The key event in early Bay Area conservation campaigns was an effort to protect the redwoods in a deep canyon astride Mount Tamalpais, west of Sausalito and Mill Valley. A wealthy Republican landowner named William Kent stepped up to buy the woodlands for $45,000 in 1905, just before they would have been bought by a water company intending to clear-cut the timber and then flood the valley for use as a reservoir.[7] Kent had inherited substantial wealth from his family's meatpacking business in the tough stockyards of Chicago. He used much of his inheritance to buy land all over Mount Tamalpais. A substantial portion of these lands became today's state park, and the Kent family name was soon attached to nearby schools, woodlands, and the town that still bears the family name, Kentfield.

In 1903, Kent chaired a crucial strategy meeting with federal officials, including Gifford Pinchot, later head of the US Forestry Bureau, and San Francisco mayor James Phelan. They convened at the modest Ross cabin of the Lagunitas Club. Kent had grand ambitions; at this Marin County gathering, he announced the formation of the Tamalpais National Park Association. It was a five-year struggle before just one small piece of these lands, Muir Woods, was secured as a national monument. Three-quarters of a century would pass before Kent's dream of integrating a preserve on Tamalpais into the national park system was realized. As with Point Reyes, the campaign involved both local and federal support and relied on both the grassroots activism of membership organizations and the grasstops lobbying of VIPs, as is evidenced by Kent's correspondence with President Roosevelt. These letters speak to us more than a century later, as does the defense Kent offered to his wife for this extravagant purchase: "If we lose all the money we had and saved the trees," Kent explained, "it would be worthwhile, wouldn't it?"[8]

When President Roosevelt deftly used the new powers granted him by the 1905 Act for the Preservation of American Antiquities to secure the redwood grove, he proposed naming the place Kent Woods. The donor demurred, insisting it carry the name of his fellow Bohemian Grove and Pacific Union Club member John Muir. Roosevelt's written response gushed with admiration for Kent's selfless act: "You are right. It is enough to do the deed and not to desire, as you say to 'stencil one's name' on the benefaction."[9] Muir in turn heaped praise on Kent's gift of the oldest remaining stand of redwoods in Marin County as "the best tree-lover's monument that could be found in all the forests of the world."[10]

Kent was elected to the House of Representatives in 1910 as a Progressive Republican (later becoming an Independent.) He became the chief House sponsor of 1916 legislation creating the NPS, the present-day guardian of the seashore at Point Reyes. Kent's Washington home became a virtual war room for the team pushing for the creation of the NPS.[11] Kent had numerous allies in this quest to better equip the US government to conserve, protect, and expand its parklands, including industrialist Stephen Mather and his key aide, Horace Albright. As the definitive study of the administrative history of Point Reyes notes, the NPS was established in 1916 in large part owing to the efforts of Kent, the Sierra Club, and San Francisco Bay Area activists—forces that had been bitterly split by the decade-long fight to flood Hetch Hetchy in the Sierra Nevada mountains to meet the water needs of the growing San Francisco population. During the period from 1901 to the 1916 establishment of the NPS, the total number of national parks nearly tripled, rising from five to fourteen.[12]

Kent drew support from Republicans in these efforts. Republican Party champions from Andrew Mellon to John D. Rockefeller were instrumental in donating land for national parks and funding the government studies to prepare and manage them. Mellon's foundation later paid for the Depression-era nationwide NPS survey that first identified Point Reyes as a possible site for a national park. The Rockefeller family donated much of the land for Acadia National Park in Maine, and the Mellon family helped support the national seashore at Cape Hatteras, North Carolina. The latter was a set-aside that took almost twenty years after congressional authorization before it was finally opened after having been redesignated a "National Seashore *Recreation Area*" (emphasis added) by Congress in 1953 to make clear the intent of adding roads, parking, and marinas. This remote shoreline also benefited from substantial efforts by the New Deal–era Civilian Conservation Corps (CCC). The CCC used unemployed workers to build berms to protect against beach erosion on the Carolina Outer Banks and to plant grasses to hold sand dunes for future recreation opportunities.

By contrast, the Democratic Party since the post–Civil War Reconstruction era had remained an awkward combination of urban ethnic machine politicians and prairie populists, joined by the white supremacists of the Jim Crow South. Democrats in Congress were deeply suspicious of park initiatives from Yellowstone to Yosemite, proposals pushed by railroad interests and viewed by Democrats as a threat to homesteaders and miners.[13] Northern Democratic Party politicians of the pre–World War II era, such as patrician Franklin Roosevelt, invariably reached for Southerners such as Texan John Nance Garner to provide regional balance to their national ticket —as John Kennedy would a generation later with Texan Lyndon Johnson.

National party politics played a limited role in local policymaking; Kent was able to champion several initiatives key to preserving the coast north of San Francisco. Kent also took the lead in creating the Marin Municipal Water District (MMWD), which built a series of reservoirs on Mount

Tamalpais's north and east slopes, thereby creating not just water resources but also thousands of acres of preserved parklands. Kent's work to protect open lands in Marin County also benefited his family's real estate holdings. He had ambitions to profit from a rail line not just to Muir Woods but from Sausalito over Mount Tamalpais to the beaches at Stinson, Bolinas, and Point Reyes. These commercial interests do not diminish Kent's accomplishment: protecting Mount Tamalpais from unlimited development provided both local and national benefits.[14] As poet Gary Snyder and artist Tom Killion observe, "Tamalpais was blessed with a unique situation, in that one of its largest landowners, indeed the owner of many of the most popular hiking areas in the higher terrain, was an ardent preservationist himself."[15]

A similar dynamic benefited Point Reyes. When the battle to preserve the seashore was joined in earnest, however, the landowners on the peninsula were dairymen and investors, not the conservationist who owned much of Mount Tamalpais. Initially, local support for creating a park from private lands at Point Reyes was tepid; the movement would require pressure and guidance from the federal legislators who sponsored the legislative proposals. Point Reyes was to be a park initially pushed by federal officials, whereas Mount Tamalpais was most decidedly promoted as a park by grassroots hiking clubs and local landowners led by Kent.

Muir Woods is just 10 miles from the Golden Gate. After the Kent purchase, it rapidly became a magnet for tourists and day trippers. A rail line was extended most of the way to the site to hasten visitors to the grove in Redwood Canyon. Today, after heading north over the Golden Gate Bridge on Highway 101 and through the rainbow-topped Robin Williams Tunnel above Sausalito, drivers are warned by flashing road signs, "Muir Woods Parking Full." The popularity of this surviving grove remains so substantial that, more than a century after it was saved from logging, reservations are required to park and walk among the old-growth trees.

After Teddy Roosevelt's presidency, hiking clubs continued to support conservation in Marin County. Hunting was banned on Mount Tamalpais soon thereafter due to a campaign led by the hiking and conservation clubs. A natural amphitheater below the three peaks of the Mount Tamalpais summit saddle was transformed into a local club's site for theater productions. William Kent attended the first performance of what became an annual "Mountain Play"—it was on his land, after all—in 1913. The site was reinforced as a Greek-style theater with stone seating by the CCC under the administration of Franklin Delano Roosevelt; the CCC would also build and upgrade dozens of hiking trails around Mount Tamalpais.

The fight to preserve Mount Tamalpais laid the foundation for the Point Reyes battle to come. Both efforts grew from a local political culture that revered open spaces. As Snyder and Killion note:

> Proximity of the mountain's wildlands to San Francisco's metropolitan area, with its outdoor enthusiasts, eminent universities, and eloquent public figures, gave the cause of preserving Tamalpais an unusual degree of political support both locally and nationally.[16]

The experience of hiking along the ridge lines in Marin from Mount Wittenberg and Inverness Ridge at Point Reyes to the slopes of nearby Mount Tamalpais is captured in the authoritative work, *Tamalpais Walking*. This work highlights the power of early Marin hiking clubs in setting the environmental agenda. Here is how Snyder described his first hike in the Marin hills, in 1948:

> It made you feel remote from the city so quickly, close to San Francisco, yet so far. And it had oceanic vegetation on one side, then there was this Mediterranean scrub (on the other), which was really kind of beautiful.[17]

Snyder moved to a cabin above Mill Valley and traveled the Marin trails with great frequency. A favored companion, author Jack Kerouac, made Snyder's character—and the mountain trails alongside the pounding Pacific—central to his early novel of the coming Beatnik generation, *The Dharma Bums*.[18]

Women in Leadership: "Garden Club Lobbyists"

The hunting and hiking clubs at Point Reyes and on Mount Tamalpais established by wealthy men from San Francisco played an important role in the early conservation movement in Northern California. In many key parts of the story, however, women were the best organizers, the most generous donors, and the most effective park advocates. Women had a very limited public role in American politics before World War II. Behind the scenes, they were often the catalyst for environmental policy action. As early as 1900, before women had national voting rights, Laura White had initiated the campaign to save California's redwoods via the California Federation of Women's Clubs.[19]

A generation later, Caroline Sealy Livermore was a conservation trailblazer in the Bay Area. Livermore was an active organizer who created neighborhood associations with modest titles such as the Marin Conservation League and the Marin Art and Garden Club. Then she repurposed these groups as the women became effective lobbyists for local causes. These groups pressed Marin County officials to create a county wide zoning ordinance, no small feat in a region where politics was dominated by the men who led banks, ranches, and housing developments.

When a particularly sensitive piece of land in Marin County would be threatened, Livermore would move swiftly with other women prominent in Marin society to organize local "associations," even if the association in question consisted solely of her garden club members.[20] This was a model similar to the one that would be used by Barbara Eastman in the early months of the Point Reyes National Seashore Foundation, whose files reveal extensive coaching by—and coordination with—Members of Congress and Park Service officials.[21] Livermore would use her contacts and family means to buy open spaces out from under the threat of development. Over the course of four decades, she led the effort to prevent the filling in and paving over of Richardson Bay, between Sausalito and Mill Valley. She used family funds to help buy key parts of Angel Island, blocking persistent state highway department efforts to build a massive freeway and bridge from San Francisco to Marin via Angel Island. She then donated the land for a state park. Similarly, Livermore led an effort to buy Shell Beach on Tomales Bay on the eastern edge of the Point Reyes Peninsula. A parallel Marin Conservation League effort between 1935 and 1945 led to the creation of Samuel P. Taylor State Park on nearly 3,000 acres, including the redwood groves lining parts of Lagunitas Creek. As historian John Hart notes, this key post–World War II effort created yet another "buffer" along Sir Francis Drake Boulevard between the surging housing developments in central Marin County and the primarily agricultural lands near Tomales Bay and the Pacific coastline in West Marin. Ranching families on the peninsula also created some limited beach access for the public—Joe Mendoza and Judge Edward Butler bought key parts of Drakes Beach and gave them to the county. Margaret McClure from the McClure ranch gifted the beach which bears the family name to Marin County as well. Both are now part of Point Reyes National Seashore.[22]

Pressures on Marin County Open Spaces

With the new bridge to San Francisco completed in 1937, and through San Francisco across the Bay Bridge to Oakland, Marin's splendid isolation was about to end. The Marin County lands were immediately open for housing developers looking to meet the demands of auto commuters.[23] (A third bridge spanning the bay was completed in 1953, connecting Marin's San Rafael county seat to Richmond and the Oakland-Sacramento freeway Interstate 80.)

The World War II years would bring swift changes. After the Japanese surprise attack on Hawaii, lands in the modest Marin harbor of Sausalito were promptly seized by the US government to build shipyards. The nearby cities of Richmond, Oakland, and Vallejo saw a dramatic expansion of shipbuilding. On the Tiburon peninsula in Marin, US Navy contractors made submarine and torpedo netting, which was soon deployed across the Golden Gate from Sausalito to the San Francisco Marina. Women were brought into the defense contractor workforce to help staff around-the-clock shifts. These contributions are memorialized in the Rosie the Riveter/World War II Home Front National Historical Park standing today near the Richmond shoreline a few miles east of Marin's Point San Quentin.

The review of this history should not obscure the fact that, while Marin County and the Bay Area are now known for their liberal politics, many of the region's leaders embraced notoriously racist policies into the 1950s. The leading San Francisco Democrat of the progressive era, James Phelan, served as San Francisco's mayor then as a US senator. Phelan's Senate re-election campaign slogan was "Keep California White!" Phelan's virulent racism and relentless hostility to Asian-Americans sparked protests from US allies in Tokyo during World War I. Kent led national efforts to enact measures excluding Asians and his son William Kent, Jr., developed the 350-home Seadrift community at Stinson Beach, just south of PRNS, with racist covenants barring Blacks and Asians. The family attached similar racist covenants to lands developed as Kent Woodlands, which remained in place well into the 1950s. Pinchot of the Forest Service served for years as an advocate for eugenics societies that, along with Teddy Roosevelt, embraced the theory that Black people were biologically inferior. California laws of the time barred home ownership in most neighborhoods for Chinese Americans and interned prospective Asian immigrants for lengthy periods on Marin County's Angel Island, the so-called "Ellis Island of the West." Then World War II led to the detention of more than 100,000

American citizens of Japanese ancestry, who were imprisoned in remote inland camps. There was no comparable prison detention program for immigrants from other Axis powers, the very White Americans of German or Italian descent.

Marin County finally accepted a sizeable Black community in 1942 when the rush to expand shipbuilding capacity in Sausalito brought hundreds of Black workers from the south. They were to reside in public housing hastily built in an isolated new town named Marin City, which was originally 80 percent White. It was "the only integrated project in the Bay Area," as author Richard Rothstein notes. "The project was not integrated purposely; the first buildings were dormitories for single men, and the shipyard's rapid expansion left no time to separate the races."[24] Small pockets of public housing in Richmond and San Francisco's Western addition grew over subsequent decades to house Blacks in segregated and substandard conditions for generations. As Rothstein details, this segregation in public housing was a direct consequence of local, state, and federal government policies.[25] After the war, White workers living in Marin City left the substandard housing and moved elsewhere in the Bay Area. This was an opportunity few Blacks enjoyed due to restrictive real estate covenants and bank redlining. By 1960, with the housing deteriorating, the isolated Marin City was 90 percent African-American. Marin County has remained for generations the least integrated region of an otherwise ethnically diverse Bay Area.[26]

The traffic of day trippers increased considerably with the opening of the Golden Gate Bridge. So, too, did the pressures to develop the land to house commuters. With the growth of the scouting movement and the renewed growth of hiking clubs in these years, the foot traffic on Mount Tamalpais became so voluminous that clubs stationed marshals and the county had sheriff's deputies posted on the trails on busy weekends to keep order. The rise of the automobile brought more paved roads in Marin; Sir Francis Drake Boulevard was extended from Point San Quentin opposite Richmond clear out to the Point Reyes lighthouse above the open Pacific.

The new road over Mount Tamalpais was realigned in a compromise to limit its impact on the mountain. The State of California joined the cause, and a $6 million state parks bond won voter approval by an impressive 3-to-1 margin, in part to buy Tamalpais lands. The state also received a study conducted by wilderness advocate Fredrick Olmsted, Jr., on the possibility of creating a state park on the Point Reyes Peninsula. The coalition in support of the state bond campaign for Mount Tamalpais included conservationists and commercial interests throughout the state. The Kent family donated more lands and a grassroots campaign run by the hiking clubs raised more than $30,000 to officially open Tamalpais State Park. When this park was joined a half century later with Point Reyes National Seashore (PRNS), Muir Woods, and the Golden Gate National Recreation Area (GGNRA), it provided a nearly uninterrupted stretch of parklands along dozens of miles of the Pacific Ocean shoreline. This greenbelt of parklands helped make the Bay Area such a sought-after place to live, work, or visit. Mount Tamalpais was thus one critical piece of the puzzle that made the park at Point Reyes a reality.

World War II and the Cold War in Point Reyes

The near destruction of the US Pacific Fleet by the Japanese at Pearl Harbor in December 1941 put the California coastal cities—especially San Francisco—on high alert. The Bay Area remained at the time the most important region on the West Coast, still eclipsing greater Los Angeles as a center of commerce, finance, and transportation. It was home to the two great universities and research centers west of the Mississippi, the University of California at Berkeley, and Stanford University.

The state became known as "Fortress California" amidst expectations of an imminent Japanese attack. Soon massive concrete bunkers were carved out for long-range Navy artillery that dotted the Marin Headlands, supplanting naval batteries in the hills that dated all the way back to the Civil War. Army troops were deployed at Point Reyes to protect RCA and ATT trans-Pacific communication facilities and at Lake Ranch to monitor the coastline. The Point Reyes Peninsula's Abbott's Lagoon and parts of Tomales Bay were repurposed for pilots practicing dive-bombing maneuvers. Rodeo Valley and the headlands west of Sausalito became home to the US Army's Fort Cronkhite. Angel Island became a key army mobilization facility; more than 300,000 troops transited its Fort McDowell en route to the war in the Pacific. With the Japanese surrender on September 1, 1945, the traffic reversed; more than 57,000 troops passed through the Marin facility while heading "home for Christmas" in the last four months of 1945.[27]

This military presence served again to buffer Point Reyes from commercial development. The same phenomenon would occur throughout the early years of the Cold War, when Hercules missiles with nuclear warheads were prepared for launch from aircraft stationed in Marin and Nike missile sites dotted the Marin Headlands. The army flattened the summit of Angel Island to accommodate the helicopters servicing the missiles. Advanced radar systems were poised atop Mount Tamalpais on a section of the summit that was also decapitated by the US Army Corps of Engineers; the air force deployed sophisticated radar arrays atop the leveled west peak. The local military bases they helped defend included the nuclear submarine facility at Mare Island in Vallejo, 30 miles east of Point Reyes; Travis Air Force base, east of Vallejo; and the enormous Alameda Naval Air Station, where aircraft carriers docked, in nearby Oakland.

After the Soviet Union tested an atomic bomb in 1949, the United States built up defenses for strategic sites throughout the country. With the region housing a substantial number of military research facilities and bases, Bay Area defense was a high federal priority. Hamilton Air Force Base in Marin County deployed F-89 Scorpion jets, each of which carried two missiles armed with nuclear warheads. Each missile had an explosive capacity almost as large as the bomb detonated over Hiroshima. They were ready to take off to meet any incoming Soviet bombers at less than sixty seconds' notice.[28]

Surging Population Challenges Conservation Efforts

None of these defenses would serve, however, to contain the exponential growth in population that threatened to bring development to Mount Tamalpais and Point Reyes after World War II. The population of the state had nearly doubled in less than a generation. In Marin, the pressures on open land were intense. Marin had some 15,000 citizens in the 1940 census. By 1970, its population had exploded to over 200,000. In just two generations after World War II, the county's population ballooned by fifteen times to some 250,000 by the beginning of the twenty-first century.[29] Explosive population growth in the region would bring land use policy fights to a head after World War II.

No other US state has dealt with anything like the successive surges in population that headed to California in four mass migrations. The first was the 1849 gold rush, which sparked the tenfold growth of California's population in less than a decade. The second and third population waves led the California population to increase from 5 million to 10 million in just twenty years, between 1930 and 1950. These mass migrations began with the Depression and the Dust Bowl, when refugees from Oklahoma to South Dakota turned west in a struggle captured by Salinas author John

Table 2.1   California Population Trends, 1850–2020

1850	93,000
1860	380,000
1880	865,000
1900	1,485,000
1920	3,427,000
1940	6,907,000
1960	15,717,000
1980	23,668,000
2000	33,872,000
2020	39,538,000

Source: US Census data (totals rounded to nearest 1,000)

Steinbeck's *The Grapes of Wrath*. These migrations then accelerated during World War II, which brought hundreds of thousands of workers into California to build planes and ships.

After World War II, many veterans continued to head west for jobs in aerospace, building planes and rockets. The state invested in public schools and universities that were among the best in the nation. "Environmental concerns were rooted in the vast social changes that took place after World War II," as historian Samuel Hays observes. "Evolving environmental values were closely associated with rising living standards and levels of education."[30] Private research companies, working with US Department of Defense support, developed National Aeronautics and Space Administration (NASA) hardware and invested in information technology in both the San Francisco Bay Area and greater Los Angeles. Between 1950 and 1970, the state's population doubled *again*, rising to 20 million. The state's population experienced phenomenal growth throughout the century, with a fourth wave of migration coming especially from Asia and Latin America; it peaked near 39 million in 2020, as indicated in Table 2.1.[31]

California thrived at the outset of the post–World War II "Wonder Years."[32] Government funding supported progrowth policies. Citizens needed places to live, water for homes and agriculture, and roads for their cars to transport them from suburban subdivisions to city jobs. California newspapers, including the Bay Area's *San Francisco Chronicle* and the *San Rafael* (later the *Marin*) *Independent Journal*, invariably supported the push for more freeways and housing while opposing efforts to "lock up" lands for parks and recreation.

These infrastructure investments, in turn, facilitated suburban housing developments through the coastal hills and deltas. This suburban sprawl

San Francisco Chronicle

THE VOICE OF THE WEST

Charles de Young Thieriot, Editor and Publisher
George T. Cameron, Publisher 1925 to 1955
Founded 1865 by Charles and M. H. de Young

PAGE 32   Wednesday, March 22, 1961   CCCCAA

Eleventh Hour For Pt. Reyes

POINT REYES National Seashore Park, one of the most imaginative public trusts ever conceived, goes before a House Interior subcommittee this week with the hopes of innumerable Californians that Congress will make it come true.

The Chronicle urges the creation of this splendid recreation area where, it is said, a million could swim, hike and camp without crowding. Lying only 30 miles from San Francisco, it is superbly suited to the needs of a great metropolitan region. And Congress should realize, as the National Park Service warned three years ago, that this is the eleventh hour as far as the opportunity or possibility of preserving the Point Reyes region is concerned.

Point Reyes is in Marin county, and Marin county's Supervisors are begging Congress to pinch back on the park. By this action they are shortchanging the future of the people of a metro-

San Francisco Chronicle cartoon about Point Reyes. Courtesy of Hearst Corporation.

was unrelenting in the Los Angeles Basin and most of the San Francisco Bay Area. Greater urban density was resisted by consumers and builders, and suburbs spread far into agricultural lands and woodlands. Wetlands were paved over. Hilltops were leveled. Bays once teeming with wildlife were filled. By midcentury, fully one-third of San Francisco Bay had been cut off from natural tides, filled with silt or repurposed for agricultural use or salt ponds, or filled in for homes and freeways.[33]

Across the state, only one-fifth of the dramatic California coastline was accessible to the public. Proposals circulated to transform the large delta north and east of the Golden Gate—San Francisco and San Pablo Bays—into a concrete river channel surrounded in places by industrial and military facilities or by houses on paved-over marshlands. The US Army Corps of Engineers invested in construction of an enormous bay model to demonstrate the challenges of this "Reber Plan."

Ironically, as the head of the Marin County Planning Department, Felix Warburg, lamented, it was sometimes the cohort of "newcomers" among the World War II veterans settling in the state who fought most aggressively against local powers to preserve the land: "The people who have lived here all their lives are the first to destroy what is here. The 'newcomers' know what they have here and they want to save it. Then they are branded a whole lot of terms like 'conservationist' said in a derogatory way."[34]

While the battle between developers and environmentalists was approaching an inflection point, so too were the modern Democratic and Republican Parties undergoing a process of transformation. California trends often presaged the future of other states. Here, the California element of the Point Reyes story also had national implications that political scientists can see more clearly with the benefit of historical perspective. Until the 1950s, most leading conservation advocates in the United States were Republicans, conservationists who gave meaning to the political term "conservative." Several of their most prominent leaders came from great wealth. It was a central tenet of the Protestant ethic—and of conservative politics in general—that one should accumulate wealth and then conserve the inheritance for future generations.

Balancing citizens' needs for housing and resource extraction with the preservation of wilderness and open spaces has long been a struggle in the United States. This tension was by no means unique to the Point Reyes battle. It had existed since the first national parks were created at Yellowstone and Yosemite in the late nineteenth century. The battles where conservationists did prevail, including the creation of Yosemite—which was first protected by *state* legislation—and Glacier National Parks, involved remote areas far from population centers. Several campaigns had early conservationists' support. They were also backed ardently by commercial interests, the railroad magnates who often owned both the tracks to these sites and the hotels conveniently built within their boundaries.[35]

One of the first major American battles to preserve a wilderness area close to the reach of urban day trippers occurred over Point Reyes. This struggle took place in an era when both major political parties in California agreed on one key principle: growth. Growth was a shared faith, held with near religious zeal in the California politics of the time. Managing growth required massive government infrastructure investments in freeways, dams, power transmission lines, and aqueducts. These projects transformed once rural areas outside major metropolitan areas into bustling suburbs from which commuters would travel to city jobs in their private automobiles. Throughout the post–World War II era and into the administrations of Democratic governor Pat Brown (1959–1967) and Republican governor Ronald Reagan (1967–1975), there was political consensus in California: it was the job of government to pave the way for the relentless development of housing, water, and transportation infrastructure needed for the ever-growing state population.

Finding housing in California for the influx of people was not an abstract concern. No other state in the union has been blessed with the variety of natural resources found in California. The state's history is one of balancing efforts to exploit these resources with the need to protect public health and the environment. This is one of the many reasons that California has been at the forefront of most environmental regulation battles, for example, adopting the California Environmental Quality Act, legislation that paralleled the National Environmental Policy Act. As the definitive history of American environmental politics notes, "California was often the lead state, originating policies in coastal-zone management, environmental impact analysis, state parks, forest management practices, open-space planning, energy alternatives, air pollution control, and hazardous waste disposal. Often environmentalists sought to apply California's innovations to the rest of the nation."[36]

California regulators and legislators ultimately went beyond federal requirements in setting strict auto emissions standards to combat air pollution and to protect the state's 1,100-mile coastline. Other states and federal authorities, and even some foreign nations, have adopted nearly identical standards. Haas School of Business professor David Vogel offers context for this growth of California's regulatory infrastructure: "California's attractive geography gave it the potential to be a desirable state in which to live, invest, work, and vacation. But without effective government regulation, that potential would have been squandered."[37]

The challenge of finding the right balance between development and preservation has often been exacerbated in the Golden State by the inflow of new immigrants. Successive waves of immigration from other parts of the United States and from foreign nations have repeatedly challenged politicians. Immigration has also divided the electorate and made land use planning a source of division and centuries of litigation as the definition of "the public interest" has been contested for generations.

Point Reyes Becomes a Prime Development Target

The intense pressures after World War II for housing development in the rolling hills north of the Golden Gate Bridge grew each year. Developers were eager to build on the large tracts of open land in Marin County, on the slopes of Mount Tamalpais, and on the hills at Point Reyes, extending all the way down to the Pacific shoreline.[38]

As the US military pulled back from some of its World War II–era defensive positions in Marin County, developers were ready to step into the resulting vacuum. Real estate companies plotted out spots for large housing blocs at Point Reyes, stretching from Tomales Point to Inverness Ridge, and groups of homes in a new subdivision were started on the hillside above Limantour Beach. The pasturelands and timbered slopes of Point Reyes were ripe for land speculation. Wealthy San Franciscans still frequented hunting lodges built in the Point Reyes meadows and old-money families with names like Hertz, Spreckels, Kelham, and Tevis controlled choice parcels. Hunting clubs cut a road for car campers clear through Bear Valley and along the cliffs above the Pacific coast. Logging companies built a mill in the Olema Valley to harvest some of the abundant Douglas firs along Inverness Ridge. Fleets of San Francisco–based trawlers harvested salmon and crab in Drakes Bay, complementing the commercial oyster operations begun in the 1930s in Drakes Estero.

By the middle of the 1950s, the pressure to build more housing throughout the Bay Area as well as on the Point Reyes Peninsula had led planners on the NPS regional staff to revive a 1930s regional staff proposal to explore the creation of a shoreline recreational park with a small footprint. This beachhead would be augmented with new freeways and housing subdivisions endorsed by the Park Service staff at various junctures. There was limited engagement by state and federal planners with the few dozen ranching families who had lived at Point Reyes for several generations, people who had labored for years on the land before gaining titles to properties from the Shafter holdings.[39] Mindful of pressure from Congress, early NPS discussions about Point Reyes emphasized the need for auto access for city dwellers. In these initial designs, parts of the Limantour wetlands would be paved over for shopping centers, parking lots, a golf course, a polo field, and a marina for power boats. Public recreation opportunities for the bourgeoning middle-income families of the region were emphasized; the notion of re-creating a wilderness experience for visitors would come only years later. The price tag suggested by one early NPS study was $35 million for recreation-related improvements.

Plans endorsed by the Board of Supervisors pushed for two new freeways connecting West Marin to the growing cities east of Mount Tamalpais. A Golden State Parkway would run west over Mount Tamalpais parklands astride the Bolinas Ridge clear up to the Sonoma County coastline. In Olema, a vast concrete interchange at the park entrance would join it to a 30-mile extension of Highway 17 from San Quentin Point on San Francisco

Bay all the way to Point Reyes. Permits for housing construction along the west-facing bluffs at the seashore were approved by Marin County officials. Efforts by environmentalists on the Planning Commission to oppose them were voted down handily by county officials, with the Board of Supervisors overruling the more conservation-minded Planning Commission.

Point Reyes was viewed by regional planners and housing developers as a prime target for the expansion of the growing suburbs of San Francisco. The Marin County Board of Supervisors staff estimated in the early 1960s that the county population east of Mount Tamalpais along the San Francisco Bay would grow from 25,000 to 250,000 by 2000—which it did. The same county planners projected that 66,000 residents would be housed in West Marin by 2000, where only a few hundred families were resident in 1960, before the national seashore was created at Point Reyes.[40] As a consequence, land deals proliferated.

Developers' stakes began to appear at several key locations in West Marin. On the slopes just above the miles of beaches at Limantour, the first eighteen of several thousand planned private homes were completed. The dam holding back population expansion from the Point Reyes Peninsula had finally burst. The same suburban sprawl that plagued greater Los Angeles and filled the peninsula south from San Francisco all the way to San Jose was flooding into Marin County. The impact of these developments on the dream of a pristine national seashore would be profound. The ensuing struggle would shape generations of environmental politics.

The die, it appeared, had been cast. Soon, very soon, the sprawl of highways, asphalt parking lots, and commercial developments that ran from Huntington Beach to Santa Monica, and the housing subdivisions that carved the hills south of San Francisco in Daly City, would come to Point Reyes and the Marin Headlands.

CHAPTER THREE

Mr. Miller Goes to Washington: The Fight in Congress for Point Reyes

Clem and Katy Miller and family, 1956. Courtesy of the Miller family.

Clement Woodnutt Miller was an unlikely hero for Marin County environmental activists of the 1950s. Miller was an Eagle Scout and a World War II army officer yet something of a dreamer, who had majored in art history in college. His appearance at his first local meetings was not that of the grizzled political veteran who is expected to prevail in running a long legislative gauntlet.

Miller was from the East Coast and had been employed as a field examiner for a local branch of the National Labor Relations Board. Frustrated by his board's convervative tilt, he quit and tried his hand as a gardener, beginning at the Redhill Nursery in San Anselmo. After taking some evening classes at the College of Marin, he went out on his own as a landscape designer, without significant financial success. He would show up at local Democratic club meetings not in a politician's suit and tie but in the scruffy work clothes of a man of the soil.

His wife, Katharine Southerland Miller, was similarly unpretentious. She had left Bryn Mawr College at the age of nineteen to marry, then moved west with her husband. Over the next decade, they would become the parents of five daughters. They had grown up in the same circles in Wilmington, Delaware, though "Clem" was nine years older. "Katy" was similarly outgoing yet unassuming, active, she recalled years later, on the local nursery school committee. Neither appeared a likely architect for the complex lobbying scheme that featured Washington bargaining sufficient to secure two major legislative victories over the course of a decade. Clem would lead the first successful charge. After his death, it would ultimately fall to Katy to lead a second crucial battle to secure the enduring victory seven years later.

What was unstated, and not known to many of their new Marin County neighbors, was that public service as a calling had been respected in both of their families for generations. Katy was the daughter of lifelong Republicans. Her father had served as state attorney general and then become chief justice of the Delaware Supreme Court. Clem's grandfather Charles Miller had been elected governor of Delaware, and his uncle Thomas Woodnutt Miller had served one term representing Delaware as a Republican in the US House of Representatives in 1915 and 1916.

Clem Miller graduated from Williams College in rural western Massachusetts, surrounded by the Berkshire Mountains; he and Katy were first introduced on the beach at Rehoboth, on the Delaware coast. Miller was a decorated veteran whose army unit had seen extensive combat with the Germans, including more than one hundred consecutive days on the front lines in Holland and Germany. The early weeks of the American occupation of Germany in the spring of 1945 had deeply disturbed him; he had been assigned to a military police unit and witnessed the starvation among survivors of the Nazis. He was in San Diego in August 1945, about to be redeployed to the Pacific to join the Allied invasion of Japan, when the use of two atomic bombs hastened the Japanese surrender. After being discharged in California in November 1945, he returned home to Delaware. He felt out of place in Wilmington, however, at loose ends and ready for a fresh start. After he and Katy married, the young couple made their way west and were soon Marin County residents, living in a home on Redwood Avenue in the old logging town of Corte Madera on the east side of Mount Tamalpais.

On weekends, the Millers would often load their daughters into the family station wagon and drive the narrow, winding Sir Francis Drake Boulevard north of Mount Tamalpais out to the Point Reyes Peninsula. Sometimes they were accompanied by their friend Margaret Azevedo, a local political leader, or their Ross Valley neighbor George Collins, who served as the regional chief for the Division of Recreational Resources and Planning in the San Francisco office of the National Park Service (NPS). On days when they visited the girls' favorite spot, McClure's Beach, Katy would pick wild watercress from the beachside creek. McClure's Beach had public access, but when they visited other parts of the peninsula, they had to pass through a series of ranch gates and private property fence lines to reach the shoreline.[1] Clem was an avid bird watcher and an amateur naturalist; in addition to regular Point Reyes visits, he would take the family on trips to Atlantic beaches as distant as Rhode Island and North Carolina's Outer Banks.

Collins and the Millers would talk about how some of the land at Point Reyes might be preserved and greater public access granted. The national seashore idea, Katy recalled in a revealing 1990 oral history interview, was "part of the discussion forever and a day. It was so obvious that that land was so incomparable, and it was miraculous that despite the development that had gone down south on the [San Francisco-San Jose] Peninsula, this [Point Reyes] was completely unspoiled."[2] Their rolling discussion of a shoreline recreation area found its way into a regional study of potential national seashores that Collins's San Francisco office sent to the NPS in Washington, where it risked languishing at the end of the Eisenhower years.

George Collins would retire from the Park Service in 1960, but not before he had deftly planted the seed of the Point Reyes park idea with those who would realize the vision of a national seashore. Collins later recalled that when NPS staffers saw the escalating land prices along the California coast, "we decided we weren't going to lose Point Reyes to anybody."[3] While still on the NPS payroll, Collins coordinated efforts to rally local environmentalists, recruit board members to a foundation lobbying for the creation of a national seashore, and pitch the idea to Marin County officials. Building upon a 1935 regional staff study that had languished within the NPS for decades, the first public proposal of a seashore preserve came from the NPS in 1958. Collins used personal funds to rush printed copies to potential allies. Then he continued to push the seashore proposal as a consultant to the campaign.

Clem Miller embraced the ideas Collins shared. Miller was an idealist, relatively untarnished by partisan politics. He had become a liberal, influenced by his NLRB work and his championship of the working man; he and Katy embraced New Deal social programs opposed by their parents. He had even written a lengthy college paper questioning why all the fountains and statues in Wilmington exclusively honored White male business and political leaders.

Unburdened by any experience in politics or legislative practice, Miller sensed an opportunity for public service as change came to Marin County. He ran for the Larkspur–Corte Madera School Board in 1954 but lost. Then he joined a local committee charged with recruiting a sacrificial lamb to run for the US House of Representatives against popular Republican incumbent Hubert Scudder. When no promising candidate agreed to run on the Democratic ticket, Miller volunteered.

Miller lost that 1956 race for Congress by a substantial margin. This race was run in a clumsy fashion, as Katy later conceded: "The first campaign was very, very amateur. I swear the nucleus was our Larkspur–Corte Madera Cooperative Nursery School. . . . Clem didn't think he had any real qualifications."[4] (Clem Miller later reinforced the point in the foreword to his book about Congress, noting how little he had known about legislative practice.)

Then Miller surprised the cynics by announcing immediately after his November 1956 defeat that he would campaign again over the next two years for the same seat representing Marin County and California's north Pacific coast in Congress. He redoubled his efforts, packing local meetings with supporters, earning respect from party officials, and building a base from which he could run throughout the geographically large district. When he ran his third race for public office in 1958, he was aided by a national Democratic wave in an election in which President Eisenhower was a lame duck.

This time, Clem Miller won. He rode a tide in 1958 that swept in many new Democrats from northern and western states, several of whom were from the spreading suburbs. This new cohort in Congress was full of ideas for government initiatives. They were the vanguard of a group the national press would come to call "the New Frontiersmen" after the election of America's youngest president, John Kennedy, in 1960. Miller, who was very much a polymath with an agile, curious mind, proved to be a prototype.

As a congressman-elect traveling to Washington in December 1958, Miller would for the first time in his life serve in a legislative post. He decided that his top goal was to get on a committee where he might pass a House bill to help protect the shoreline at Point Reyes.

The Transformation of California Politics

The 1958 election of Miller to represent California's First District (dubbed "the Redwood Empire") would prove to be a bellwether. California was viewed as a reliably Republican state through both Eisenhower presidential victories in 1952 and 1956. Richard Nixon was the lucky beneficiary when a moderate World War II hero, Dwight Eisenhower, was enlisted by Republican leaders to run for president. Eisenhower's advisers pushed the general to recruit a young anticommunist navy veteran, freshman senator Nixon of California, to balance the national ticket ideologically and regionally.

Beginning in 1958, however, California moved from a reliably Republican state to one where Democrats were ascendant. The influx of immigrants from other parts of the United States, Mexico, and Asia began to change its political dynamics. Suburban Republican voters were no longer tethered to the national party. A few moderate Republican politicians, men such as Peter Behr of Mill Valley and Pete McCloskey, a marine veteran from Palo Alto, advanced the traditional environmental values of old-fashioned Teddy Roosevelt–style conservatives. Goldwater Republicans and much of California's Inland Empire were unabashedly pro-development and supported private land rights. A political transformation was about to occur in the single generation that also saw the birth of the Point Reyes National Seashore (PRNS). California's congressional delegation would flip from solidly GOP to reliably Democratic.

The Long March to Victory, 1959–1962

Collins and the Millers discussed the Point Reyes seashore idea at a time when NPS planners were suddenly eager for such proposals. The original idea for creating a *national* park at Point Reyes was floated internally through an NPS staff study in 1935, when Conrad Wirth and Emerson Knight in the San Francisco planning office wrote glowingly of its potential.[5] The report noted that it was something of a "miracle" that the pristine seashore so close to a major city was not already being developed as the Golden Gate Bridge construction was proceeding. The NPS study did not cite any cultural significance of the existing ranches on the peninsula while optimistically asserting that the ranchers' objections could be overcome when residents weighed "the great need of this breathing spot generations hence."[6] The 1935 report stated that all the ranches could be acquired to create a park on the peninsula for an estimated cost of $2.4 million. The study did not express any idea that the ranches—which many tenants had only recently bought from the Shafter heirs—would be allowed to remain or were part of a unique "cultural heritage." This was in the Depression era, when federal park initiatives, such as the creation of Shenandoah National Park in Virginia, anticipated state condemnation with prompt seizure of all lands sought for federal purposes.

The concepts floated by Knight and Wirth were very much on Miller's mind when he campaigned for the House seat in a district that ran north from the Golden Gate Bridge all the way to the Oregon border. The Point Reyes national seashore idea was not featured, however, in either of his first two congressional campaigns. Collins had been assigned by Washington to identify possible West Coast sites for a national seashore area. By the late 1950s, finding and protecting remaining open spaces amidst exploding suburbs was becoming a national concern, impacting areas from Long Island's Levittown to the greater Los Angeles Basin and the Southern California coastline from Long Beach to Malibu.

The continued economic growth of those postwar years and the relentless consumption of suburban lands for housing increased the demand for outdoor recreation. "An expanding middle class enjoyed unprecedented economic prosperity and leisure time," historian John Leshy notes. "Americans had confidence in their governmental institutions and were optimistic about the future."[7] Yet the federal budget for parks had not kept pace with demand.

The NPS budget had been cut 80 percent during World War II. Annual park visits grew from 358,000 in 1916—with most of these visitors coming by train—to more than 50 million in 1955.[8] The NPS aggressively promoted the idea of renewal with a ten-year, $1 billion funding proposal entitled "Mission 66," designed to be completed in time to celebrate the upcoming fiftieth anniversary of the NPS in 1966.[9] The NPS secured private funding for a study of possible Gulf of Mexico and Atlantic seaboard parks, issued in 1955 as *A Report on Our Vanishing Seashore*. Studies of the West Coast and Great Lakes were added in 1958. The seashore initiatives were not a central element of Mission 66, yet they could prove especially helpful for eastern legislators long irked by the fact that NPS money often went to the many parks west of the Mississippi. Several legislators from eastern states began to pitch locations for new national lakeshore and seashore recreation areas on the Gulf of Mexico, at Great Lakes sites such as the Indiana Dunes (already made a *state* park in 1927 but later expanded with federal funds), and at Cape Cod, Massachusetts.

Miller in Washington: Lobbying the Congress
After Miller won in the wave election of 1958, Marin County residents suddenly had a new Democratic governor, Pat Brown; a new Democratic senator, Clair Engle; and Miller, a freshman Democrat representing a county where Republicans, ranchers, home builders, and conservative voters had long held sway. These developments represented a marked political shift portending change in California.

After arriving in Washington, Miller sought and secured a seat on the House Interior Committee. Wayne Aspinall, a feisty curmudgeon from Colorado's Front Range, had finally risen to seize the gavel and serve as committee chair. Stuart Udall, a junior Democrat from Arizona, also sat on the committee with Miller.

Miller told his new legislative assistant, former Santa Rosa journalist Bill Duddleson, that saving Point Reyes was his top legislative priority.[10] He began working closely with the new junior California senator, Clair Engle. While still in the House in 1958, Engle had introduced a bill during his Senate campaign calling for a $15,000 federal study of the economics of the Point Reyes seashore idea. Miller put considerable time and thought into the effort. He traveled to North Carolina's Outer Banks twice to learn how local support had aided in the two-decade-long effort to create a national seashore at remote Cape Hatteras. He also reached out to legislators from other states to look for allies beyond California who might help him secure federal funding for a Marin County park. Miller soon joined with Senator Engle to introduce identical House and Senate proposals calling for authorization of a seashore park at Point Reyes.[11] The freshman Senator Engle outlined the stakes: "If we act sensibly and foresightedly now, while the opportunity remains, we shall have preserved for America priceless heritage to be enjoyed many times over, not only by our generation, but also by those which follow."[12]

The joint Engle-Miller proposal introduced in July 1959 anticipated a park of just 28,000 to 35,000 acres without specifying boundaries or identifying necessary federal appropriations for land purchase. It did not address the matter of the fifty-nine ranch families who owned the lands in question, nor did it authorize any federal funds for their purchase. The Engle-Miller strategy was to start small and then expand later, tactics embraced by a key early conservation champion, Senator Richard Neuberger of Oregon, who regularly counseled allies, "Let's bet on a train that's going somewhere; we can get it to go farther later."[13] A similar tactic of incrementalism had worked at Yosemite and Yellowstone, as it ultimately would for subsequent parkland protection efforts in California's Redwood National Park and the Golden Gate National Recreation Area.

Miller's bid faced stiff headwinds in the House from the start. The first problem was that for generations, the position of the House Democratic leadership had been that parks were provinces of privilege. National parks, this position held, should be created only from remote lands already owned by the federal government. Alternatively, Democrats maintained, parklands should be donated by civic-minded millionaires, private citizens such as the Rockefellers and the Kents, whose noblesse oblige and large bank accounts afforded them that luxury. Even Franklin Roosevelt had been blunt on the matter; he had insisted that parklands be donated by states or purchased for public use by wealthy donors.

"Not a cent for scenery," legendary House Speaker Joe Cannon, the Illinois Republican, would thunder. This was also Democratic Party policy dating back to the Reconstruction era and discussions of Yellowstone and Yosemite. Democrats resisted funding for park rangers so persistently that the US Army was deployed to patrol Yellowstone Park from 1886 to 1918 until the NPS was established and recruited rangers. A House of Representatives heavily influenced by lobbyists for mining and timber interests blocked park expansion.[14] This skepticism of public funding for new parks influenced most Democratic legislators well into the twentieth century.

President Franklin Roosevelt had supported selected park efforts as part of Depression-era jobs programs. It had been an unspoken rule, however, that Republicans and wealthy donors among them served as park champions, not urban or southern Democrats. The new NPS initiative in the late 1950s supporting the idea of shoreline set-asides was part of an effort to change this thinking, yet private foundation funding was needed even for the federal government to conduct feasibility studies.

Miller's second immediate problem as the most junior of House freshman in 1959 was the antipathy of Interior Committee Chairman Wayne Aspinall. The Colorado Democrat was clear that the Miller bid would never even get a committee hearing if there was not strong evidence of local support for the initiative. The Marin County Board of Supervisors had already voted 4–1 *against* the Point Reyes national seashore proposal.[15] This was a major roadblock for park champions, as the usual route for creating parks relied on grassroots support. "Customarily, Congress develops an appetite for action on an issue only when it feels enough pressure from constituents," longtime Sierra Club Executive Director Michael McCloskey observed. "Then it usually looks to the interest groups that embody the hopes of those constituents to do much of the work."[16]

The local ranchers proved to be a powerful grassroots interest group with an effective lobbyist. They organized as the West Marin County Property Owners Association and hired a well-connected local attorney, Bryan McCarthy, to represent the sixteen largest ranches that owned more than 19,000 acres at Point Reyes. McCarthy was a tough, garrulous lawyer who had worked his way through Berkeley law school with a janitorial job at an auto dealership. He was an ardent believer in the American dream and eagerly represented his ranching clients, most of whom had worked their way to ownership after serving as Shafter tenants. Having secured titles before World War II and labored through tough times to improve the dairies, they were infuriated by the prospect of Washington bureaucrats evicting them. As NPS critic Laura Alice Watt notes, "From the beginning, there was almost no enthusiasm for the national seashore proposal from residents of West Marin. The impetus for protecting the area primarily stemmed from San Francisco and Washington."[17]

McCarthy traveled repeatedly to Washington to lobby Department of the Interior officials and to inform key committee chairmen in Congress of the ranchers' skepticism about the park proposal and strident opposition to any federal seizure of their lands. McCarthy argued that if the ranches were condemned and the lands seized by the federal government, the ejection of cows would cause the northern coastal prairie lands to be overgrown by scrub brush and invasive species. When he testified before a congressional committee, he angrily mocked the NPS's concern about the "vanishing seashore." McCarthy suggested that the national seashore proposal was a monumental power grab that threatened capitalism, free enterprise, and private property rights: "Do you know who is *really* vanishing today? It will be the vanishing private property owner, the vanishing dairy rancher, the vanishing man who built your country."[18]

Landowners pleaded with legislators to prevent the federal government from condemning lands; they pointed out the negative impact that such a federal "lockup" could have on the Marin County tax base and growth capacity. The politics of Marin were just beginning to change. Even though the number of ranches in all of Marin County had decreased sharply after World War II, from 200 in 1950 to just 100 by 1970, the ranchers and developers still dominated county land use planning and had an outsize influence on local politics.[19]

The ranchers' concerns had been given little consideration in initial NPS studies, yet they garnered sympathy from the major Bay Area newspapers, especially the Marin County paper of record, the conservative-leaning *San Rafael Independent Journal.* The local Point Reyes Station paper led its coverage with the statement by the ranchers that a federal "seizure" would "rip the backbone out of Marin County's $12 million a year dairy industry."[20] When Miller's field director, Bill Grader, reached out to the ranchers in a town hall–style forum held with the West Marin County Property Owners Association on July 9, 1959, they blistered Miller's position. A weathered transcript of these proceedings preserved in the official Point Reyes Archives details the pounding that Grader endured. Prominent rancher James Kehoe, who owned a key shoreline tract, condemned the proposal as he questioned Miller's motives and support: "For the life of me, I can't see how you are going to do this thing . . . first it was 22,000 acres, then 28,000. Now Mr. Miller comes up to be the big guy and he asks for 35,000 acres. I think it is wrong! If put to a vote of the people of Marin, I doubt whether this damned park would pass."[21]

A rancher whose family had helped secure limited public access to Drakes Beach, Joe Mendoza, claimed that the whole park idea was being pushed by "just a few people" and singled out Caroline Livermore's Marin Conservation League. County officials remained concerned about the potential loss of tax revenue if thousands of privately held acres were removed from the tax rolls. Grader absorbed the beating without much debate, though he maintained for the record that the Miller congressional office mail was running seven or eight to one in favor of the proposed national seashore.[22]

In fact, Congressman Miller and his district staff were scrambling to create the appearance of local support for what was initially a Washington-driven park proposal. Miller's congressional papers and the PRNS Foundation files show Miller and Grader coaching Barbara Eastman and Joel Gustafson to jump-start the local support effort, with Collins—while still employed by the NPS—recruiting foundation board candidates. The PRNS Foundation board did not even hold its first formal meeting until January 1960; it remained for a time what the cofounders later conceded was a "paper organization."[23] Miller lamented in an August 11, 1959, note to Eastman, "I am convinced that the Park would be in their [the ranchers'] own best self-interest. This is apparently impossible to put across."[24] He also cautioned allies that spring that "we are trying to proceed with the greatest deference to all local interests."[25]

Miller's Interior Committee chairman, Wayne Aspinall, is a fascinating figure in the Point Reyes story. Aspinall's political demise in 1972 serves as a key postscript. His career in Congress embodied the change that was occurring in national politics as one consequence of the rise of the environmental movement. He ascended in the politics of twentieth-century Colorado as a man of the countryside. He was proud to support the extractive industries in Colorado and throughout the nation. He heaped scorn on state and federal bureaucrats who came between landowners and what he saw as their unfettered rights to use their land for profit regardless of the consequences. Aspinall had a particular animus toward decisions made by "city folks" about how people living in the country could use their land.[26] Miller and Udall were junior members of the House Interior Committee in 1959, whereas Chairman Aspinall knew how to use his leverage. He was a brilliant legislative poker player who was good at raising the ante with whomever he did business, as his subsequent dealings with Miller, the Sierra Club, Lyndon Johnson, and Richard Nixon would demonstrate.

After issuing the upbeat press release about the introduction of a bill for a park at Point Reyes in July 1959, Miller knew a great deal of hard work lay ahead. One way of measuring the effectiveness of this rookie legislator is simply to list the tasks before him at this juncture. Miller needed to secure (1) a House hearing, (2) House passage of the bill authorizing the PRNS, (3) Senate passage, (4) support from fiscally conservative Republican

Barbara Eastman, PRNS
Foundation, 1960.
Courtesy of the Point
Reyes National Seashore
Archives.

President Eisenhower to fund land purchases while prices escalated, and
(5) NPS support for the unique public-private partnership that the park at
Point Reyes would require.

From the perspective of a half century later, Miller's challenge had an
even greater degree of difficulty. In 1959, there was a major push by the
NPS to provide more parks for places *east* of the Mississippi, not out west,
where Yosemite, Yellowstone, and the Grand Canyon drew so many tourists. Four senior legislators in the Senate took the lead, introducing a measure to provide national seashore status to some of the remaining imperiled
shorelines. Led by Senators Neuberger of Oregon and Douglas of Illinois,
their proposal called for five new national seashores.[27] The push for a park
at Point Reyes was being challenged in the Senate blueprint by a proposal
to establish a California park at the Channel Islands off Santa Barbara, 350
miles to the south. The greater Los Angeles area had by then surpassed
the San Francisco metro region, and the Southland's growing population
gave it added political clout. Among the many challenges for Miller was
the need to move Point Reyes to the front of the line against this strong
contender from the Santa Barbara region of his home state.

Congress Comes to Marin: Grassroots Lobbying

Making Point Reyes the California favorite, however, would be meaning-less if Miller could not get even a House subcommittee hearing on the proposed national seashore for Marin County. Thus, Miller's endeavors to spur local grassroots efforts and create favorable publicity for the seashore proposal proved crucial.

Miller prepared for the battle by tactfully reframing his argument in Marin to emphasize the *economic* benefits of conservation. The creation of a federal park in the West Marin region "would keep land values up," Miller explained in televised interviews preserved in archives.[28] This tying of environmental politics to land values and quality of life—not just to bio-logical diversity and public health—would prove key for many subsequent victories by environmental activists in other parts of the nation. Economic considerations had been a reason for powerful Democrats to resist park expenditures. Critics viewed such uses of public funds for outdoor recre-ation, hiking, and boating as elitist. Cynics noted that creating parks often increased the value of assets held by a wealthy minority, whether they were local landowners, savvy investors, or business leaders who would profit from bringing guests to newly established parklands and housing them.

The first public congressional hearing on the Point Reyes seashore pro-posal was finally held by the Senate in Marin County on April 14, 1960, in the large Olney Hall at the College of Marin in Kentfield. A total of fifty-eight witnesses were heard, and another forty submitted testimony for the hearing record. NPS director Conrad Wirth appeared in Marin to re-prise his 1935 staff report, pointing to the richness of the Point Reyes land-scapes and fragile ecosystems. He also cited the 1958 NPS study, though its insistence that "there has been relatively little development in the entire [PRNS] area" upset ranchers, several of whom had invested in their farm properties since buying Shafter lands.[29] Miller made good use of his field trips to Cape Hatteras, explaining the danger of cost escalation. He testi-fied that the park had great promise while pledging to support the ranch-ers: "I believe the salvation of the area will be a park, but I won't stand for anything that doesn't safeguard the ranchers."[30]

Supervisors from Marin and Sonoma County joined the congressional delegation for a helicopter tour; supervisors Vera Shultz and Leigh Shoe-maker were required to change from dresses to pants before army officials would allow them to ride in the helicopters. The helicopters rounded the southern tip of the Point Reyes Peninsula at Bolinas just as the fog lifted.

The *Independent Journal* front-page coverage captured the mood with the headline that appeared the morning of the hearing: "Nature at Prettiest: Solons Impressed by Beauty of Pt. Reyes."[31] Shoemaker testified that preservation was their duty: "We have a moral obligation to look out for future generations."[32] A leader of the new PRNS Foundation, Joel Gustafson, similarly warned in his public testimony that "the nation can have an area that would be invaluable for public enjoyment . . . or we can let this jewel be carved by the bulldozer and smeared over by asphalt."[33]

Park opponents pleaded to keep the federal government out of their lands, as they would in subsequent House hearings.[34] Aspinall had "life or death power" over the Point Reyes bill, Duddleson recalled, and gave some of the pro-park witnesses a hard time.[35] The hearings were enlivened by the passionate presentation of the ranchers' lobbyist, Bryan McCarthy. His testimony assailed the park proposal with a list of a dozen alleged flaws in the plan, including the assertion that "the Park is unnecessary. Marin already has enough parks."[36] Douglas S. Hertz, a wealthy investor from the Point Reyes Land and Development Company who held 1,100 acres on Inverness Ridge in a parcel that included two miles of prime shoreline frontage, matched McCarthy's bluster, testifying that the proposal for a federal park was "an impending boondoggle of immense proportions, developing in our own backyard, at a frivolous, ill-conceived waste of money."[37] McCarthy earned Miller's scorn; his district director, Bill Grader, alleged that the consistent misrepresentation of facts earned McCarthy a place in the ever-affable Miller's "Bastard File." Yet McCarthy would later be proved right about one key point: the $14 million price tag cited by federal officials in 1960 would ultimately grow to exceed $54 million.

In the wake of the first 1960 field hearing, legislative action in Congress stalled in the run-up to the national election. One unusual development over the course of the next year, however, proved to be an initial breakthrough. A complex series of local disputes led to an attempted recall of an anti-park member of the Marin County Board of Supervisors. For the first time in California state history, such a county recall vote succeeded, and the new supervisor, Peter Behr of Mill Valley, was a park proponent. Miller's aide, Duddleson, argued later that this recall campaign and Behr's arrival on the board proved to be a local "tipping point" that began to turn the tide of local officials from public opposition to support of the seashore proposal.[38] Miller subsequently wrote that after the surprise recall of a supervisor and his replacement by Behr, he was able to "flip" one more vote

Zena Mendoza Cabral
preparing to testify, 1961.
Courtesy of the Point Reyes
National Seashore Archives.

on the county board to create a new majority in support of a park at Point
Reyes.[39] This evidence of local support for the park would later be cited
in the key 1962 House committee report endorsing Miller's bill. It was essential. Failure to reverse the board's 4–1 vote against the national seashore
proposal would have locked in Aspinall's opposition.

Miller was able, over the course of his first term in Congress, to demonstrate to the regional press and to his Washington colleagues that there was
no clear consensus among park opponents. The environmentalists were
able to divide their opposition and point to a few converts among landowners in the area, some of whom grudgingly accepted a future national
seashore presence as inevitable.

The election of Senator John F. Kennedy of Massachusetts to the White
House in November 1960 by a razor-thin margin over Vice President Nixon
of California had altered the national political dynamics further in favor
of the Point Reyes seashore park proposal. Nixon had carried nearly every
state in the West, including California. Senator Kennedy's lonely fight for
a national seashore at Cape Cod was now a White House priority. Kennedy's selection of Miller's friend and Interior Committee colleague Stuart
Udall to become secretary of the interior proved to be another source of
remarkably good luck for PRNS advocates. Udall's role would turn out to
be another key to success.

Kennedy's staff moved with dispatch to revive his Senate proposal for a national seashore at Cape Cod and to transform it into an action item for what proved to be a difficult first year in office. As President Kennedy's White House team in 1961 pressed Chairman Aspinall to move the Cape Cod bill, there was a push from Secretary Udall and NPS Director Wirth to create regional alliances. One anecdote recalled by Udall in an oral history is especially revealing. In February 1961, the new Department of the Interior team was completing a major conservation plan to embrace national seashores and new wilderness areas. When department leaders saw that the draft White House speech for President Kennedy singled out only Cape Cod, Udall recalled that it would appear "rather narrow and selfish for the President to recommend [only] Cape Cod in his home state." Udall and the speechwriters decided, "Let's make it national, let's have him recommend two others, one on the Gulf Coast and one on the Pacific Coast." Here is where Miller's friend from the Interior Committee pushed Point Reyes ahead of other West Coast competitors.[40] President Kennedy's statement embracing the Cape Cod bill, delivered on February 23, 1961, explicitly called for a comparable park on the nation's west coast—not at the Channel Islands, but at Point Reyes.[41]

The Cape Cod National Seashore Act was signed into law on August 7, 1961, with a cap of $14 million in federal funds authorized for land acquisition—the same cap that would be applied to Point Reyes. This modest beachhead in Cape Cod proved, as a Massachusetts paper noted, to be an important "breakthrough in the cause of U.S. preservation." Over the next five years, the NPS cobbled together a sinuous shoreline park from local and state lands while devising flexible options for existing homeowners to convey their land to the NPS. "A great public project that seemed hopelessly visionary when first proposed became a reality in Washington," historian Daniel Lombardo observed. "[It was] the finest victory ever recorded for the cause of conservation in New England."[42] Kennedy was quick to note at the White House signing ceremony that he hoped for more such coastline parks, especially including the California proposal—now Point Reyes—and one advanced by his Texan vice president, Lyndon Johnson: Padre Island. Cape Cod proved to be the most valuable precedent for Point Reyes advocates; indeed, the formal statement that Kennedy read the next year at the Point Reyes bill signing employed nearly identical language in many places.[43]

The 1962 Compromise Legislation

As 1962 opened, the Miller team was fighting to prevent the US Army Corps of Engineers from dredging in Drakes Estero and dumping the spoils in the marshlands and sand dunes along Limantour for the 3,500 homes planned by developers for the site.

"Delay 'em to death" was the strategy adopted by park supporters.[44] After the success in placing Behr on the Board of Supervisors led to success in flipping the vote of another supervisor, William Gnoss, Miller wrote the board a new plea on January 12, 1962, noting that all the changes he proposed to make to the legislation would be to the advantage of Marin property owners and asserting that "establishment of this major unit of the National Park System in Marin County would benefit all segments of the Marin economy. . . . Preservation and development of this seashore playground will make all of Marvelous Marin an even more attractive county in which to live and work, as well as one of the nation's major tourist attractions."[45]

Within twenty-four hours after Supervisor Gnoss moved from no to yes on the park, Miller had personal letters hand-delivered to House Interior Committee leaders bearing the news that "the Board's adverse vote against the Park of 4 to 1 last year [sic] has been completely turned around due to real grass roots support." Miller also rejected the claim that the ranchers had not been adequately consulted: "It does not seem possible to me that the ranchers or their representatives have any justification to complain that they have not been heard."[46]

Miller and Engle then made a series of carefully calculated compromises. These compromises proved essential to secure the proposal for a park at Point Reyes before Congress adjourned sine die in October for the midterm elections, yet these same compromises from 1962 remain the subject of bitter dispute and litigation more than half a century later.

The local politics of the time had a substantial impact on decisions made in Washington by federal officials in the early 1960s. In the Bay Area, the city of Berkeley's proposal to fill in more acreage and wetlands along its waterfront—increasing the city's size and expanding its tax base—was meeting with surprisingly effective opposition. The effort of the fledgling Save San Francisco Bay Association (Save the Bay) to block the Berkeley move was one of the original grassroots environmental campaigns of the era. It was modeled after Caroline Livermore's Marin "associations," which

Limantour subdivision development plans. Courtesy of the Point Reyes National Seashore Archives.

often consisted of only a few women activists from her Marin Art and Garden Club.

The Berkeley group evolved into a series of Monday-morning meetings in the kitchens of its three original organizers, Kay Kerr, Sylvia McLaughlin, and Esther Gulick. They were the well-connected spouses of the University of California chancellor, a University of California regent, and an economics professor, respectively. In an oral history interview, McLaughlin recalled looking out her windows in the East Bay in 1961 and watching garbage trucks dumping their loads in the tidal marshes near present-day Emeryville.[47]

The San Francisco Bay was known at the time as "the nation's largest open sewer." The city of Berkeley proposed filling in more prime waterfront acreage upon which to build homes and roads. A proposal called the Reber Plan was also advanced that proposed to shrink the bay and convert the shallow northern and southern arms into freshwater lakes with a series of dams. The US Army Corps of Engineers produced a schematic of the bay reduced in many sections east of the Golden Gate to a narrow shipping channel lined with industrial and military port facilities right to the edge of the remaining "San Francisco River."[48] The women reached out to other Bay Area environmental organizations, secured mailing lists, and then generated letter-writing campaigns, petition drives, and calls to the Sacramento and Washington offices of decisionmakers. They were effective in mobilizing the very pro-business newspapers in the region to come out, somewhat surprisingly, against Berkeley's latest bay fill proposal.[49] Within four years, their Save the Bay membership had grown to eighteen thousand; elected officials took note.[50]

Harold Gilliam, the *San Francisco Chronicle* columnist, provided coverage of the public land issues even as he made the awkward transition from an unbiased reporter to an unabashed advocate of environmental causes. Gilliam explained his transformation simply. As a young man, he had grown up in Los Angeles and watched the Hollywood Hills being leveled and parts of the Pacific coastline in West Los Angeles filled with apartment towers. As he noted, it appeared that "the developers had all the power. . . . I was sure when I came to the Bay Area, the same thing was going to happen here. I looked across the Bay at those open [Marin County] hills and thought 'wow, how have those hills lasted so long? They won't last much longer.'"[51]

The Berkeley-led Save the Bay group generated a genuine grassroots groundswell. It had much in common with the PRNS Foundation launched by Barbara Eastman, Margaret Azevedo, and other park backers. The archival records make the provenance of the PRNS Foundation clear, however: the Point Reyes group was formed at Miller's behest, specifically to show Chairman Wayne Aspinall that there was local support for a national seashore.[52]

Congressman Miller was explicit on this point. He had written to Bill Grader, his district field director, on March 5, 1959, just two months into his first term in Congress, warning, "It is necessary that we begin to take some steps in our office to push this matter if the local people are unable or unwilling to do it. At the same time, I want to retain the concept of local autonomy in West Marin. We want to give the impression that everything is emanating from there."[53]

In this battle, the grassroots activists were being organized to fuel grasstops lobbying, in their initial efforts targeting prominent local opinion leaders who would in turn directly press key federal officials. Like Caroline Livermore's associations, the local group supporting a Point Reyes park had few members at first. It gave legitimacy, however, to Miller's quixotic effort to create a national seashore in West Marin through its lobbying campaign.

Eastman had played a lead role, along with Livermore, in raising funds for a small state park on Tomales Bay, adjacent to the proposed PRNS boundaries. Especially striking is that even as freshman federal legislator Miller was pushing an initiative in Washington, he was anxiously backfilling to create the appearance of local support for what was initially a top-down initiative. This was precisely the reverse of how many other national parks and seashore efforts were launched.

Miller took care, his files make clear, to discourage constituents from pressuring Chairman Aspinall, with whom he labored to maintain an ever-respectful working relationship.[54] The proposal to create a national seashore at Point Reyes, however, had drawn the support of the Sierra Club. This group was just emerging as a powerful lobbying organization with a growing nationwide membership recruited in part through efforts to protect lands and waterways in Utah, Colorado, and Arizona. It had previously been a primarily West Coast group, rather top-heavy with scholars, biologists, hikers, and wealthy professionals—many of them Republicans—as it had been since its founding by Muir and others in 1892. Yet Miller's campaign for Point Reyes engaged the club in an era when it was spreading its wings under its ambitious executive director, David Brower, to take on more national environmental causes, ranging from opposition to more dams on the Colorado River to the Mineral King fight in California's Sierra Nevada Mountains. Sierra Club membership—spurred in part by the local efforts of such groups as the PRNS Foundation and the Save the Bay start-up—swelled fourfold from 27,000 to 113,000 by 1970. Membership would then soar to 500,000 by 1980.[55]

The wide circulation during the 1960s of Ansel Adams's and Nancy Newhall's Sierra Club book, *This Is the American Earth*, and Rachel Carson's surprise bestseller, *Silent Spring*, spread new environmental awareness, as historian Douglas Brinkley ably chronicles. Conservation was now a cause that was making its way into mainstream media and onto network television, shaping expanded coverage of what was then still called the "ecology" issue. As Carolyn Merchant explains, "[Carson's] book was both an environmental and popular success. The book identified the environmental impact of pesticides (especially DDT) including the concentration as they move up the food chain and insects' development of genetic immunity requiring still stronger pesticides."[56] The literature was further enriched by the publication of Secretary Udall's conservation book *The Quiet Crisis* and the launch of what he later termed the "third wave" of environmental activism; Udall accurately credited Teddy Roosevelt for the first such wave, and rather generously suggested that FDR had led a "second wave" of environmental activism, albeit one financed not by Congress but rather by Republican donors and with Civilian Conservation Corps sweat equity.

Point Reyes advocates thus had Kennedy, Udall, and Wirth in place in Washington as federal champions for the park cause. Together with Miller and the PRNS Foundation, they continued inviting key legislators from Washington on field trips to Point Reyes. Participants on both sides of the debate tell in their oral histories of the remarkable luck park champions once again had, this time with the weather. While the ranchers and local editorials against the park often portrayed the area as desolate, windswept lands "nobody would want to visit," whenever the Washington visitors came to see Point Reyes, winter rains and spring-summer fogs miraculously lifted.

The rains held off, and it seemed that on every VIP visit, the visibility stretched for miles—they could see clear to the lighthouse from atop Inverness Ridge. Nevada senator Alan Bible teased the ranchers during one sun-splashed April visit for having claimed that the weather was too bad for a park. The weather gods, proponents claimed, favored the establishment of a national seashore at Point Reyes.

The visits by members of Congress and petitions were not new tools. Even the railroad lobbyists of the nineteenth-century campaigns had used the former strategy to push for national parks at Yosemite and Glacier, while the Hayden Expedition funded by Congress to map the Yellowstone region in 1871 had included such "political boys" as the son of Charles Dawes, the chair of the House Ways and Means Committee, who repeatedly earmarked federal funds to support Hayden's work.[57] What came to be known as "green politics" proved good for many in business; this phenomenon was in evidence well before Miller reframed the Point Reyes fight as one to protect not just nature but land values as well.

A third element introduced into the Point Reyes fight by the Sierra Club was more novel. This brainchild of David Brower was a tactic that he employed successfully in other conservation campaigns. He designed and assembled on a rush basis for Sierra Club publication a glossy book titled *An Island in Time* that was full of seductive color photographs of the stunning landscape. Then he had the books delivered to all 535 members of the Eighty-Seventh Congress.[58]

Brower had recruited *San Francisco Chronicle* columnist Harold Gilliam to write portions of the text after Gilliam had authored an eloquent 1958 piece for an issue of the monthly *Sierra Club Bulletin* devoted to discussion of the PRNS proposal. Many other sections of the 1962 *An Island in Time* text added without attribution were authored by Brower. A year later, Gilliam stepped away from his career as a journalist to become a speechwriter for Secretary Udall and later a historian whose narrative shaped the study of Point Reyes.

In early 1962, Kennedy White House staff members were actively looking for follow-up action after their Cape Cod win. With the Point Reyes legislation stalled, land prices in West Marin were climbing and the developers were pressing ahead with their subdivisions. Benjamin Bonelli, the lead investor for Drake's Bay Estates and the planned subdivision of 3,500 homes being built above Limantour Beach, continued to assail the Miller proposal to remove all dwellings built after the summer of 1959, when the first House-Senate bill had been introduced. "This is an attempt to confiscate the land," Bonelli argued, "by intimidating people into not buying."[59] That spring, Bonelli began running ads on the front page of the Marin County daily newspaper urging buyers to secure spots in the Point Reyes subdivisions while falsely alleging that Congress was "about to adjourn" and the seashore proposal was "washing away in Washington."

Congressman Miller was furious about the ads. He privately assailed the newspaper, writing Gustafson with the lament that "most responsible newspapers adhere to a policy of excluding misleading, deceptive and inaccurate advertising in the interests of protecting their readers. In my opinion, acceptance of these recent Drake's Bay Estates subdivision ads violates any reasonable standard."[60] The issue was even raised on the floor of the House of Representatives, where the leading Republican conservation advocate, John Saylor of Pennsylvania, assailed the Bonelli scheme as "a way to make a fast buck."[61]

Miller could not move forward with Aspinall, however, until a deal was cut to temper the opposition of ranchers. Here, the reverence with which Point Reyes enthusiasts and environmental activists remember Miller and Engle needs a reality check. Each man proved to be an effective politician who would take considerable risks to advance his legislative objectives. Miller was a relative novice at governance, but he made a political veteran's crucial calculation at this juncture. In hindsight, this move can be seen as brilliant, even though it invited decades of future challenges in Congress and the courts.

Miller was under pressure from the Senate. Engle and California's Republican senator Thomas Kuchel struggled to obtain support from the powerful Senator Bible of Nevada. Bible chaired both the subcommittee that appropriated annual funding for the NPS *and* the authorizing committee that would need to pass legislation authorizing the PRNS. Kuchel then double-crossed Miller by reneging on a pledge not to include in the measure a special allowance for a dozen private lots in Duck Cove on Tomales Bay. Miller and Engle decided that it was wiser to take a partial victory than to hold out for an ideal measure. They would accept a compromise in order to pass a Point Reyes bill for a modest-sized seashore park before Congress adjourned in the fall of 1962, when all legislative proposals not enacted would expire. The controversial bipartisan compromise engineered by the two California legislators in 1962 favored the existing ranches while securing a foothold for the national seashore. It led to decades of litigation. It also saved the national seashore proposal and Point Reyes forests from falling. The compromise ultimately prevented and reversed the subdivision of future parklands. Quite simply, it saved Point Reyes as we know it today.

Proponents agreed in 1962 to pass a bill for a larger park of up to 53,000 acres but one that left one-third of the parklands as what was termed a "pastoral zone." These lands could be maintained in agricultural use by private owners or purchased by the government and then granted back on multiyear leases to tenant ranchers who committed to limiting their land use to agriculture. Aspinall's Interior Committee report was clear on this point.[62] So was the congressional newsletter sent by Miller to constituents on August 24, 1962, declaring that "the compromise boundary line between the ranching area and the public-use areas is drawn with the intent of permitting every dairy ranch in the peninsula to remain in operation—forever, if that is the desire of the owners."[63] The last newsletter sent by Miller's to constituents in October 1962 similarly asserted that "every dairy ranch on the Peninsula can remain in operation under private ownership so long as present or future owners desire—and so long as the natural or pastoral scene is preserved. . . . The oyster and fishing operations, like the dairies, will be encouraged to remain so long as they wish to continue present compatible activities."[64] The Senate committee led by Bible issued a similar report, noting that the sponsors' legislative intent was a compromise that allowed for "continued use for ranching purposes in a manner that would satisfy the preservation objective."[65]

Each of the compromises adopted by the legislators was designed to counter and dilute the opposition of ranchers. They also sought to safeguard the commercial interests of the small towns, Bolinas and Inverness, bordering the new parklands. Miller worked to shape the proposal to generate sufficient local support to free the seashore proposal for final congressional action.

Miller Counts the Votes

What Miller did next was so unusual that it has few precedents in the modern Congress. Miller had made friends easily and was popular with Washington colleagues on both sides of the political aisle. In the summer of 1962, the cheerful novice embarked on a Don Quixote–like challenge. He decided that he would personally conduct his own whip count on the bill. The system of party whips used by Democratic Party majorities in Congress in the 1960s had a dozen senior legislators serve as deputies on the whip's team. Each member so deputized was responsible for gathering intelligence from up to two dozen of his or her party caucus members. Each of the whip team deputies would then assemble his or her individual count and report back to the party leadership with an initial vote count and indications of where opponents had footholds.

Miller decided in 1962 that he would poll all 434 fellow members of the House of Representatives personally, face-to-face, one at a time, and ask them to vote for his bill. He set out to do so through weeks of roll-call votes, when he could buttonhole both Democratic and Republican members as they entered the House chamber. As Duddleson recalled at the NPS dedication ceremony for the Clem Miller Environmental Education Center, Miller "undertook the unusual labor of talking to every Member of the House."[66] By the time the bill was moved to the House floor, Congressman Miller was able to assert to Aspinall not only that he had the votes to win but also, rather optimistically, that as a result of the large carving-out of a pastoral zone compromise, local opposition "has swung around either to acceptance or to outright approval."[67]

The resulting public law did not spell out precise park boundaries. It did not specify the length and terms of leaseback operations for the ranchers. The sponsors privately conceded that the law did not provide nearly enough funding to acquire beach access and prime parklands; the paper trail is clear on this point. The park champions knew the initial $14 million authorization was inadequate. They felt they could not ask in 1962 for more than a $14 million cap on federal funds, however, as this was the precedent set in the Cape Cod bill. An appropriate analogy is that they decided to pass a bill granting citizens the deed to a checkerboard, but they secured only enough funding to acquire title to the red squares. The other half of the squares would remain privately managed lands and would require continued negotiations and substantial future federal appropriations to secure right-of-way access to the coastline. The strategy was consistent with Senator Neuberger's counsel; it was a classic adoption of incrementalism.

The hard parts of the complex Point Reyes lands issues were finessed with this 1962 compromise. The ranches could stay for an indefinite period, although the local leaders on both sides of the effort, George Collins and Bryan McCarthy, conceded in later oral histories that they assumed interest in continued ranching would "dissipate" and the ranches would be phased out in a generation or two.

The park would initially have a Swiss-cheese footprint. It would rely on untested theories and inconsistent assumptions about how this public-private partnership would work. It gave little guidance to the local NPS rangers, who were immediately placed in the midst of continuing conflicts among ranchers, developers, environmental activists, county officials, and park expansion advocates.

This was then and remains today the single most complex land use arrangement that NPS professionals are asked to administer. There was no model for this plan to mix commercial businesses and thousands of manure-generating cows with two million annual visitors in a national seashore within an hour's drive of a metropolitan region of seven million people. As Secretary Udall explained, "The Park Service had very little experience in this. They had to tool up and get a whole system of land acquisition set up. The local people always fought national parks."[68] When the full House first took up the Miller compromise bill on July 23, 1962, Rules Committee member Bill Avery (R-KS) made clear the precedents they were about to establish: "The issue today is not simply authorizing Point Reyes as such. The House is passing judgment on a package of recreation and conservation areas and the Point Reyes National Seashore Park [sic] was first on that list."[69] The record confirms that legislators and executive branch officials were, in fact, keenly aware of the precedents they were setting with policies created for PRNS.

A Patchwork Park

It was to be a patchwork park for a time. The cows would reign in some parts, but parklands and seashore access would be set aside for the public in others. NPS allies at the time cited a similar experiment that the NPS had used in the Everglades. As Director Wirth explained to Secretary Udall, in Florida, "a donut" of private inholdings had initially been allowed to coexist inside the new national preserve. Yet the PRNS pastoral zone represented a similar "donut hole" in the geographic center of the Point Reyes Peninsula. The 1962 compromise at Point Reyes proved to be a recipe for bitter dispute.

The Point Reyes origin story continues to be colored by the selective accounts of history advanced by litigants. Environmental activists who favor continued expansion of the wilderness areas and the "rewilding" of most of the Point Reyes Peninsula insist that this 1962 accord of convenience was just a *temporary* deal to secure the beachhead. Proponents of this position maintain that some parties to the legislative compromise language hoped to move, at a later unspecified date, to eject the ranchers after their initial leases expired.

Miller was facing a challenging reelection campaign in a swing district; he was intent on getting the national seashore started with an authorization and deferring lease issues for later resolution. The legislative history is clear here: the original 1935 proposal assumed that all the ranches would be acquired by the government. The 1959 proposal also assumed that the government would gain ownership of all the shoreline properties with full power to condemn and purchase private lands. Then, in 1962, out of political necessity, the sponsors agreed that some lands would remain privately owned dairy and beef cattle ranches—a patchwork design. As Collins details in his 1979 oral history interviews, the NPS stepped in after state officials visited Point Reyes to evaluate its suitability for a state park—they left within an hour, concluding that the fog and wind would make the place undesirable for a park. Collins later confirmed with state authorities that the remaining ranches on the Point Reyes Peninsula were not essential to the state's economy; officials treated the ranchers with wary respect while privately assuming that the ranch families' time on the land would be limited by attrition rather than by any federal policy action.[70]

The 1962 compromise created the still awkward visuals of a national seashore with more than 33,000 acres of wilderness but one whose creeks, lagoons, and marshlands are routinely fouled by cow manure. Litigants

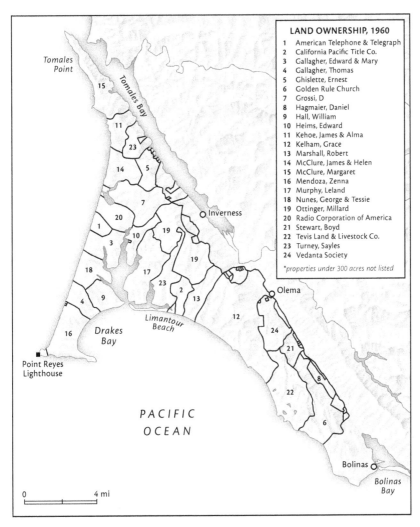

LAND OWNERSHIP, 1960

1 American Telephone & Telegraph
2 California Pacific Title Co.
3 Gallagher, Edward & Mary
4 Gallagher, Thomas
5 Ghislette, Ernest
6 Golden Rule Church
7 Grossi, D
8 Hagmaier, Daniel
9 Hall, William
10 Heims, Edward
11 Kehoe, James & Alma
12 Kelham, Grace
13 Marshall, Robert
14 McClure, James & Helen
15 McClure, Margaret
16 Mendoza, Zenna
17 Murphy, Leland
18 Nunes, George & Tessie
19 Ottinger, Millard
20 Radio Corporation of America
21 Stewart, Boyd
22 Tevis Land & Livestock Co.
23 Turney, Sayles
24 Vedanta Society

properties under 300 acres not listed

Owners of Point Reyes lands, 1960. Courtesy of Erin Greb Cartography.

have disputed the degree to which five thousand cows contaminate nearby waters, yet some Point Reyes waters have registered exceptionally high fecal counts for years. Tests conducted in subsequent decades revealed high pollution levels at multiple points in the public park waters.

When one drives to the end of the road at Point Reyes today, one views the alive-and-well dairy and beef operations of commercial ranches with gates and fence posts. Sir Francis Drake Boulevard and Pierce Point Road pass directly through the detritus of messy barnyard operations on several ranches. It is a realistic pastoral scene, but the vast amounts of cow manure are jarring for first-time visitors who are expecting open spaces from which most signs of human habitation have been removed. US environmental policies have gravitated over several decades from a conservation focus to a restoration effort, where the rewilding of special preserves is more the goal than the British concept of parks as public spaces and peopled areas.

The 1962 legislation proved essential to gain seashore access and to start the process of buying future parkland from the fifty-nine different land-owners with whom the Department of the Interior would have to do business as the new park neighbors.

The number of owners would balloon over the course of the decade as land speculation soared and developers bought into the game.[71] One ranch had already been subdivided into more than 600 lots, of which 104 had been sold by the time the 1962 bill passed; eighteen homes had been completed in the massive subdivision going in just above Limantour Beach.

It helped immensely that Miller's friend Udall ran the Department of the Interior and had President Kennedy's ear and trust, although Kennedy had limited interest in and little time for environmental policy and politics. It also helped that the man who had worked on the first NPS study of Point Reyes, Wirth, was now director of the NPS. The cliché is true: in politics, relationships matter. They often prove more consequential than tidy bureaucratic organizational charts or procedural precedents. The Point Reyes story repeatedly bears out this point.

The White House Ceremony

The run-up to the 1962 election was worrisome for Kennedy partisans. The midterm elections presented opportunities for voters to express frustration with the gap between the new administration's rhetoric and the reality of making tough choices while governing. The Kennedy White House was pushing for every possible advantage. One key was to hold suburban House districts such as Miller's, swing districts where party control of Congress was often decided. The September 13, 1962, signing ceremony for the Point Reyes bill was part of this deliberate White House political process.

As the cameras rolled and the official White House photographer snapped black-and-white photos, President Kennedy gave a brief speech. He praised the "outstanding scenic and recreational characteristics of the area," noting that Point Reyes was "readily accessible to millions of our citizens, and its establishment as a National Seashore will pay vast dividends in the years to come." President Kennedy then noted the urgency of the situation with an ad lib repetition, declaring that

> the enactment of this legislation indicates an increased awareness of the importance of prompt action—*and I emphasize that particularly with the population increases and these areas disappearing under that pressure*—and the necessity for prompt action to preserve our nation's great natural beauty areas to insure existence and enjoyment by the public in the decades and centuries to come. This is especially true about those areas close to the major centers of population.[72]

Kennedy placed the Point Reyes initiative in the context of his broader park agenda; he was working with NPS Director Wirth and Secretary Udall on their Mission 66 plan of park expansion and improvement funding (see Key Documents in Appendix). When propelled forward later in the decade by President Lyndon Johnson, this funding would ultimately add a total of 1.7 million acres to the nation's parklands while emphasizing not just wilderness preservation but also robust outdoor recreation and commercial concessions. Point Reyes, Kennedy stated, was just one step in what was to be a long-term Kennedy-Johnson effort to create new parks and national seashores. "The creation of Point Reyes National Seashore," as John Hart notes, "proved to be a catalyst for many additional acts of preservation."

The bill signing was a happy occasion for most. It was billed by all parties to the compromise as a win-win situation. Senator Engle graciously insisted that Congressman Miller, at first barely visible next to Senator Hubert Humphrey, come from the back row and stand just behind the president for the photographers.

Look closely again at the photograph of the event. There on the right is a lobbyist: David Brower of the Sierra Club. On the far left is House Interior Committee Chairman Wayne Aspinall, whose objections had to be overcome to make this crucial step. Staffers recall that efforts were made by Miller to keep the two men physically apart because they disliked and distrusted each other. Indeed, part of Miller's strategy in pushing for the creation of the PRNS Foundation had been to ensure that Aspinall did not come to view the park proposal as "another Brower Sierra Club project."

"Then it became law before our eyes," as Miller wrote in his September

Clem Miller in his congressional
office, 1962. Courtesy of the
Point Reyes National Seashore
Archives.

1962 newsletter to constituents, "a fitting climax to years of effort by many
people who worked to save the beauty of this magnificent 'Island in Time'
for our and future generations."[73]

In the following days, Miller campaigned for reelection and was widely
hailed for his major accomplishment in stewarding the Point Reyes bill
into public law. It was a heady time for the sophomore legislator and former landscape gardener. He had found a top New York publisher for a
collection of the folksy letters home he pounded out weekly on his manual
Olivetti typewriter. The book, *Member of the House: Letters of a Congressman*, was to be released the first week in October. Early reviews from the
likes of Washington reporter David Broder sang its praises.

Triumph Turns Tragic

Then, just three weeks after the bill signing, the forty-five-year-old chief
sponsor of the measure, Clem Miller, was dead.[74] Miller was lost in a plane
crash along with his Marin County–based pilot as he campaigned along
the rugged California coast. The plane went down in thick clouds between
Eureka and Crescent City en route to a meeting with logging groups in a
sparsely populated area where voters were unlikely to support his reelection. It was the first time Miller had chartered a private plane to barnstorm

in his vast Redwood Empire district. He left a young widow and five daughters. President Kennedy sent the family to California and back on a special US Air Force plane for the funeral, which was held in a driving rainstorm at Point Reyes.[75] The Miller family was able to negotiate with a private landowner to later inter the congressman's remains on future parklands on a majestic bluff beside the Coast Trail near the Bear Valley Trail terminus at the Pacific Ocean.

Back in Washington, beginning on October 16, 1962, President Kennedy was soon embroiled in the Cuban Missile Crisis, an existential threat that placed military defenses on high alert in Marin County, in the Bay Area, and throughout the nation. The nation's young president and father of two children was assassinated the following November in Dallas, even as his White House staff was completing plans for a long-delayed presidential visit to Point Reyes.[76]

The lead Senate champion of the Point Reyes initiative, Clair Engle, was crippled by a stroke in 1963 and died in July 1964. Survived by his wife and daughter, the first-term senator was only fifty-two years old.

The Struggle to Secure the Park at Point Reyes

With the park's three most visible champions gone and most of the land designated for a federal park still privately owned, subsequent years brought litigation and delay. As a leading critic of the seashore administration correctly notes, "Point Reyes National Seashore ran into trouble almost as soon as it was authorized. Even before the [1962] bill's passage, some congressmen remained unconvinced that the Seashore could be established with the proposed budget."[77]

At the time of the bill signing, the federal government owned less than 1 percent of the lands in question—primarily the land under the lighthouse at the point secured by the 1857 appropriation after much haggling with the Shafters, who had repeatedly jacked up the price to taxpayers. By the mid-1960s, the nation's economy had stalled and inflation was growing. The Department of the Interior spent the balance of the new Land and Water Conservation Fund (LWCF) down nearly to zero. Escalation of US troop involvement in the Vietnam War divided the country's electorate into bitterly opposed camps. Bipartisan collaboration on domestic programs grew increasingly difficult.

The deaths of Miller, Kennedy, and then Engle within eighteen months of the 1962 bill signing devastated park champions. Four years later, the final California veteran of the 1962 Point Reyes legislative compromise, the Republican Senate whip Tom Kuchel, was gone from Congress. The GOP Senate deputy leader was blindsided from the political right, defeated in a contentious 1966 California Republican Senate primary election by ultra-conservative state Superintendent of Schools Max Rafferty.

The NPS began trying to buy out some of the ranchers at Point Reyes. The promise of a new park, however, made these inholdings ever more valuable, even as the ranchers' annual property taxes escalated dramatically. In some sections, land values increased nearly tenfold over the course of the decade. Land speculators were buying ranch lands in the Olema Valley and inside the projected park boundaries. The investors would lease lands back to the ranchers and then hold out for ever-increasing cash offers from the NPS to buy title to their lands, effectively fleecing taxpayers. Within years, this escalation factor would be a key argument for more Point Reyes land acquisition funding from Washington. While progress was stalled, the Johnson administration nevertheless held a ceremony to mark the semi-official opening of the seashore on the eve of the 1966 midterm election.

Population pressures elsewhere in Marin throughout the 1960s raised questions as to whether the vision of national seashore proponents for the Point Reyes Peninsula would ever be realized. Over the course of the decade, Point Reyes was relegated to the back of the line in Washington, behind park proposals and urgent maintenance projects in dozens of other states whose needs had yet to be met.

Local conservationists were making some headway beyond the Point Reyes fight, however, in both the Bay Area and Sacramento. Their progress would prove highly significant for the future of the PRNS. A fight to block development at the southern end of the Point Reyes Peninsula, in the Bolinas Lagoon, ended when Mrs. Roger Kent and Huey Johnson outmaneuvered the Bahia Baulines development corporation by flipping the swing vote of Supervisor Ernest Kettenhoefen. Kent and Johnson then deeded the key land on Kent Island for a county park. Their deal checkmated the investors, who had planned a powerboat marina with slips for 1,500 vessels and a hotel astride the Bolinas Lagoon.[78]

In nearby Berkeley, the Save San Francisco Bay Association had grown its membership and won support in 1965 for the creation of a temporary body, the San Francisco Bay Conservation and Development Commission (BCDC). This body was a regionwide organization that ultimately gained the power to block individual counties from taking actions that would

Secretary Udall, Mrs. Johnson, and Governor Pat Brown, 1966. Courtesy of the Point Reyes National Seashore Archives.

harm others along the shoreline of the expansive San Francisco Bay and Sacramento River delta. When California's new Governor Reagan balked at signing a bill to make the BCDC a permanent body, environmental lobbyists launched a petition drive. The Bay Area activists then circled the large state capitol building in Sacramento with a miles-long chain of petitions from BCDC supporters. The anti-big-government Reagan soon signed the bill.[79] This petition drive tactic would later be copied by the PRNS champions to secure more funding. Soon the BCDC was successful in first halting and then actually reversing the impact of bay fill proposals, restoring some wetlands, and barring new fill projects.[80]

Despite some wins by environmentalists, by the end of the decade, as one history notes, "the situation at the Point Reyes National Seashore was appalling. Only ten scattered parcels of land included in the park had been bought, the $14 million land acquisition fund was used up, the Inverness Ridge was being logged, and dairy and beef ranches inside the proposed park boundaries were being surveyed for building lots."[81]

Marincello: A Park Vision Eclipsed?

As NPS efforts to buy the Point Reyes lands ground to a halt, another major land use fight reared its head in southern Marin County that would ultimately have a great impact on Point Reyes. This related battle proved to have profound implications for both the national seashore effort and the Sixth US Army headquarters at San Francisco's Presidio near the Golden Gate. In this struggle over the proposed new city of Marincello, the Marin County Board of Supervisors once again sided with housing and commercial developers.

In 1964, Pittsburgh developer Thomas Frouge announced plans to build a vast planned community in a valley just beyond the north wall of the Golden Gate at the southern end of Marin County. Joining forces with investors from Gulf Oil, Frouge bought from the California State Lands Commission more than 2,000 acres west of Sausalito alongside the former US Army outpost at Fort Cronkhite, adjacent to the abandoned sites of World War II naval artillery bunkers and Cold War–era Nike missile sites. The new city developers proposed initially to build fifty high-rise apartment-bloc towers and single-family tract homes for up to 100,000 new residents all over the valley and on the hillsides just inland from the Marin Headlands.

Critics feared that the new city would blow open the hills and shorelines of West Marin for other competitors. They also claimed that it would clog and overwhelm traffic on the Golden Gate Bridge. Marin County desperately needed housing for its exploding population, however, and Frouge pointed to the success of the new planned community of Reston that his team had developed out in the Virginia cornfields alongside the new Dulles Airport. His Marin County plan to develop a new city also had many modern elements designed to create public spaces and local jobs.

The scope of the project was reduced to an initial target population of 30,000. Objections of dissenters on the Marin County Planning Commission were overridden.[82] On November 12, 1965, the Marin County Board of Supervisors voted to approve the plan for Marincello. Ground was broken, and an impressive adobe-tiled archway was constructed in the Sausalito hills just north of the Golden Gate Bridge and a few miles south of Mount Tamalpais' summit and Muir Woods. This was to be the grand entrance to the enormous new planned city. A freeway off-ramp to Marincello from Highway 101 was built, and more interchanges were planned for the north end of the Golden Gate.[83]

Once again, it appeared that the die had been cast and the young environmental movement was too late to preserve open spaces at Point Reyes and the Marin Headlands.

CHAPTER FOUR

The Battle That Had to Be Won Twice

Point Reyes was saved through a combination of exceptionally clever lobbying techniques and repeated streaks of good luck. Fortune favored those who were champions of the park cause. The campaign featured targeted lobbying both inside Congress and at the local level. This over-under challenge for advocates would focus on gathering signatures on petitions at the grass*roots* level while carefully targeting grass*tops* efforts to sway decision-makers in Washington. The climax of the Point Reyes National Seashore (PNRS) story unfolded over the course of nearly a decade, from 1962 to 1972, leading to a vast expansion of the northern California greenbelt along the Marin Headlands north and west of the Golden Gate.

The election of Richard Nixon as president in November 1968 began a series of events that forced developments at Point Reyes to a head. Their resolution led not just to victory for the PRNS vision and a tripling of the acreage in the park from its original 1959 proposed size but also to a series of land use decisions that impacted the entire San Francisco Bay Area. The results of the fights for Point Reyes and for a new national recreation area centered on the Golden Gate and the San Francisco Presidio also portended a profound change in the politics of California and, ultimately, in the environmental protection movement nationwide.

After Richard Nixon, the former vice president and California senator, lost narrowly to John Kennedy in the 1960 presidential race, he then failed in his 1962 California gubernatorial political comeback bid. Nixon had angrily announced his retirement from politics in a November 1962 morning-after press conference, telling the journalists they wouldn't have him "to kick around anymore." Nixon nevertheless continued to work for Republican Party causes and campaigned for candidates in the 1966 mid-term elections. Then he ran again for the White House in 1968 with his advertising team promising a "new" Nixon. Ads produced by an expensive Madison Avenue agency featured not the hard-right anticommunist Nixon of Joe McCarthy days but rather the profile of a cheerful healer, a man who could restore normalcy to a divided nation. For voters appalled by the urban riots of those years and the violence at the Democratic National Convention in Chicago in 1968, Nixon was a safe choice. Candidate Nixon in 1968 was more moderate than the overtly racist George Wallace. Nixon appeared to many centrist voters to be better able to check the more extreme voices from the anti-war left who were tearing the Democratic Party apart between the McGovern wing and the Lyndon Baines Johnson (LBJ)–Hubert Humphrey establishment. Nixon also appeared more moderate than the hardline Goldwater faction of the GOP right, who were suspicious of Nixon's ties to the Nelson Rockefeller moderate wing of the Republicans.

The Context of the Times and the LBJ Environmental Legacy

The United States in December 1968 was greatly changed from the country that had greeted celebrants on that happy September 1962 morning when the White House ceremony launched the PRNS. After the Cuban Missile Crisis in October 1962 and the assassination of President Kennedy in 1963, the nation had suffered through the subsequent escalation of the Vietnam War, the murders of civil rights workers, inflation, and recession. The San Francisco "Summer of Love" mood in Golden Gate Park had fallen into darker times with urban riots and the spring 1968 murders of Dr. Martin Luther King, Jr., and Senator Robert F. Kennedy.

In the interim, much progress had been made in advancing an ambitious national environmental policy agenda. After he assumed the presidency, Lyndon Johnson kept Stuart Udall at Interior. Together, they ramped up a push to pass Kennedy programs that had previously been low priorities. Banking on a pledge that Kennedy had extracted from Chairman Aspinall hours before departing for the fateful Dallas trip in 1963, Johnson and his allies succeeded in finally passing the Wilderness Act in 1964. By then, Chairman Aspinall, a favorite of Rocky Mountain extractive industries, and the Sierra Club's David Brower were sworn enemies. In 1964, when Brower was pushing for action on the sweeping Wilderness Act, Aspinall blocked him for months, tangling repeatedly with his friend John Saylor, the ranking minority member of the Interior Committee, an ardent environmentalist, and a Pennsylvania Republican.[1] Aspinall's tactics yielded major concessions as the Coloradan sought to appease private landholders and to limit the use of eminent domain to seize private holdings for park-lands. A national commission to review all use of public lands was created with Aspinall at the head, free to pursue his agenda of making greater commercial use of public lands.

The same day in September 1964 that he signed the Wilderness Act, LBJ signed legislation creating the Land and Water Conservation Fund (LWCF). The LWCF would prove crucial in 1970 for the full funding of the land acquisition and expansion of Point Reyes. These proved to be critical pieces, as they provided the federal government with a new mission—to expand the National Park Service (NPS) network, especially east of the Mississippi and along shorelines—and provided a stream of dedicated revenue for these federal land purchases. Indeed, the Johnson record on environmental legislation would ultimately far exceed the accomplishments of any predecessor, including Teddy Roosevelt. LBJ succeeded in expanding nearly three dozen national parks; thirty-two of these were within easy driving distance of major American cities, as noted by the authors of *The Green Years: When Democrats and Republicans United to Repair the Earth*: "The total included five national seashores, six national recreation areas, the first national lakeshore as well as additional national monuments, national historical sites, and national memorials that were established."[2]

Oil Spills and Rivers Afire: Politicians Discover "Ecology"

California political campaigns were especially turbulent during these years. Pundits began to cite California politics as offering previews of national battles to come. California was deemed a bellwether in terms of both political trends and changing cultural norms. The Free Speech Movement in Berkeley was at its peak. Anti–Vietnam War demonstrations were numerous, often regaled by rock stars based in Marin County, including the Grateful Dead, Janis Joplin, Carlos Santana, Quicksilver Messenger Service, Steve Miller, and the Sons of Champlin. National media closely covered the rise of the Black Panthers in Oakland as well as the hippie communes in the Haight-Ashbury district of San Francisco.

In 1966, the state's Republican Party contested primary election split had allowed a liberal Bay Area Democrat, Alan Cranston, to win Kuchel's

Senate seat in an off-year election that Republicans otherwise dominated. This was the same election that gave Ronald Reagan the California governorship in his first bid for office as a Goldwater-style conservative.

Marin's Board of Supervisors was becoming greener as well, though some of the newer board members who were more environmentally sensitive, such as Peter Behr, were still Republicans. Cranston's fellow California senator, the affable Republican and former Hollywood entertainer George Murphy, grew alarmed about his own 1970 reelection prospects. Clem Miller's successor in the First Congressional District was Don Clausen, a gregarious Republican official from the timberlands north of Marin around Eureka. Clausen found it increasingly difficult to find common ground with both his moderate GOP base in Marin and his conservative, small-government timber industry allies up the north coast.

Clausen and Murphy were also drawn into the fight over a proposed new Redwood National Park 100 miles north of Point Reyes. Boundaries for this proposed new park were being negotiated in what proved to be a long and difficult fight. Members of Congress from the other forty-nine states grew resentful of California for receiving so much federal money for national parks. This was a serious problem for the California delegation, as Point Reyes was already over budget. The resulting Redwood National Park initially looked like a wickedly gerrymandered congressional district map. The public lands footprint for the first ten years of the park's existence looked like a string bean, connecting existing state parks while incorporating a sliver along Redwood Creek, where some old-growth redwoods survived, even as continued timber cuts on private land on slopes above threatened the watershed.[3] The fight over the Northern California park for redwoods stirred up anti-California sentiment in Congress just when Point Reyes needed an infusion of more federal support.

The California delegation and NPS officials were also drawn into a major national battle over a Sierra Nevada park occurring at the same time as the Point Reyes and Redwood Park battles. When the US Forest Service solicited bids in the early 1950s to create a ski resort at Mineral King, a remote valley just south of Sequoia National Park, the venture initially won the support of the Sierra Club. It promised greater auto access to a new ski resort for an industry that was booming after World War II—but the new road would have to be cut through a national park. The winning bid was from none other than Walt Disney, and the wildly successful creator of films and entertainment resorts was determined to see Mineral King become a model ski resort. After reversing its initial backing, the Sierra Club team in San Francisco went all in against the Mineral King development—in contrast to the second Point Reyes fight, where the club had given only limited support. The Mineral King fight became a major test for the Sierra Club, as it led conservationists towards a strategy that embraced litigation as a central element in campaigns to secure and protect parklands. While the club lost its battle in appeals court, it ultimately won the war to block the Mineral King development. The Supreme Court decision in *Sierra Club vs. Morton* established a key precedent for standing that has been used by environmental organizations ever since. The battle also left one of the Mineral King development's prominent political backers, Senator George Murphy, eager to find a cause where he could be on the side of environmental activists, an opportunity he soon realized with Point Reyes.

The Mineral King and Redwood National Park challenges arose at the same time that a nascent environmental movement was pushing Congress for action. This pressure led to the adoption of a series of congressional initiatives in the latter half of the 1960s that began to reshape resource management and the protection of American lands, air, and water. With beginnings of local activism around such issues as saving San Francisco Bay from pollution, the filling of the vast Sacramento River delta, and the severe air pollution afflicting many cities—especially Los Angeles, San Jose, and Denver—grassroots citizen groups fighting separate battles began to coalesce across the nation and grew into a wider movement.

The swift post–World War II expansion of suburban home construction nationwide along with the soaring use of automobiles had an increasingly apparent cost to the environment. *Time* magazine featured the polluted Cuyahoga River fire in Cleveland on its influential weekly cover. Then, on the eve of Nixon's presidency, the traumatic year of 1968 ended with the *Apollo 8* circumnavigation of the moon. The astronauts' somber Bible reading of Genesis on Christmas Eve was accompanied by live television pictures of the blue planet rising from the far side of the moon. One photo by William Anders, *Earthrise*, had as great an impact as any photo or environmental publication in history; it altered the consciousness of many citizens. The accumulated impact of these events greatly changed voter attitudes. Pollsters tracked these sweeping changes. Politicians took note.

One of the key events that changed the political dynamics for the PRNS was a major oil spill offshore from Santa Barbara on January 28, 1969. The blowout came just eight days after Nixon was sworn in as president and continued into February, coating 40 miles of beaches on the Pacific coast from Goleta to Ventura. Oil as thick as half a foot spread over 800 square miles of the fragile coastline, much of it in surfing spots celebrated in popular Beach Boys songs. It was the largest oil spill in American history—later surpassed by the *Exxon Valdez* disaster in Alaska and the Deepwater Horizon blowout in the Gulf of Mexico.

The Santa Barbara disaster forced the new Nixon administration to pivot swiftly; officials even considered a freeze on all offshore drilling. This was, as David Vogel notes, "a highly dramatic and photogenic environmental disaster."[4] Images of this disaster, which released the equivalent of two million barrels of oil along the Southern California coastline, dominated the national evening news broadcasts for days.

The politics of the time had changed. Parks and conservation issues had been reframed. The civil rights and anti–Vietnam War protests had proved effective in changing policy in part because they were highly visual actions. With rivers afire and oil spills leading the television news, environmental activists similarly benefited from using visual images to lobby for new policies.

Eleventh-Hour Victory for Marincello Opponents

Even as parts of a shoreline park were cobbled together amidst the dairy and beef cattle ranches at Point Reyes, by the late 1960s, it appeared that the fight to protect the slopes of Mount Tamalpais just south of the park and the Golden Gate headlands at Marincello had been lost. What happened next, however, became part of the legend activists would cite when discussing Point Reyes and San Francisco. It was celebrated most recently in such films as the award-winning documentary *Rebels with a Cause*, which suggested that it was always grassroots activism that protected Marin's open spaces.

Like the Mineral King critics, the opponents of Marincello went to the courts. An informal alliance formed among three local attorneys, Douglas Ferguson, Bob Praetzel, and Marty Rosen, who had hiked the trails at Fort Cronkhite. They decided to sue. They based their suit not on the content of the well-received, professionally packaged Marincello proposal but on the allegation of a process foul committed by Thomas Frouge, his Gulf Oil backers, and county staff who had rezoned the land and hastily permitted the project. Bay Area newspapers had endorsed the Marincello construction plan—even the local alternative weekly, the *Pacific Sun*, had given it grudging editorial support. Marincello builders had already broken ground. In their haste to press ahead, however, they had failed to observe the letter of the law. Public notification requirements were cut short during the licensing proceedings, allowing only six days for public review instead of the statutorily required ten.

Despite their suit, the project opponents could not obtain a temporary injunction to freeze construction. Permitting delays were attributable to an internal struggle between the developer and his financiers at Gulf Oil, who sought to diversify their holdings with real estate investments. These disputes, combined with the growing chorus of environmental activists and inflation, made the projected costs rise. Then suddenly, in January 1969, Frouge died. The three local attorneys pressing the case against Marincello subsequently secured court relief; the California Supreme Court ruled that the Gulf investors would have to start their public hearing process back at square one with a new environmental impact statement. A consumer boycott was also started by Marincello opponents: hundreds of Gulf Oil credit cards were cut in half and mailed to the head of Gulf's consumer sales.

When Huey Johnson, then the western director of The Nature Conservancy, once again visited Gulf headquarters to explore a resolution, he was met by a furious head of consumer sales seated behind a pile of the destroyed Gulf credit cards. After blistering Johnson, the Gulf executive informed him that the company strategy was still to wait out the environmental lawyers. Gulf's attorneys believed that their opponents would soon run out of money.

Johnson recalled that he then laughed and told the Marincello financiers, "You don't understand two things. One, they [the environmental lawyers] are working for free. And, two, they are *crazy.*"[5]

Fearing the prospect of lengthy delays, bad press, and a consumer boycott and missing their key partner, Frouge, the Gulf leaders agreed that day to abandon the project and sold the land to Johnson, who made a personal $100 down payment on the spot. With $6.5 million from The Nature Conservancy, the valley and hilltops were preserved and restored. These are today a part of the Marin Headlands in the Golden Gate National Recreation Area. Combined with Muir Woods and the Mount Tamalpais watershed and state park, these public lands now stretch all the way north to buffer the border of the PRNS and south to the Presidio and Ocean Beach in San Francisco.

Point Reyes Becomes a White House Political Opportunity

From the moment he took the oath of office in January 1969, Richard Nixon faced a series of significant challenges. Having won the White House with only 43 percent of the popular vote, he faced strong Democratic majorities in the House and Senate. With inflation picking up steam and the Vietnam War dividing the country even more than the culture wars and the San Francisco–based "hippie" awakening, the midterm elections looming in 1970 became a major concern for Nixon and his senior staffers, H. R. Haldeman and John Ehrlichman. Nixon delegated most day-to-day refereeing of cabinet-level issues on domestic policy to his longtime campaign aide Ehrlichman, a Seattle native who had previously been involved in public lands issue as an attorney.

Tapes and internal memoranda from the Nixon White House, as well as oral history interviews with Nixon advisers, reveal how the Nixon team polled voters on the new "ecology" issue. The president's political advisers were worried about surging support for new environmental protection measures. The front-runner for the Democratic nomination to challenge President Nixon, Senator Edmund Muskie, a Maine Democrat, chaired hearings on the Santa Barbara disaster and the need for more environmental protection measures. These proceedings drew a large turnout of journalists and national television coverage.

The environment had simply not been a topic in the bitter 1968 presidential campaign. By 1970, however, support for environmental protection was surging, and polls showed growing citizen anxieties about pollution. The widely respected Harris opinion polls of the era showed voter concern about air and water pollution jumping from 28 and 35 percent, respectively, in 1965 to 69 and 74 percent in 1969. Similar results showed a jump in voter concern about pollution as one of "the most important problems facing people here in the United States," leaping from 1 percent in early 1969 to 25 percent just two years later.

The usually staid *Public Opinion Quarterly* summed up the sea change: "A miracle of public opinion has been the unprecedented speed and urgency with which ecological issues have burst into the American consciousness. Alarm about the environment sprang from nowhere to major proportions in a few short years."[6]

The environmental movement was also being celebrated in popular culture during these years, often in songs with San Francisco Bay Area roots.

Table 4.1 National Polling Data on Environmental Issues: Most Important Domestic Problems

Q: Aside from the Vietnam War and foreign affairs, what are some of the most important problems facing people here in the United States?

Problem	May 1969 Survey	May 1971 Survey	Change
Inflation/cost of living/taxes	34%	44%	+10%
Pollution/ecology	1	25	+24
Unemployment	7	24	+17
Drugs/alcohol	3	23	+20
Racial problems	39	22	-17
Poverty/welfare	22	20	-2
Crime/lack of law and order	15	19	+4
Unrest among young people	6	12	+6
Education	5	8	+3
Housing	0	6	+6

Source: Opinion Research Corporation, "Public Opinion on Key Domestic Issues," mimeographed (Princeton, NJ, May 1971), 17. May 1969 and May 1971 polls based on 1,508 and 1,506 interviews, respectively.

Table 4.2 Polls on Environmental Issues: Increase in Public Concern about Pollution, 1965–1970

Q: Compared with other parts of the country, do you think the problem of air/water pollution in your area is very serious or somewhat serious?

Year	Sample Size	Air	Water
1965	2,128	28%	35%
1966	2,033	48%	49%
1967	2,000	53%	52%
1968	2,079	55%	58%
1969	2,168	69%	74%

Source: Hazel Erskine, "The Polls: Pollution and Its Cost," *Public Opinion Quarterly* (Spring 1972): 121 (Opinion Research Corporation).

These included Malvina Reynolds's lyrics (covered memorably by balladeer Pete Seeger) lamenting the ugly housing tracts being built in Daly City ("little boxes on the hillside, and they're all made out of ticky-tacky, and they all look just the same") and Jesse Colin Young's "Ridgetop" paean to Point Reyes and Inverness Ridge.[7]

The Point Reyes cause had faltered over the course of the 1960s. Demand for housing and exponential population growth had driven real estate prices ever higher in Marin County and in nearby San Francisco, Berkeley, and San Jose. With the Los Angeles Basin experiencing similar growth, many of Southern California's suburban beach towns, from Manhattan Beach to Ventura, welcomed freeways and high-rises. Much of the San Francisco Bay shoreline south down the freeways through Silicon Valley to San Jose was filled in with high-tech industry facilities and housing tracts during these years.

The few parcels the NPS managed to buy at Point Reyes in the 1960s had limited shoreline access. Early visitors to the park had to pass through gated private properties to reach some beaches. The resulting checkerboard mix of public and private land froze wilderness access and park development.[8] With the Point Reyes seashore's three champions dead and the nation's economy in a slump amidst the Vietnam War escalation, completing the job at Point Reyes was a low priority for federal officials more than 2,500 miles to the east. As Clem Miller's former aide Bill Duddleson later recalled, by 1969, "the Point Reyes National Seashore seemed doomed to diminishment or destruction" with only ten scattered parcels secured by the NPS in seven years and only one-third of the 84 miles of peninsula coastline in public hands.[9]

The NPS began internally exploring new ideas for funding the park. These staff proposals did not enter the public domain until a crucial May 13, 1969, House hearing. The Department of the Interior staff under the Nixon administration and NPS director George Hartzog proposed selling 10,000 acres of prime Point Reyes parklands to housing developers. Hartzog was being criticized harshly by both park supporters and ranch families. His stated goal was to raise funds sufficient to create a small shoreline set-aside.[10]

Nixon was lobbied on the proposal by members of Congress, his California supporters, and his own domestic policy counsel. Soon, he chose a different course. By January 1970, Nixon was issuing a very pro-environment State of the Union message and warning his staff to protect him on

the environmental issues being pushed by his likely Democratic challeng-
ers. His very unusual "Special Message to the Congress on Environmental Quality" was out of character with many of his actions. It read like a
speechwriter's clarion call for environmental activism:

> At the turn of the century, our chief environmental concern was to con-
> serve what we had—and out of this concern grew the embattled but always
> determined "conservation" movement. Today, 'conservation' . . . [means]
> we must also restore what we have lost. We must go beyond conserva-
> tion to embrace restoration. . . . This task is ours together. It summons
> our energy, our ingenuity and our conscience in a cause as fundamental
> as life itself.[11]

The Nixon message was either a commitment to a new activist agenda
or a calculated political marriage of convenience. Given the subsequent
Nixon administration slowdown on the environmental agenda, historian
Samuel Hays concludes that "the strategy reflected political expediency
rather than agreement with environmental objectives. . . . (The message)
was remarkable, in view of the president's lack of sympathy for the environmental movement."[12]

White House documents make clear that Nixon was eager to court California votes and hoped to boost Republican prospects in the wake of the
Santa Barbara oil spill and mounting concerns about plans for Earth Day,
the first national push by environmental activists. Nixon staffers feared
that environmental activists would make common cause with civil rights
and anti–Vietnam War protesters, both decidedly anti-Nixon grassroots
movements. The Santa Barbara spill had left a profound impression on
the public, a development swiftly captured by pollsters. White House aide
John Whitaker recalled the near "hysteria" after Santa Barbara, saying that
the oil spill disaster proved to be "the match that lit a conflagration."[13]
Santa Barbara "was the seminal event that environmentalists had sought,"
historian J. Brooks Flippen argues. "It shocked Americans, placing environmental protection on the front burner in a way that it had never been
before, turning a concerned public into an activist one."[14]

This was the backdrop against which the Point Reyes funding issues
were presented to the White House. Oral histories and documentary evidence from the sustained citizen lobbying that have recently been recovered reveal in remarkable detail just how Nixon was deftly lobbied on the

Point Reyes issue by Bay Area Republican leaders. They were led in public by Marin County Supervisor Peter Behr.[15] The campaign was initiated, financed, and orchestrated, however, by Clem Miller's widow, Katy Miller Johnson.

A key role was also played by Republican Congressman Pete McCloskey and by his close friend and onetime Stanford Law School classmate John Ehrlichman, who was President Nixon's domestic policy counsel. Ehrlichman later became notorious for his deep involvement in a series of crimes that came to be called "Watergate." Prior to his White House tenure, Ehrlichman had worked as a Seattle attorney and helped block a major development on islands in the Puget Sound. In the White House, Ehrlichman worked with one of his deputies, a geologist named John Whitaker, to press President Nixon to get out in front on some of the environmental issues Democrats were seizing.

Nixon's rhetorical flourishes notwithstanding, the president was by no means a natural environmental activist, Ehrlichman explained years later in an interview with former Miller aide Duddleson.[16] Therefore, the case for Point Reyes funding that Ehrlichman put to the president was made on overtly political grounds. The president was essentially told, *Do this to help your own reelection prospects. Do this to help reelect Senator George Murphy. Do this to avoid getting run over on environmental issues by Democrats.*

Richard Nixon: An Environmental Champion?

In the end, one man made the most crucial move late in the final act to save the park at Point Reyes: Richard Nixon. Scores of activists, lawyers, local officials, and politicians and a half-dozen presidents were involved in the complex battle to create the largest national seashore on either coast. Each group of stakeholders maneuvered over the course of a half century to secure and defend this achievement.

In the simplest retelling, Richard Nixon, distrusted by many of the Northern California liberals who championed a park at Point Reyes, was the person who carried the day. There is deep irony in this fact. Nixon's core supporters, going back to his first run for statewide office in 1950, were conservative Orange County developers, home builders, bankers, and men who built freeways. It was President Nixon, however, who committed the federal funds to buy the lands necessary to complete the park at Point Reyes. It was Nixon who signed H.R. 3786, making the Interior Department Authorization Act of 1970 public law.[17]

The key question is *why? Why did Nixon sign the Point Reyes funding measure? What changed the political dynamics to convince him this was both in the national interest and a move that would advance his political agenda as Republican Party leader?* Richard Nixon in 1969 was facing a Congress in which there were few domestic policy initiatives he could fund without not just acquiescence but also active support from the powerful Democratic committee chairmen he dealt with.[18] The legislator who most forcefully pressed Ehrlichman at the White House for Point Reyes funding, moderate Bay Area Republican McCloskey, just months later broke with the president over Vietnam. McCloskey even ran against Nixon in the 1972 presidential primaries, shattering the friendship between McCloskey and Ehrlichman. They did not speak for many months, but their enduring friendship was patched up after McCloskey visited Ehrlichman in federal prison, where the latter served eighteen months for his part in the Watergate cover-up.[19] The ironic twists here warrant closer analysis.

Park Service Misstep Revives Point Reyes

Nixon was moving in the first days of his presidency to cut the federal budget across the board. This was Nixon's promised bid to shrink the size of the government, as other conservative presidential candidates of the era, including Eisenhower, Arizona senator Barry Goldwater, and California governor Ronald Reagan, had pledged to do.

Point Reyes park advocates were told by Nixon administration officials in 1969 that even if Congress appropriated the funds needed for land purchases—and even if this appropriation was signed into law by the president—the Nixon administration would "impound" or simply refuse to spend them. Such was the new Nixon administration's fervor for cutting the budget. With the price of the remaining private lands at Point Reyes escalating rapidly, finishing the park purchases became like trying to bail water in a leaking boat. The NPS leaders in Washington began to cast about for other options to secure enough land to create a viable park. The subsequent May 1969 proposal by the new NPS leadership under Director George Hartzog proved to be so contentious that it made finding a resolution to the ongoing controversy about Point Reyes in the political interests of all parties.

Building upon the still controversial 1962 deal and NPS staff options quietly developed in the intervening years, the May 1969 NPS proposal was for another hybrid compromise.[20] If citizens wanted a national seashore,

Hartzog informed Congress, the NPS would have to sell much of the park-lands already acquired to raise the money needed to buy beach access. As reported in a May 1969 front-page story in the *San Francisco Chronicle*, many of the Point Reyes lands under NPS control would be sold and subdivided under the new proposal that Hartzog unveiled in his Capitol Hill testimony. Adding to members' alarm were actions at Lake Ranch, the "crown jewel" of the future park, where May testimony revealed that bulldozers were daily carving roads for subdivisions, and at Tomales Point, where Duddleson learned of extensive engineering studies that were being completed for a large number of private homes.

The NPS initiative suggested that $10 million could be raised by re-selling some of the lands that the federal government had only recently bought, including the timber-rich lands on Inverness Ridge, for subdivision and the construction of tract homes. The NPS was already under fire from both camps. It had alienated the ranchers, while developers and land speculators had driven up the ranchers' tax bills. It had also disappointed environmentalists by pushing ambitious "mixed use" recreation and development plans for Point Reyes while failing to purchase key tracts of land. Thus, the Hartzog proposal was advanced by Washington officials as a solution that was both financially practical and consonant with the new Nixon administration's small government budget–cutting moves. It was utterly tone-deaf, however, in terms of its politics.

Katy Miller Johnson Enlists Allies to Revive Point Reyes

In the audience that day in May 1969 were Bill Duddleson and Miller's widow, Katy Johnson. They were joined by Katy's second husband, Stuart H. Johnson, Jr., who had previously served as counsel to a senior member of the House Judiciary Committee. They had been tipped off about the Hartzog plan by Congressman Jeffery Cohelan, a Berkeley Democrat. The full implications of the Hartzog proposal were unclear at first. During a lunch break in the congressional hearing, however, the Johnsons approached the witness table and looked closely at some of the charts the NPS had prepared.

When they saw what the new NPS proposal entailed—including subdivision of Inverness Ridge, a golf course, a polo field, and power-boat anchorages in Drakes Estero—they were stunned. Once they heard more details, "we just couldn't believe it. We came back to our house and we were just staggered," Katy Johnson recalled. "I was in a cold rage."[21]

Katy had not stayed involved in Point Reyes land use issues since 1962. Days after Clem Miller's funeral in October 1962, the Kennedy White House had sent a senior congressional relations official to her home in a vain attempt to recruit her to run for her late husband's seat in Congress. (A majority of voters had ultimately selected the name of the deceased Clem Miller on that November 1962 ballot, four weeks after his death, before Clausen won a special election early in 1963 after the seat was declared vacant.) Katy Miller declined the invitation to run for Congress but instead began working part-time for the House of Representatives with the Democratic Study Group. By 1969, Katy had remarried, given birth to a sixth daughter with her second husband, Stuart Johnson, in Washington, and often also had three stepchildren in residence. The May hearing with Hartzog shocked her into action.

In short order, from their Washington base, she and Duddleson began to reassemble the coalition of Point Reyes supporters from 1962. Their first act was to draft and for Katy to send to every Democratic and Republican member of the House Interior Committee a copy of her letter to California congressman Harold "Bizz" Johnson (no relation) assailing the proposal. (See Key Documents in the Appendix.) She then called on top Interior Committee members one by one, seeking their help in blocking the NPS proposal and securing more funding. She began to push to the national press the story of the NPS proposing to sell public parklands while enlisting environmental leaders from around the country. These supporters included former secretary of the interior Stewart Udall, who joined the board of the new Save Our Seashore at Katy's invitation, while declaring, "It is a scandal of historic proportions if the American people, at the peak of our affluence, admit that we lack the foresight and wherewithal to preserve this great Seashore intact for ourselves and future generations."[22]

The resulting controversy was heard deep inside the Nixon White House, where opposition to the Hartzog proposal was soon pushed by Congressman McCloskey. As Ehrlichman later recalled, "When I read this business about the National Park Service advocating subdividing a portion of the allocated areas to condos and golf courses, I probably flipped. It's preposterous. . . . McCloskey had done an effective job framing the issues in a way that appealed to me."[23]

The alarms over Hartzog's proposal prompted Katy Johnson to lead an all-out effort to try to block the NPS plan. As she recalled in the *Rebels* documentary, her status as Miller's widow gave her a considerable entrée with the California congressional delegation and even with the irascible Aspinall. Here, a great irony is once again revealed by the record—the key victory to save the national seashore at Point Reyes and to secure funding after more than a decade of effort was won in large measure because of the near universal opposition to this unwelcome NPS proposal. A further irony was that while the California seashore park proposal had been embraced by John Kennedy, it was his longtime foe, Richard Nixon, who would take the crucial follow-up step necessary to secure the park at Point Reyes. In fact, neither man prioritized environmental issues in his House and Senate careers, and there is no evidence that either ever set foot on the Point Reyes Peninsula.

Katy Johnson visited House members in person with a plea to save the park Clem Miller had fought to create. Her letter explaining the stakes to Congressman Bizz Johnson became a key lobbying tool.[24] Her persistence with Aspinall paid off. The chairman and his staff director soon saw the utility of having her lead the charge to persuade Nixon to agree to more funds for Point Reyes—which they hoped to use as leverage to gain the release of LWCF accounts impounded by the Nixon administration. Katy Johnson charmed Aspinall; soon he and his staff were converted to supporting her cause. They began to coach her on how to sway their fellow committee members, all the while increasing Aspinall's leverage with the White House.[25] She was especially forceful in arguing that selling parklands would set a terrible precedent for all national parks and seashores: "Dearly as Clem loved Point Reyes, and would have been horrified at commercial subdivisions inside its boundaries, he would have felt far greater dismay at the possible establishment of a far reaching disastrous precedent."[26]

Her argument resonated with Congressman McCloskey. He knew the Point Reyes lands well from family hikes and sought to put his party back on the right side of this California environmental issue. McCloskey badgered his longtime friend Ehrlichman during their daily commute from Virginia in a White House limousine, a critical yet nearly invisible grasstops lobbying campaign.

McCloskey wrote formally to Ehrlichman on September 16, 1969. The letter reads very much as if the two men had rehearsed the language and drafted it together for the president's eyes: the congressman was trying to help Ehrlichman come up with the most effective issue framing with which to sell the president the idea that the White House should intervene to increase the land acquisition funds for Point Reyes. (See Key Documents in the Appendix.)

"Dear John, Here's a starter," McCloskey opened his letter before continuing, "The only man who can save Point Reyes National Seashore is the President. He is running out of time." He then laid out the political benefits they had rehearsed in the carpool: "If you move this time, why not let a few of us know in advance so that we can properly give the President credit where it is due. It might also help to have the President announce that due to the efforts of George Murphy, Don Clausen and [San Francisco Republican] Bill Mailliard, he is taking this step to preserve a priceless national heritage."[27]

Ehrlichman used McCloskey's letter and mounting evidence of Behr's campaign appearing in national newspapers to set in motion a key White House meeting with the president. There would then be a scheduled follow-up White House press conference featuring the beleaguered Senator George Murphy of California as an environmental champion.

Aspinall and Saylor Roll Nixon

This decisive meeting took place in the Oval Office on November 18, 1969. The purpose was made clear in talking points prepared for the president: to convince Congress to increase the authorized ceiling for funding Point Reyes fourfold and then allow Senator Murphy to announce it so that he could take credit back home in California. Aspinall was belatedly added to the all-GOP meeting when White House aides made it clear that his support was the sine qua non of their gambit to help Murphy.

The two key people in the Oval Office meeting when the deal was cut to fund Point Reyes land acquisition were Richard Nixon and Wayne Aspinall. The White House excluded its own ranking member of Aspinall's committee, Republican John Saylor, who was an opponent of such "pork-barrel" politics. Saylor represented a suburban Pennsylvania district and had often done combat with the more pro-development Aspinall; Saylor consistently decried political patronage playing a role in park policy.

Neither Nixon nor Aspinall was a committed environmental leader. Both had earned the enmity of environmental lobbyists and the Sierra Club. In fact, when the US House Committee on the Judiciary voted later to impeach Nixon, key votes against him came from the same type of moderate Republican members who had implored him to fund Point Reyes.

The paths of the president and Chairman Aspinall crossed that day because presidential counselor Ehrlichman and Ehrlichman's aide John Whitaker had convinced Nixon that more funds for Point Reyes might help save the flagging reelection campaign of Senator Murphy and would boost Nixon's reelection prospects in Northern California. As chair of the House Interior Committee in a solidly Democratic Ninety-Second Congress, Aspinall was not inclined to help California Republicans. He had not had a complete change of heart simply due to the importuning of Clem Miller's widow. Yet Aspinall felt the growing strength of environmental advocates; he sensed growing support for more parks and sought to ensure that he would have the resources as chairman of the Interior Committee to play the lead role in granting his colleagues' wishes for funding. His price of doing business with Nixon was insistence that the LWCF accounts used throughout the nation to purchase parklands be fully replenished by Nixon administration officials. This would enable Aspinall to wield his power to help dozens of House colleagues whose park funding requests were languishing under Nixon's budget-cutting moves.

Support for using public funds for parkland acquisition had not previously been considered good politics. By 1969, however, members of the House and Senate in both parties were lining up for federal dollars to expand more than three dozen parks in home districts and states around the nation. These parks, it was clear to most by 1969, both added to quality of life and increased local home values while bringing more jobs to accommodate visitors. Polls from that era show that in 1965, less than one-third of Americans made environmental protection a significant issue; the figure had increased to more than 70 percent by 1970.[28]

Nixon warned his staff to make sure they protected him on the emerging environmental issue. Yet, in private conversations, Nixon disparaged the cause, bluntly telling Ehrlichman that "if we have to pick between smoke and jobs, we are for jobs."[29] He belittled "rich backpackers who could afford to take weeks off work" for wilderness treks and told a Ford Motor Company executive that "environmentalists are a group of people that aren't really one damn bit interested in safety or clean air."[30]

The paper trail inside the Nixon Library is unmistakable regarding the fact that Aspinall and Saylor gamed the president for weeks after the November 1969 Oval Office tête-à-tête. As Ehrlichman recalled, the Colorado Democrat and Pennsylvania Republican "upped the ante," just as Chairman Aspinall had done in his Wilderness Act negotiations with President

Johnson. Aspinall and Saylor refused to push for a full House vote on the bill quadrupling Point Reyes funds, H.R. 3786, until the administration made a broad public commitment to request another $75 million to fully fund the LWCF in 1970 and then increase it to $300 million in 1971. To obtain this result, Nixon's staff had to come up with not just the $7.5 million for the next year's land acquisition efforts at Point Reyes but also funds for nearly a dozen other projects Aspinall and Saylor backed, from Padre Island, Texas, to Lake Mead, Nevada. Aspinall had already extracted a pledge that the Nixon administration would earmark another $7.5 million for the PRNS in 1971 and then $38.5 million in the next year to finish the job of purchasing the lands of the Point Reyes Peninsula as prices continued to escalate.[31]

Once the deal to fund more purchases at Point Reyes was announced at the White House on November 18, however, Saylor came out foursquare *against* it. It would take several more weeks of lobbying and a public commitment by the Nixon administration to fund all the backlogged LWCF projects before it would move forward. Katy Johnson recalls lobbying Saylor in the interim:

> Saylor was totally outraged and said that it [the initial Aspinall-Nixon deal to fund only Point Reyes] was a blatantly political move . . . I don't know if he said it was to help a sitting senator's re-election campaign, but he knew it was. It was completely unfair to the rest of the country . . . it was absurd to single out one park in order to save one Senate seat of the same party as the president. I mean, it was ridiculous . . . his [Saylor's] intransigence eventually brought him exactly what he wanted.[32]

Saylor declared that the Point Reyes deal "isn't going anywhere . . . a press conference takes place at the White House and suddenly we find the principles which over the years have guided funding of the national park program thrown out the window in . . . a strictly political procedure."[33]

Saylor reversed himself only after the Nixon administration agreed to completely restore all impounded LWCF accounts and to spur parkland and national seashore acquisition efforts nationwide. The White House allowed Saylor to make the announcement that the Nixon administration was reversing its position and would now support an increase in LWCF resources. On February 10, 1970, the veteran Republican pulled from his jacket pocket in the well of the House chamber a letter from the Nixon administration affirming this commitment.[34] This was a classic example of both pork-barrel politics and sound policy. The additional funds, Department of the Interior and Bureau of the Budget leaders in the Nixon administration grudgingly wrote, would come from unobligated LWCF balances from prior years and revenues from user fees suddenly now made available to support parklands purchases across the country.

Saylor announced the new administration proposal on the House floor on February 10. Then, *the very same day*, the House adopted the long-stalled measure increasing authorized spending for Point Reyes to $57 million. The bill sponsors back in 1962 had known the $14 million cap placed on federal costs for Cape Cod and Point Reyes was insufficient. Bryan McCarthy, the West Marin ranchers' lobbyist, had told a US Senate hearing in 1961 that the park would costs taxpayers more than $50 million. Here was confirmation that the original price was 400 percent greater than the amount advertised by sponsors, including the NPS. The 1970 measure also carried a House amendment lobbied for by Katy Miller Johnson that became an important national policy precedent; the Ryan amendment explicitly prohibited implementation of NPS director Hartzog's plan to sell some of the Point Reyes land, a plan that had proved so incendiary that it had helped rally park supporters.[35]

President Nixon signed the bill in an April 2, 1970, White House ceremony. He pointedly snubbed the California Democrats in the House and Senate who had authored the measure and pressed the Point Reyes cause, none of whom were invited to the photo opportunity. The setup was complete when the White House political aides had Murphy at the president's elbow right before the president signed. Nixon paused dramatically, pen in hand, and turned to Senator Murphy to ask, "This bill is *yours?*"

The ever-gracious Murphy then fumbled his line, instead gushing his reply: "It's really *yours*, Mr. President."

Hours later, California's junior senator, the Democrat Alan Cranston, issued a puckish press statement: "I am delighted the President has signed my Point Reyes bill and the people of California and the nation will thus be able to enjoy this unique national asset. That I was not invited to the White House for the formal signing is of no consequence to me."[36]

A battle that had begun in 1959 and advanced with the first 1962 compromise victory led by Clem Miller was thus won again in 1970. The second victory was won because of the tenacious leadership of Katy Miller Johnson, securing a quadrupling of federal funds for land purchases at

Point Reyes and a renewal of the LWCF to pay for acquisitions and improvements for dozens of national parks and seashores across the country, thereby ensuring a remarkable legacy for the determined public policy battle over Point Reyes.

Clem and Katy Miller and family, 1962. Courtesy of the Miller family.

CHAPTER FIVE

Who Saved Point Reyes?

To understand why the Point Reyes National Seashore (PRNS) survived and grew so remarkably, one must dissect the case. Public policy case studies can be analyzed effectively by looking at "the four P's": process, precedent, personality, and party. The same analytic constructs used in civics classrooms can be applied here to help see how policy advocates secured victory at Point Reyes.

When effective lawmakers and lobbyists begin to map out a new issue campaign, they invariably work early in the effort to define success. Some imagine a future date, when the team is celebrating "victory." Then they ask, *What exactly is it that we won?* Speculate how that result might be achieved, and you have the outlines of an issue campaign blueprint, a key benefit of reimagining a public policy challenge by working the problem backward.

In the Point Reyes battle, success rested on four strong pillars. First was the locking up of the land through Marin County prohibitions on subdivision and further commercial development. Second was the provision of federal funds to purchase title to the lands in question. Third was the removal by the National Park Service (NPS) of existing commercial infrastructure that compromised natural habitats and was incompatible with park purposes. Fourth was the expansion of park boundaries to build buffers around the most fragile ecosystems. The importance of this last step was influenced by similar challenges at Mineral King and Redwood National Park, where environmental activists insisted from the outset that a park is not secure if its watershed remains subject to commercial exploitation.

The coalition of environmental groups in the Point Reyes campaign enjoyed extraordinary successes, and the reasons the victory proved to be significant for activists were that it helped create key precedents and secured a steady funding stream for years of parkland purchases nationwide. To use a football metaphor, it served as a pulling guard. The blocking by Point Reyes champions opened such a big hole in the defensive line that it helped many subsequent park initiatives to break through and score funding. After the 1962 act created the PRNS, dozens of environmental protection measures poured forth over the course of the decade. After the 1969 Santa Barbara oil spill and the release of park acquisition funds achieved by Point Reyes champions in 1970, a steady funding stream for national parks and seashores was finally secured with bipartisan support. For the next decade, even conservative Republicans, such as Richard Nixon and his successor, Gerald R. Ford, deemed the political costs of opposing such environmental initiatives prohibitive.

The 1962 law had authorized a park in theory, but at that point, the US government controlled only 123 acres at Point Reyes. The park grew in subsequent decades to encompass not only the 28,000 acres in the original proposal but more than 71,000 acres. Then it was joined in 1972 to an even more ambitious plan, the Golden Gate National Recreation Area (GGNRA). The GGNRA today covers *another* 82,000 acres on adjacent lands (including state parks on Mt. Tamalpais) and in thirty-seven noncontiguous sites to the south and east.[1]

Process Shapes Outcomes: Mapping the Stakeholders

The lawmaking process that shaped this history began and ended with Congress using its Article I power of the purse, its constitutional authority to initiate and approve most annual federal spending. President Nixon had tacked to the political right on most issues in the divided nation since his January 1969 inauguration; he was zealously cutting the federal budget during his first months in office. He was already in hot water with Congress by November 1969 for refusing to spend funds that Congress had appropriated. This "impoundment" was cited as an issue in the subsequent House move to impeach Nixon. The Nixon administration's illegal impoundment of funds led to a raft of legislation, including the creation of the Congressional Budget Office, so that Congress could match the quantitative skills of the newly reorganized executive branch Office of Management and Budget, an empowered version of the old Bureau of the Budget.

Process was key because the Point Reyes advocates needed to win over *five* separate groups of stakeholders between 1959 and 1970, each of whom had an effective veto. The first set of stakeholders consisted of local officials. If the Marin County Board of Supervisors had been dead set against a park, it likely would have been able to block it. Indeed, when Miller first approached Chairman Aspinall in 1959 about moving his park proposal, Aspinall declined, noting that the Marin Board of Supervisors had already voted 4–1 against the plan for a federal park. The state of California could also have blocked the park. After he took office, Governor Reagan could have stalled the federal effort to buy all the Point Reyes Peninsula lands, called for another study, or pledged to use some state funds to create a small park along a shoreline strip that would have allowed construction at Drake's Bay Estates and housing blocs atop Inverness Ridge to proceed.

Miller was able to create some divisions among the landholders with the 1962 compromise to create a pastoral zone to permit inholdings of ranchers that could later be bought by the NPS. By the second round, the fight for full funding in 1969, some of the leading ranchers in the area, the Mendozas and Boyd Stewart, *supported* a revised national seashore plan that would require all the ranchers to sell but would allow them to retain leases within the park so long as they kept the lands in agricultural use and did not damage the parklands through incompatible practices. Ranchers were thus able to pocket the large sale prices, avoid the soaring property taxes as the land values skyrocketed, and then work their lands under multiyear leases while enjoying cut-rate grazing-fee deals with the NPS. Boyd Stewart's 1970 Senate testimony acknowledged this change of heart after noting the initial opposition:

> The ranchers in Marin County, whom I have been asked to represent here by the Board of Supervisors, feel as everyone else does that this park ought to be completed. . . . Those of us who have loved this land for years and seen it through its many moods and seasons, recognize that this treasure can no longer remain ours to enjoy exclusively. Its beauty and grandeur must be shared with all Americans. . . . We recognize that dairying with the necessity of confining large herds of cattle tightly into pastures is not compatible with public ownership of the land.[2]

The latter observation was an acknowledgment that critics of continued ranching would subsequently cite in litigation that stretched over a half century.

The second key group of stakeholders in the process was the executive branch bureaucracy, specifically the NPS. The archival record here reveals inconvenient facts, crosscurrents that are rather startling. Yes, the idea for a park at Point Reyes had first been floated by the NPS. It was Knight and Wirth's 1935 NPS study that contained the outline of the park idea that was picked up by George Collins when conducting regional planning for the NPS in the late 1950s and then advanced by Congressman Clem Miller and Senator Clair Engle in the legislation they introduced in July 1959.

NPS staffers took seriously, however, the recreation part of their mission. Prior to the adoption of the 1964 Wilderness Act, the NPS was 100 percent committed to making parks more accessible for cars with new roads and freeways. Recreation, not wilderness preservation, was their priority. They produced studies in the early 1960s that proposed shrinking the Point Reyes National Seashore footprint while inviting in substantial commercial developments, including golf courses, freeways, and a powerboat marina in the wetlands. One 1964 NPS study even proposed spending $35 million to develop recreational infrastructure for a park that still had not secured the funds needed to buy the lands involved. This initial NPS plan for recreation at the PRNS was, as historian John Hart notes, to create "a park for cars, cars, and *more* cars" with a four-lane highway to Limantour and a cliff-top parkway down the pristine shoreline to Bolinas with marinas for powerboats and marshes filled in for dune buggies.[3]

The NPS's May 1969 proposal to sell much of the Point Reyes lands to fund a small shoreline strip for the remaining seashore launched the petition drive to "save Point Reyes from bulldozers." The campaign was publicly led by the Nixon campaign's Marin County reelection chairman, Peter Behr, who was preparing to run for a California State Senate seat and eagerly seized the issue. Behr was brilliantly recruited by Clem Miller's widow, Katy Miller Johnson, who flew to California in August 1969 to make the request personally. "I saw that we weren't going to get anywhere without an outpouring of opinion from California," Johnson explained, so she appealed directly to Behr. Together they would rally Bay Area groups led by the Marin Conservation League and other organizations that could extend the reach of grassroots support beyond just a Marin County base.[4] Soon Behr was working the national media as well, arguing that adopting the new NPS plan would lead to "a conservation tragedy."[5]

Behr responded to Katy Johnson's urgent lobbying with a handwritten letter dated August 14, 1969. In this letter, Behr agreed to lead the lightning-quick campaign and detailed his proposed strategy. The document still reads today as a clever and disciplined plan. (See Key Documents in the Appendix.) Behr focused on the delivery of voter petitions to the White House in time to alter the 1970 LWCF budget.[6] Johnson quietly contributed $2,000 of her personal funds to hire a staffer from the Marin Conservation League to coordinate an all-out ninety-day grassroots effort. Soon Save Our Seashore (SOS) folding card tables staffed by volunteers gathering signatures appeared outside grocery stores throughout the San Francisco Bay Area. Yet Johnson's appeals to national conservation leaders initially received pessimistic responses. These included ardent conservationist Lady Bird Johnson's letter of September 9 (after Katy had enlisted LBJ's spouse to lobby the Nixon White House) reporting that "prospects are not good" for more Point Reyes funding from the Nixon administration.[7]

The third key group of stakeholders in the process was leaders in the House of Representatives. President Nixon could issue campaign-season proclamations embracing national parks and seashores, but such White House statements would have no practical effect if Congress did not approve the funding. The Marin County House seat in 1969 was back in Republican hands. Miller's successor, Don Clausen, was a member of a beleaguered House minority caucus, outnumbered in 1969 by a Democratic margin of more than fifty seats. While the authorizing committee chaired by Aspinall had great power—these were in the days before the appropriations subcommittees seized most of the funding power—Aspinall was using the Point Reyes issue to help try to win a bigger fight over funding for parks nationwide.

"He came at the President pretty hard on the problem," Ehrlichman's deputy John Whitaker reported to Budget director Mayo in a November 20 memo about the Oval Office meeting between Nixon and Aspinall. (See Key Documents in the Appendix.) As Whitaker had explicitly warned in a memo to Ehrlichman the previous week, the Democrats were poised "to make political hay out of it." If Nixon vetoed the parks bill, Whitaker wrote Ehrlichman, it would come "at great political expense . . . the political pressure on this one is extremely high. For example, Congressman Don Clausen now has 250,000 petitions [sic] for purchase of the park."[8] Senator Murphy would claim that there were 600,000 signatures. (SOS files indicate that there were, in reality, 423,585 petition signatures as of November 25, 1969.)

Aspinall was aided immeasurably by Congressman McCloskey, who was back-channeling the White House in his daily commutes with Ehrlichman. McCloskey would lecture his friend about the natural beauty of Point Reyes and its fragile ecosystems. The issue was raised to the level of senior Oval Office staff, Ehrlichman conceded, "because Pete McCloskey pounded on me."[9]

Ehrlichman and his wife had helped raise McCloskey's first child in Palo Alto when McCloskey was deployed to the Korean War within weeks of her birth. Their families had grown up together. As Ehrlichman explained in 1991, McCloskey succeeded in convincing him to push President Nixon only when the congressman reframed the pitch to focus on California politics.

The fourth set of stakeholders who proved to be key to the process was in the Senate. Aspinall could not deliver if his Senate colleagues across the table in the inevitable House-Senate conference committee on the interior spending bill did not go along with the deal. Here, the paper trail can be misleading. It is true that the new liberal California senator, Alan Cranston of Palo Alto, was on board. The freshman Democrat Cranston testified before the Senate committee, eloquently advancing the park cause: "This strange and unique triangle of land must be preserved. There's nothing quite like it anywhere on earth. To allow it to be lost through private development would be a crime against nature and a tragic disinheritance for the future of our people."[10]

Support from the openly anti-Nixon Cranston, however, was not decisive. It would normally have been a reason for the Republican White House staff to *oppose* the request. Cranston enlisted Murphy as a cosponsor of his Point Reyes bill, while Behr and McCloskey pushed the embattled Republican senator to write Nixon in support of the Point Reyes park. Also of significance for the White House was the support of the Senate chairman of both the authorizing and appropriating subcommittees with jurisdiction over national parks, Alan Bible of Nevada. Bible remained irked that Congress had been "misled" in 1962 about the real costs of acquiring lands for the PRNS. His support for the 1970 deal came with a caveat: he argued that the commercial ranches should be allowed to remain, a position that would be cited by litigants in years to come: "These cattle people and dairy people have been long in that business, that their dairy should be permitted to continue said business. That's a promise the Federal

Government has made, and I think the Federal Government has to keep that, but also I am very much aware that speculators are moving in, and they are the ones that worry us."[11]

The fifth key stakeholder in the process was Richard Nixon. The president could have vetoed the funds, effectively killing the vision of a peninsula-wide park at Point Reyes. He was eagerly vetoing many bills favored by Democratic chairmen in his first two years in the White House. He relished these opportunities to highlight his fiscal conservatism while gamely battling inflation. Nixon did not fund Point Reyes as a favor to the Democrats and Cranston. Events in California and across the nation made his calculated political move toward more environmentally sympathetic positions a more attractive political proposition.

President Nixon supported funding Point Reyes to advance his own self-interest in trying to hold on to the Murphy Senate seat for the GOP. Nixon saw a chance to secure a Republican Senate majority in the 1970 election. Prospects would diminish greatly if the GOP lost the second California Senate seat. Nixon also hoped to improve his standing in California as he prepared to run for reelection in 1972. When interviewed decades later by Bill Duddleson, Ehrlichman candidly commented, "Richard Nixon was not your natural birds, bees, and bunnies man. He had to be persuaded that this was not only right to do, but that it had a payoff down the line in political terms. Point Reyes helped to demonstrate that, in unmistakable terms, to him . . . he never saw this many people mobilized in quite this way."[12]

"Was it the *first* such demonstration?" Duddleson asked.

"It was the *best,*" Ehrlichman responded, underscoring the degree to which the Point Reyes precedent changed political dynamics.[13]

White House staff had warned Nixon that the Democrats were poised to "hijack" the parks issue. Leaving nothing to chance, Ehrlichman's deputy Whitaker prepared talking points for Senator Murphy to share in the White House press briefing room after the November 1969 Oval Office meeting, noting that "Point Reyes is unique in the sense that there are higher pressures for real estate development and escalating values here than in any place in the country."[14] (See Key Documents in the Appendix.)

Early in his presidency, Nixon had delegated most of the day-to-day environmental portfolio to Ehrlichman. The two met each working day to go over a list of action items. In one such November 1969 discussion,

President Nixon passed back a story from that morning's *Wall Street Journal* that he had marked up; it commended his administration for moving forward on the Point Reyes bill. The article noted that the GOP was losing moderate suburban voters who were said to be animated by the health and quality-of-life issues raised by the new environmental awareness. Such reporting clearly reinforced the president's view that helping Murphy on Point Reyes funding was good politics.[15] Indeed, there was remarkably extensive national press coverage of the fight over Point Reyes throughout the fall of 1969.

Katy Miller Johnson and her team in Washington succeeded in pitching the story of Point Reyes for feature stories in the *New York Times, Washington Post, Los Angeles Times*, and other top national newspapers. The narrative they presented fit right into the context of the times and the new environmental awakening. The Point Reyes story was also covered extensively in the San Francisco Bay Area; a detailed article by Harold Gilliam titled "The Crisis at Point Reyes" was featured in the Sunday edition of the *San Francisco Chronicle* of October 12, 1969, and the *Pacific Sun* published fifty thousand copies of a special edition on the SOS campaign that was thick with letters and testimonials from local voters and elected officials of both major political parties appealing to Washington leaders.[16] Katy Johnson's success in generating national press altered the political calculus in Washington in a manner strikingly similar to contemporaneous battles over parklands at Mineral King and Redwood National Park.

Nixon was a shrewd political veteran. He was especially adept at seizing and framing issues at the top of the public mind, such as his 1968 campaign as the "new Nixon" who was committed to "law and order" at a time of rising violence and cultural upheaval. Nixon was pivoting systematically to shore up his political bases, looking to the 1970 midterm elections. Acceding to the request from Aspinall and Saylor could be a two-for-one. It would reinforce Nixon's image as a leader sensitive to environmental concerns, especially along the nation's vulnerable coastlines. It would also help shore up the Murphy Senate seat in Nixon's home state. While California's affable Ronald Reagan was completing his first term as a popular conservative governor, by 1970, Nixon could see that in many respects, California was turning toward the Democrats. The 1958 election's blue wave altering the state's congressional delegation had not been an aberration.

Nixon was lobbied on the Point Reyes issue by Republican loyalist Behr. Ehrlichman described the significance of Behr's role colorfully:

He (Behr) personified the local effort, the citizen effort and really sold me on the bona fides of this. I'd take McCloskey's word for it, but McCloskey is kind of a wild hare. . . . Behr sort of cemented the respectability of this for all the people he represented, by the way he presented himself. He came to [Nixon's Southern California Western White House retreat] San Clemente. . . . It wasn't just a bunch of Washington people cutting a deal.[17]

Therefore, Nixon backed the deal with Aspinall and Saylor and then took credit for the initiative with Murphy. "Ehrlichman had some interest in the seashore," Katy Johnson recalled. "It was obvious that the president really had none and was only interested in the politics of the situation."[18] Behr revealed years later that the grassroots campaign he had led in late 1969 was specifically designed to persuade Nixon to act in the hope of saving Murphy's seat: "The whole campaign was directed at George Murphy. It was apparent that he needed Northern California support in his upcoming election and he could be a key player to influence President Nixon. But this was not divulged at the time."[19] Behr continued, "Murphy had in fact gone in to see the president and said 'Dick, I've *got* to have it.' Murphy was the one who won the president over."[20]

Irony abounds here; George Murphy was not actually a White House favorite. Nixon told his staff that he thought the senator was a lightweight entertainer from Hollywood who lacked the gravitas of his predecessors. Nixon officials tried repeatedly at the president's request to entice Murphy to step down and clear the way for Health, Education, and Welfare secretary Robert Finch to seek the California Senate seat.[21] In reality, Senator Murphy had very limited involvement in the congressional consideration of the Point Reyes issues beyond the letter he sent to Nixon and his appearance in the White House briefing room in November 1969. Senator Murphy was nevertheless set up by all parties—local and federal, House and Senate, White House and Congress—to receive the largest share of the public credit.

Nixon had been briefed on the Point Reyes funding issue by Whitaker and Ehrlichman. Decades later, Duddleson disputed how strong an advocate Ehrlichman had remained, recounting the fact that McCloskey and Ehrlichman had a brutal shouting match about Vietnam policy in the car pool one morning in the autumn of 1969 and severed contact for years thereafter. Yet the record is clear that Nixon was briefed extensively by his top domestic policy staffers and chose to move. The Nixon Presidential

Library has memos written by Ehrlichman pushing the Point Reyes cause weeks *after* the big October 1969 anti–Vietnam War march in Washington that sparked McCloskey's split with the White House. For example, on November 25, 1969, Ehrlichman wrote Whitaker a memo titled, in all capital letters, "POINT REYES NATIONAL PARK CONDEMNATION" to direct the Department of Justice and the US attorney general to aggressively back the PRNS effort via additional resources for federal land condemnation to gain title to the remaining peninsula lands still held by ranchers. (Condemnation is a complex legal process by which the government can, in limited instances, seize private land needed for certain public purposes.)

"I would like to see these cases vigorously prosecuted and thoroughly prepared," Ehrlichman instructed Whitaker, "and I think our best chance of getting that result is with a skilled condemnation attorney on our side."[22] Duddleson explained why: "Nixon had not run well in the Bay Area. . . . Nixon was aware of the Point Reyes situation and eventually he also became aware that it had great voter appeal. Nixon was very, very good at knowing which way the wind was blowing . . . a new wind was blowing. It was called the environmental movement, and Nixon was not on board. . . . Aspinall had him."[23]

None of the five key stakeholders exercised a veto. The local politics had been changed by years of grassroots activism, beginning with the Mount Tamalpais hiking clubs and continuing with the Save San Francisco Bay Association activists in Berkeley. This platform was built upon in the 1960s by champions of a national preserve at Point Reyes. Its crowning moment locally came in November 1969 with the SOS campaign initiated and launched by Katy Johnson and the grassroots petition drive designed by Peter Behr.[24] Behr mastered the process part of the puzzle by adapting some of the lessons learned by the Save San Francisco Bay and Bay Conservation and Development Commission campaigns led by local activists. Both Johnson and Behr grasped the fact that this seemingly local land use controversy at Point Reyes could be resolved favorably only in the Oval Office.

The legislative dance that began in 1959 when Engle and Miller introduced their modest measure for a small shoreline recreation area did not produce victory until the funding for Point Reyes land acquisition came through in the 1970 Department of the Interior funding bill. It took eleven years for Congress to save Point Reyes. Each step of the way, the road to success was smoothed when park champions focused on the process of how to successfully run the legislative gauntlet. Process shapes outcomes; this is a truism for effective policy advocates, although environmental activists sometimes need to relearn the lesson in the face of the danger that they will try to reinvent the wheel as each new challenge arises.

Precedent: The Uses of History by Policy Advocates

Effective policy aides on Capitol Hill are eager to learn a key fact: *What happened the last time?* In other words, they need to learn who won and lost—and why—the previous time Congress wrestled with their issue. Most public laws in the United States are built upon the foundation of all that came before. They are highly derivative, incremental, and cumulative.[25] The same is true of much good jurisprudence. Many American laws are like ancient cities in the Jordan Valley. Dig into the *tel*—literally the hilltop created by the accumulated detritus of previous civilizations that inhabited the spot—and you will be able to design a more solid foundation, You can improve the odds for success as you run the long legislative gauntlet created by our constitutional system. *Who won last time? Who lost?* These are key questions that inform strategy for legislative advocates. Like bad lawyers, if they know only their own case and cannot understand their opponent's brief, well, they really don't know their own case.

In the late 1950s, PRNS advocates had little information or experience to build upon. These were wildly pro-development years. Returning World War II and Korean War veterans and their families needed housing, roads, schools, and infrastructure. Parklands and wilderness were not major issues for voters, politicians, or the authors of local newspaper editorials, the latter still being major shapers of opinion in the pre-Internet age.

An argument can be made by cynics that the hearing process and legislative dance for Point Reyes were all for show. The deal, after all, was cut in the Oval Office. *What did grassroots lobbying have to do with a White House negotiation behind closed doors?* Legislative effectiveness, some practitioners argue, is more about power than about process. Yet, as this case shows, the legislative process had to play out. The hearing record and the precedent set by a bill creating the Cape Cod National Seashore proved to be another sine qua non for success at Point Reyes. Parallel sets of efforts—grassroots and grasstops lobbying, legislative action, and executive branch deal-making—were mutually reinforcing. One was unlikely to produce success without the others. There was sufficient support in Congress to move the Point Reyes bill in 1962 and to secure the funds to create the park in 1970 because of the grassroots pressures orchestrated by Congressman

Clem Miller and, seven years after his death, the grasstops effort led by Katy Miller Johnson.

Personality: How Character Shapes Options

Richard Nixon was a brilliant politician, at least until he lost his moral compass in the feverish effort to contain leaks about the Vietnam War, efforts that led him to spy on both his political opponents and his own National Security Council staffers. Before his career in politics, Nixon was known as an exceptionally strong poker player. During his navy years, he would regularly win in dominating fashion over his shipmates.[26]

Starting as freshmen together in the new Congress in 1947, Nixon and Kennedy grew to respect each other. They worked together in Congress in the late 1940s as champions of the controversial Marshall Plan to aid European allies after World War II. Both men were veterans who supported vigorous international engagement. Each had been elected to Congress in 1946, but Nixon felt that Kennedy and his Ivy League friends got the choice invitations to Georgetown parties and editorial board discussions. After their neck-and-neck contest for the White House in 1960, Nixon decided not to challenge the election results despite the widespread suspicion of fraud in ballot counting in Chicago's Democratic Cook County. Nixon continued to have a chip on his shoulder about all things Kennedy, as his White House tapes and studies of the Nixon presidency reveal in detail. Understanding how to move Nixon on the Point Reyes issue was thus another key to success.

The mix of political personalities that together shaped the fight for Point Reyes remains ironic. As with the moon landing, at Point Reyes, Nixon was finishing a job that Kennedy had started. Peter Behr understood this dynamic; it is one reason that he had all the petitions addressed directly to the man in the Oval Office, not to Aspinall, the Senate committee chairman Bible, or Wirth at the NPS. Behr and Katy Johnson also proved adept at generating national publicity in the effort to sway Nixon. Behr even arranged to be photographed inside a bank vault for a feature story in the *San Francisco Chronicle* while melodramatically posing with thousands of signed Point Reyes petitions secured before they were flown to Washington.

Behr and McCloskey were Republican Party officials who shared the same pro-business and pro-environment perspective. It was a perspective also held by John Ehrlichman. When weighing the impact of personality on the political process, the serendipitous connection McCloskey had with Ehrlichman also proved crucial. As the *Wall Street Journal* analysis framed the environmental issue, this was an issue that Republican Party leaders needed to get right.

Ehrlichman recalled in his 1991 interview with Duddleson that Nixon's advisers were polling extensively on how the environmental issue played with key constituencies. He recalled that these polls began in earnest in the days after the Santa Barbara oil spill. This was three years before Nixon's 1972 reelection race. The urgency of the polls underscores the acute sensitivity of Nixon and his White House staff to growing environmental concerns among voters. Here is how his top domestic aide remembered their site visit: "We went out and looked at it and walked around and got our feet dirty. And we did some polling in California about offshore leasing, and that was very influential as it turned out. So, you know, this was a constant process of educating the decision maker [Nixon]."[27]

As the fight over park funds escalated with the case of Point Reyes, Ehrlichman continued to ply Nixon with polling data on environment issues: "We did some polling about jobs versus clean air, jobs versus clean water, jobs versus parks, all that kind of stuff. And it didn't turn out completely favorable on the environmental cause, but there was enough in there that we could show him that we weren't blazing a lonely trail, that there was a respectable body of public opinion that supported these things."[28] Ehrlichman noted that in the case of the GGNRA and a counterpart New York Gateway National Recreation Area, they saw to it that President Nixon "went out and dedicated them *personally* . . . the whole public recreation lands issue was cemented as respectable and viable and politically useful and all those good things. And I'm convinced that Point Reyes played a part in it."[29]

The personalities of key decisionmakers also shaped the early years of the fight for Point Reyes. When Miller won what was becoming a swing congressional district in 1958, he became a freshman with much in common with Senator Kennedy. Miller had also been educated in Massachusetts— at Williams College—and was also joined in Washington by a striking, politically aware spouse, Katy, who had attended Bryn Mawr College in Pennsylvania. Miller, like Kennedy, was a relatively young aspiring author, a man of letters who would publish his first book about public service days before he died.

Miller was widely popular among his colleagues on both sides of the political aisle, a legislator who invariably greeted colleagues with a smile. When the House held a special session in the frenetic preelection days after Miller's death, more than three dozen members personally eulogized Miller while his widow sat in the House family gallery accompanied by several of their daughters.[30] This goodwill proved crucial when Katy became the lead lobbyist for the Point Reyes funding in 1969.

Katy Miller Johnson proved to be the indispensable contributor to the second Point Reyes campaign. Her ability to call upon Chairman Aspinall and colleagues, invoking her late husband's memory to cajole, plead, and charm the chairman for funding support, proved critical to success. She had joined the cause in May 1969 with extremely limited formal education— one year of college—and enormous responsibility as the surviving parent of young daughters. Yet she was an early feminist who had read the works of Betty Friedan and was deeply committed to her mission. Recruited after her husband's death to the House Democratic Study Group (DSG) as a junior staff assistant—"a very girl Friday" was how Katy described the job—she was soon schooled in the give-and-take of the legislative process, as she recalled: "They'd have these fabulous steering committee meetings on civil rights and all these different issues and you'd watch the give and take, and when to hold the ground and when to compromise. Some of the greatest brains, like (Missouri Democrat) Dick Bolling, were just mesmerizing to watch operate . . . it was an incredible education."[31]

Johnson put the lessons she learned at the DSG to brilliant use throughout the 1969–1970 second campaign for Point Reyes. She led the letter-writing effort that stirred the House and Senate. She led the press campaign that garnered substantial national coverage while providing third-party validation of the political significance of the battle. She recruited the ambitious local GOP leader Behr, who then got to Senator Murphy. She was even a key witness before the penultimate Senate hearing, where she deftly negotiated live and on the public record with Chairman Alan Bible, eliciting commitments that the Senate bill would retain the Ryan amendment adopted by the House Interior Committee to bar any proposed NPS land sales at Point Reyes.

She claimed in letters to elected leaders that she was "a rank amateur," but the record suggests otherwise. After witnessing her strong performance in the decisive February 1970 hearing, Senator Bible concluded with a great compliment: "It's always nice to hear from you, Mrs. Johnson. You speak on the project with as much authority as any living person, because you have lived it for so many years, so I am grateful you appeared before us this morning."[32] As Ann Lage, the editor of the University of California oral history interviews about the second, 1969–1970 Point Reyes campaign, states clearly on page one of the collection, "Katy Miller Johnson, widow of Clem Miller, was the catalyst for the campaign to save Point Reyes."[33]

Clem Miller's Senate counterpart, Clair Engle, was also a Northern Californian whose personality mattered in the Point Reyes outcome. Engle was popular with his colleagues; he saw the shifting political landscape and was eager to move on the park issue early in his first term. He co-led the effort through 1962, although as a freshman senator representing the entire state, he was not able to focus on the complex process with the same single-minded purpose that Miller displayed. After Engle was crippled by a stroke in 1964, his last official act on June 19 was to be carried into the Senate chamber on a stretcher to help break the filibuster on the landmark civil rights bill and support final action. Brain surgery had rendered him speechless, but he was able to raise his thumb to signal "aye" on the cloture motion, effectively securing final passage.[34] This courageous act, more than his involvement with Point Reyes, became Senator Engle's best-known legacy.

Who among these many personalities should be credited with saving Point Reyes? Success has many parents, first and foremost among them Katy and Clem Miller. Others deserve much credit too. In making a list, one is reminded of sportswriters' poetry in recording a fabled baseball trio famous for turning double plays: "from Tinker to Evers to Chance." If we were to diagram the "save Point Reyes" play in shorthand, it would go something like this: "Wirth solicited Mellon to aid Collins to persuade Miller to enlist Duddleson to recruit Eastman and Gustafson to flip the Marin Board of Supervisors to convince Aspinall and Bible to pass the bill Miller convinced Udall to tell Kennedy he needed as a companion to Cape Cod."

More needed to be done in round two: "Katy Miller Johnson was alerted by Cohelan to recruit Behr to create SOS to lobby Cranston and Bizz Johnson to pressure Murphy while Duddleson was pushing McCloskey to press Ehrlichman to convince Nixon to sign the Point Reyes bill, but first he needed to placate Aspinall and Saylor, who freed hundreds of millions of dollars for parks nationwide as part of the Point Reyes bargain."

Party Politics Transformed
The fourth key element of any successful after-action analysis—and of any advance planning exercise by policy activists—is often examined first.

Where do the political parties stand? What exactly were the dynamics of party politics, and how did they change? In the Point Reyes case study, it was shifting party alignments that made possible sustainable success for the PRNS.

Grassroots activism on environmental issues in the 1960s, initially centered in the San Francisco Bay Area, helped change the national political calculus. Where most environmental causes had previously been led by Republicans, in the 1960s, Democrats were addressing these voter concerns with some effect, especially where suburban sprawl was fast carving up open lands. As John Lawrence, longtime aide to Bay Area congressman George Miller and then to Speaker Nancy Pelosi, notes, after the events of 1969 and 1970, "the Bay Area had become ground zero for the environmental movement. It was virtually impossible to be elected to office without a good environmental record."[35] Traditional Republican constituencies, such as the hotel operators and home builders along the Southern California coastline, could see that protecting the environment was good for business and good for land values, while offshore oil spills were both an environmental and an economic disaster. President Nixon began receiving more memos from his staff warning that the Democrats were going to "run over" the Republicans not just on Point Reyes and the specific issue of parkland acquisition but also on environmental issues more broadly. Nixon pivoted in response.

President Nixon would not have visited the San Francisco Bay Area in 1970 to trumpet his environmental credentials if he had not already witnessed the change in political dynamics after the Santa Barbara disaster and the extensive national press coverage of the fight over funds for Point Reyes. Nixon would not have traveled to California again during his 1972 reelection campaign to announce in person his support of the legislation to create the GGNRA were it not for the transformed politics of California and the nation. Nixon would not have felt the political urgency of moving forward on environmental issues had it not been for the California parks fights initiated in the San Francisco Bay Area and then accelerated by the first nationwide Earth Day.

Five different groups of stakeholders had the power to slow or block the park. None exercised a veto. Activists supporting the PRNS and other new seashores around the country helped launch a wave. This wave merged with those of the Save the San Francisco Bay Association, the campaign to protect the Marin Headlands at Marincello, and the new GGNRA campaign to begin converting the army holdings in San Francisco and Marin into public parks. These local forces helped energize a larger national wave that first crested in April 1970 with the celebration of Earth Day, an event that *The Green Years* opens with, observing, "It was the largest organized demonstration in human history."[36] After the Point Reyes success brought the doubling of funds for park acquisition nationwide, creation of the GGNRA—vastly expanding the footprint of national parks in the region—was suddenly the next big domino primed to fall. A tipping point had been reached.

In the first year of the new decade of the 1970s, environmental activists were on a roll. Their cause enjoyed extraordinary momentum. What happened next for most of the participants in this drama, and for the national environmental protection movement, was wholly unexpected.

President Nixon at Golden Gate, October 1972. Courtesy of the Golden Gate National Recreation Area.

CHAPTER SIX

What Happened Next: Point Reyes and Environmental Politics

President Richard Nixon campaigned in San Francisco just weeks before the November 1972 election. It was an unusual visit by the Southern California native to a liberal bastion. He flew by helicopter to Crissy Field at the base of the army Presidio, landing a few hundred yards from the Golden Gate Bridge's south tower, some 20 miles south of Point Reyes. The presidential party then boarded a special ferryboat for a press conference out in the bay and a victory lap on environmental issues with invited Republican leaders. It was Nixon's seventh statewide campaign in California since his 1950 Senate primary. This campaign trip to San Francisco would prove to be his last.

Nixon's 1972 reelection appeal to conservative Democrats and moderate Republicans benefited from his adept maneuvering on environmental issues. Democrats in Congress kept increasing pressures for environmental legislation after the Santa Barbara oil disaster. Nixon was signing these Democratic Party–initiated measures—and then taking credit for the proposals pushed upon him—precisely as McCloskey, Whitaker, and Ehrlichman advised in the case of Point Reyes. As activist Amy Meyer notes, "The Point Reyes campaign had taught Nixon a lesson: park support did indeed have a political payoff."[1] As Miller aide Bill Duddleson explained, with the hundreds of thousands of petition signatures and the widespread national media coverage stimulated by Katy Miller Johnson, in the Point Reyes fight, there was "the undeniable evidence of citizen concern on a massive scale."[2]

Such evidence was now apparent to all: the first Earth Day on April 22, 1970, became a far larger event than anyone expected. A group of college students launched the idea, which was then nurtured by Wisconsin Democrat Gaylord Nelson in the US Senate. The students joined to promote a national Earth Day modeled after the Arbor Day of nineteenth-century vintage. Its lead student promoter was Denis Hayes, formerly student body president at Stanford University in Pete McCloskey's congressional district. Hayes secured support from Senator Nelson and some modest grant funding. It was Duddleson—then with the Conservation Foundation—who suggested adding a House Republican for bipartisan balance with Nelson. Pete McCloskey from Palo Alto was the man Duddleson proposed.[3]

"Earth Day worked because of the spontaneous response at the grassroots," Nelson later reflected. "We had neither the time nor the resources to organize 20 million demonstrators and the thousands of local schools and communities that participated."[4] Nelson had jump-started the effort with the widely publicized joint introduction with Senator Alan Cranston on January 19, 1970, of a proposed constitutional amendment establishing that "every person has the inalienable right to a decent environment. The United States and every state shall guarantee this right."[5]

Some Nixon White House officials were alarmed by Earth Day, viewing it as an offshoot of the antiwar movement. This occurred in the same season as President Nixon's incursion into Cambodia and the nationwide antiwar protests that led to the shootings of unarmed demonstrators at Kent State University. Many of the activists involved in civil rights and anti–Vietnam War issues had similarly progressive positions on the environment. The FBI closely monitored the Earth Day event and its leaders.

Nixon was later accused by his critics of paranoia, yet there was reason for his concern. Both the civil rights movement and the anti–Vietnam War movement in the 1960s demonstrated the power of grassroots citizen action. Both movements had dramatically altered US policies. There was logic behind the assumption that if supporters of these two efforts made common cause with moderates on environmental issues, the Nixon White House would have limited options for resisting environmental protection initiatives. Nevertheless, the White House studiously ignored Earth Day. Nixon officials failed even to issue the standard proclamation. Key White House environmental policy aide John Whitaker claimed that such a move would have been considered "grandstanding," yet Whitaker later conceded ruefully that the White House inaction stood in silent contrast to Nixon declarations in the same week of National Archery Week and National Boating Week.[6]

As Denis Hayes wrapped up matters after the extraordinary Earth Day event, his team reached a decision in early May 1970 that would have a profound and enduring impact on environmental politics. They decided to repurpose the remaining $30,000 they had raised for Earth Day to be spent on political advertisements targeting twelve legislators who the activists believed had blocked environmental legislation in Congress. There was an announcement to that effect in the afternoon *Washington Star*. David Brower was about to get his revenge: Wayne Aspinall was targeted as one of the Dirty Dozen.

When breaking news of this unusual anti-incumbent campaign first ran on the news wire services, McCloskey was accosted in the cloakroom off the House floor by a furious colleague shouting, "Look at this! Look at this! McCloskey, this is *your* work!"[7] Four of the twelve members targeted by Hayes and his supporters lost their reelection bids that year. When the new Congress convened in January 1971, McCloskey later reported, attitudes had suddenly changed.

"Everybody says, 'I'm an environmentalist,'" McCloskey explained. "If you look at what happened in those next two, four years, we passed all the great environmental legislation—clean water, clear air, endangered species, estuaries . . . [those were the] golden years of environmental legislation."[8]

White House aides were closely monitoring the moves of the man they expected would emerge as Nixon's toughest challenger in 1972, Senate environmental policy leader Ed Muskie, a Maine Democrat. "Nixon always had Muskie on his mind," Undersecretary of the Interior Russell Train recalled.[9]

White House polling on the issue underscored the urgent political need to act on new environmental policy initiatives. Nixon knew he had won his home state of California in the close 1960 contest with Kennedy by only 1 percent. The "citizen concern on a massive scale" that Duddleson identified thus pressed Nixon to tack left on environmental politics through November 1972. Ehrlichman's deputy, John Whitaker, had explicitly warned on November 13, 1969, that President Nixon could get "run over by Congress on this one [Point Reyes funding] and we should therefore pick up the political credit and do so in the most dramatic way possible."[10] Whitaker stressed the urgency of the issue by suggesting that if funds were not forthcoming for projects such as Point Reyes, the president should consider a dramatic step such as canceling an Apollo moon mission in order to reallocate funds for parks.[11]

After Point Reyes

Nixon was on the defensive on environmental policy issues for much of his first term. He was not aligned with the environmental movement on many policy matters. He faced strong Democratic Party opposition because of his support for the Alaska oil pipeline and his go-slow approach to banning DDT. He was a champion of small government and private property rights. When he vetoed the first version of the Clean Water Act, his veto message cited concern over expenses and delays in issuance of construction permits while deploring alleged over-regulation by the federal government. Despite earlier concessions and the soaring rhetoric in his special Environmental Message to Congress in February 1970, Nixon was already shifting away from acceptance of a progressive environmental agenda late in his first term.

By October 1972, President Nixon was running the table on most policy issues on the national agenda, with a united Republican Party behind him. The country had become increasingly divided over cultural issues and the Vietnam War, which had spread to Cambodia and Laos. Nixon, however, was at the top of his political game. He had exploited the deep divisions within the Democratic Party. As the wind ruffled his hair during the San Francisco photo opportunity beneath the Golden Gate Bridge, he was grinning, seemingly at ease amidst a liberal Bay Area populace, confident that he was on his way to a landslide in the November election.

Nixon had in hand the surprising diplomatic breakthrough with communist China. He had negotiated two nuclear arms control agreements with the Soviet Union. In his first term, he also ended the military draft and pressed a drawdown of American troops in Vietnam. His aide Henry Kissinger announced misleadingly just before the election that because of negotiations with North Vietnam, "peace was at hand." Nixon controlled all factions of his united GOP machinery, easily besting McCloskey and a far-right candidate, John Ashbrook, in the New Hampshire primary. Nixon then won all but one of the 1,348 delegates to the 1972 GOP National Convention.

Nixon and his team had bullied, manipulated, and broken laws to gain advantage over the Democrats' candidates. His campaign staff used dirty tricks to weaken rivals, and the president's team began using government employees and illegal means to attack opponents. The Democratic campaign led by George McGovern suffered several self-inflicted wounds, especially at the Democrats' own chaotic nominating convention. Nixon, who had won only 43 percent of the popular vote in 1968, was going to win—and win big—in 1972. His national popular vote margin the week following his California campaign swing proved to be 60 percent to George McGovern's 37 percent.

Nixon's 1972 visit to San Francisco led with the announcement of his support for legislation to create the new Golden Gate National Recreation Area (GGNRA). Old news footage shows him working the reception line, where he assured grassroots leaders Amy Meyer and Huey Johnson that he was with them on the new Golden Gate park proposal.[12] The chief GGNRA bill sponsor, the Democrat Phil Burton, was not invited, just as the partisan Nixon staff had declined to invite Democrats such as Alan Cranston and Katy Miller Johnson to the White House bill-signing ceremony for the Point Reyes funds in April 1970.

Nixon was touching base with the same moderate Bay Area Republicans who he hoped would be able to limit his losses among Northern California's increasingly liberal electorate: lifelong Republicans such as Peter Behr and Sierra Club President Edgar Wayburn. Nixon also finessed a potentially tricky issue: the occupation of the former prison island of Alcatraz in the center of San Francisco Bay by a group of Native American activists. Rather than move to eject the protesters, the White House decided to wait them out. Nixon administration officials then pivoted effectively to include the Alcatraz site in the new GGNRA, effectively washing their hands of the problem.

The San Francisco visit featured the push for a new park led at the grassroots level by Meyer and Wayburn. Congressman Burton had pressed Wayburn for a complete wish list of what to include in the new GGNRA. It was Wayburn of the Sierra Club who thus added to the GGNRA proposal all the Olema Valley that he deemed essential to protect Point Reyes from freeways and housing developments.

Phil Burton was by no means an outdoorsman. He was a tough, union-backed city politician and a master of legislative effectiveness.[13] Burton slipped far-sighted language into the GGNRA measure providing that if the Department of Defense ever determined that the heart of the Presidio was excess land, those lands would be conveyed automatically to the Department of the Interior for park purposes.[14] It would be nearly two decades before this sleeper provision was activated; realizing this ambitious goal would become the principal task for the Burtons' ultimate House successor, a local Democratic activist named Nancy Pelosi.

Nixon's visit to San Francisco to trumpet his support for a new national park in the Bay Area was a direct consequence of the Point Reyes battle and the Save San Francisco Bay work by Kerr, Gulick, and McLaughlin. Support for parks had become a winning issue. The suburban sprawl expanding into the countryside threatened the quality of life for swing voters.

The magnitude of the challenge facing planners trying to expand home-ownership opportunities in Marin County and the rest of the Bay Area was not unique to the Northern California region. Data from Southern California demonstrates the nature of the pressures on Point Reyes land. Consider for the purposes of illustration how a similar challenge was addressed in Nixon's home territory of Orange County. This county south of downtown Los Angeles had grown dramatically during World War II and then grew more than three times in one decade, from its 1950 population of 220,000 to more than 700,000 by 1960. Some 2,500 different Orange County housing tracts were developed in the intervening ten years amidst the disappearing inland citrus groves and along the shoreline from Huntington Beach to Newport to accommodate the influx of new residents.[15]

Marin County had faced similar pressures, but its voters had taken a different tack, prioritizing open space over any new housing developments. Indeed, the expansion of Los Angeles suburbs and plowing under of orchards throughout the Southland was a distinct motivation for Bay Area leaders to embrace conservation over yet another suburban housing subdivision. As Mullen notes, "In trying to control the growth around metropolitan areas, Bay Area conservation groups looked to suburban Los Angeles as the foil, the example of what not to do."[16] Indeed, the antipathy that Bay Area natives have felt for decades towards rivals in Los Angeles extended beyond the many major league sports battles between the Giants and the Dodgers or the 49ers and the Rams, rival teams representing the northern and southern parts of the state. Northern California political candidates since the 1960s often gained favor by promising not to allow suburban sprawl to consume the landscape the way it had in many towns in the greater Los Angeles area, from Long Beach to Santa Monica, from the Inland Empire to Pasadena and Ventura. Historian Dewey Livingston explains that fear of becoming like Los Angeles or Long Island motivated Point Reyes champions:

Point Reyes was a great success because of a unique combination of time and place. People needed parks they could drive to. With the Marin County Board of Supervisors then still enthralled with massive subdivisions, when ideas came up to protect the Point Reyes Peninsula, people throughout the Bay Area backed them—they saw what had happened in L.A. and the South Bay and they wanted to prevent it from happening here.[17]

Changing the Politics of Parks

The full federal funding in 1970 of the National Park Service (NPS) land acquisition essential for the Point Reyes National Seashore (PRNS) was a major victory for park advocates and their grassroots allies. The ranchers also felt that most of their interests were protected. The key determinant was economic for many: those ranchers who had opposed the national seashore proposal in 1962 could no longer afford the escalating real estate taxes as the value of their lands soared. Their acceptance of tenant status was driven by the need to embrace new economic realities rather than the conversion of all the ranch owners to the preservation cause. The deal enabled them to bank sale proceeds yet remain on the same lands for decades, where they would enjoy cut-rate grazing concessions and taxpayer-funded property maintenance. Even the land speculators made out well; the value of their holdings increased annually with the park's growth. The Marin County tax base benefited from the flow of visitors to Point Reyes, which would eventually reach a total of more than two million per year as the number of national seashore visitors continued to grow (see Table 6.1).

What happened next, however, is what makes it unmistakably clear that the Point Reyes struggle was a tipping point worthy of study by political scientists. From the inflection point in 1970, when Aspinall and Saylor exploited Nixon's desire to help Murphy, Congress secured a quadrupling in funding for Point Reyes and restoration of the Land and Water Conservation Fund (LWCF) at $200 million in 1971. It also won a more than 50 percent increase in 1972 LWCF spending to $327 million. When Katy Miller Johnson was asked in 1990, shortly before she succumbed to cancer, to explain these moves, the exchange with University of California interviewer Anne Lage ably captured the implications:

LAGE: It seems that . . . Aspinall really used the Point Reyes controversy to get a lot more than you ever dreamed of.

JOHNSON: Exactly. Both he and Saylor used Point Reyes to open up the pot [of LWCF dollars] for the rest of the country. That was the way it all played out . . . I think he [Aspinall] may at some point along the line have realized that we could be a good vehicle.[18]

Table 6.1 Annual National Park and Seashore Visits, 1916–2021

Year	Total NPS Visits	Factors
1916	327,000	First year of NPS
1920	1,022,000	Increase in auto trips
1930	3,039,000	Beginning of Depression
1940	16,020,000	Eve of World War II
1950	32,706,000	Post–World War II boom begins
1960	71,586,000	Suburban growth accelerates
1970	168,135,000	500 percent increase in visits in twenty years
1980	220,463,000	Steady annual growth
1990	255,582,000	Three million more per year still
2000	285,891,000	Steady rate of growth continues
2010	281,304,000	Growth plateaus amidst recession
2019	327,000,000	Prepandemic peak in visits
2020	237,000,000	Pandemic closures reduce visit totals
2021	297,115,000	Two-thirds of pandemic losses return

After these events, even a budget-cutting GOP conservative such as Nixon was pouring large amounts of taxpayers' dollars into parkland acquisition. This was a sea change in the politics of the public lands and parks issues, a far cry from Speaker Joe Cannon's pledge that the federal government would not "pay a cent for scenery." In subsequent years, the breakthrough Point Reyes proponents achieved to open up the LWCF would yield exponential growth and striking returns (see Table 6.2).

The face of environmental politics in the United States had changed by 1972. The electoral lineup of environmental champions would change with it. Within just a few years, the environment was an issue on which Democrats, not Republicans, were out front. It remained that way for more than half a century. When the pendulum of American politics swung back, partially in response to the overzealous moves of legislators, it would produce a strong reaction.

With Muskie and McGovern defeated and the November 1972 election behind him, President Nixon swiftly marginalized his administration's three top environmental policymakers. Nixon's rhetoric and his actions reversed positions, and he flip-flopped on many environmental issues in his second term. On December 31, 1972, he took the first step, firing career civil servant Hartzog from his NPS post and replacing him with Ronald H. Walker, a political aide who served as a campaign advance man and had no professional background in park management.[19]

The backlash of national Republican leaders against environmental

Table 6.2 Land and Water Conservation Fund Spending, 1965–2020

Fiscal Year	Annual Spending (millions)	Comments
1965	$ 16	First year of LWCF
1971	$357	After PRNS deal
1978	$805	"Park-barrel" bill
1986	$168	Reagan-era cuts
1998	$969	Clinton-era peak
2010	$450	New baseline
2020	$435	Annual average

Source: Compiled from Congressional Research Service, Land and Water Conservation Fund, June 19, 2020, based on Department of the Interior annual reports to Congress.

protections after 1972 was strong. Over the rest of the decade, most national GOP leaders and local Republican primary voters began to side with industry over environmentalists in regulatory and public lands battles. This shift would prove to be most marked in January 1981, when President-elect Ronald Reagan selected James Watt as his secretary of the interior. Over time, several northern California candidates who had run for office as Republicans—such as Marin County Supervisor Gary Giacomini, Nixon education policy aide Leon Panetta, and even Congressman Pete McCloskey and state senator Peter Behr—switched parties and became Democrats. This sorting out of the political parties was accelerated by divisions over environmental policy. Moderate Republicans who placed a priority on environmental protection in several cases became Democrats. Conservative Democrats who favored deregulation and development, such as Alabama congressman Richard Shelby, moved to become Republicans.

The political center of environmental issues became ever smaller. By the time of Donald J. Trump's presidency, the Republican leader would choose to keep the post of NPS director vacant throughout his entire four-year tenure, preferring from 2017 to 2021 to work with more malleable "acting" NPS directors, as such temporary officials were more easily influenced by the pro-development politicians and former industry lobbyists staffing many senior posts in the Trump administration.[20]

Consequences for Point Reyes Policymakers

Consider the career trajectory of two people involved in the Point Reyes fight, and the inflection point in the early 1970s becomes clearer. Illustrative of the transformation in California wrought in part by the environmental activism of this time is the career of longtime Greenbrae resident

Barbara Boxer. She was a reporter for the Marin County alternative weekly newsmagazine the *Pacific Sun*. After covering such controversies as flood control in the Ross Valley and the troubled park proposal for Point Reyes, Boxer made a long-shot run against Republican incumbent Peter Arrigoni for a position on the Marin County Board of Supervisors. Boxer's first bid was a poorly funded grassroots campaign that relied on environmental activists.

Boxer lost her initial race for supervisor in 1972; however, her campaign impressed local Democratic leaders and donors. She earned party establishment backing for her next run, which she won. Then in 1982, she ran for and won a House of Representatives seat that included the Marin County portion of the district Clem Miller had represented. In 1992, she ran in the Democratic primary for the US Senate, besting establishment favorites Leo McCarthy of San Francisco and Representative Mel Levine of Los Angeles. In the Senate, Boxer rose from her modest origins covering Marin County environmental politics to become chair of the Environment and Public Works Committee, where she authored numerous environmental protection initiatives.

Boxer first won her Senate seat in the same year that former San Francisco mayor Dianne Feinstein ousted incumbent Republican Pete Wilson of San Diego. For three decades after 1992, elections for both California Senate seats were won *only* by Northern California Democrats, demonstrating the power of Bay Area progressives and environmental activists, backed now by Democratic donors from Silicon Valley to Berkeley and Pacific Heights. Northern California Senate candidates prevailed statewide despite the heavy concentration of California voters in Los Angeles and its suburbs stretching east to Ontario and south to San Diego.

Contrast Boxer's rise with the precipitous fall of a fellow Democrat deemed insufficiently supportive of environmental protection. Wayne Aspinall was precisely the type of pork-barreling pro-industry curmudgeon that young, liberal, antiwar Democrats hoped to purge from their ranks. While this major bloodletting did not peak until the first post-Watergate election in November 1974, when the Democrats elected seventy-six first-term members and created a supermajority with an edge of 291–144, Aspinall had become a target of activists.[21]

This was in part a result of Aspinall's holding up the 1964 Wilderness Act and extracting concessions from the Johnson White House that weakened the measure. The Sierra Club's David Brower never forgave him. After the nonpartisan board of the Sierra Club took issue with Brower's fiscal management and edgy politics, he was fired in May 1969. Brower then ignored his parting pledge not to "poach" Sierra Club staff and proceeded to help form two more aggressive environmental advocacy organizations, Friends of the Earth and the League of Conservation Voters (LCV). Part of their modus operandi included scoring and targeting foes of environmental protection and parks funding measures, even if the officials were Democrats.[22]

Aspinall survived his 1970 primary election after producing the long-awaited Public Land Law Review Commission report over which he had won control as an LBJ concession during the Wilderness Act debate. Aspinall's report predictably pushed the return of federal lands to private interests for mining, grazing, and timber cutting. In 1972, however, Aspinall became a featured target of the Dirty Dozen campaign directed by Earth Day cofounder Denis Hayes. With donations and precinct walkers flowing in from California to back Aspinall's Colorado primary opponent, the powerful committee chairman lost his Democratic primary to a political novice. The fact that the Democrats then lost the Aspinall seat to a Republican in the November general election did not upset Brower. The lesson for contemporaries was unmistakably clear: Democrats embraced environmental causes with gusto, while Republicans increasingly championed industry and private landowners. By 1981, when this golden era for environmental lawmaking had run its course, most Republicans would embrace the greater use of federal lands for grazing, logging, and mining, as championed by Ronald Reagan; this script was heavily shaped by Wayne Aspinall.

Did the Point Reyes fight alone cause the sea change in environmental politics? Of course not. This was a fight, however, that changed the thinking of leading Republicans for a few crucial years. The fight mobilized voters of both major parties in a highly effective manner. The record shows that after the Save Our Seashore (SOS) petitions were delivered to the White House in November 1969, the Nixon administration announced *just four days later* that the president would support the quadrupling of federal funding for the completion of Point Reyes land acquisition.[23]

Over the next two annual appropriations cycles, Point Reyes got the additional $38.5 million needed to complete key NPS land purchases at Pierce Point and Lake Ranch and then to fill in holes in the patchwork park. In October 1972, a photo opportunity was once again created just days before an election—the NPS officially "opened" the park at Point Reyes. As Huey

Johnson notes, environmental leaders knew by 1972 that the politics of the issue had shifted dramatically: "We thought, gee whiz, you know? We can affect our own destiny here and create it. And, so, people started running for office who were members of this thinking group, and they got elected, and they've *stayed* elected since then."[24]

Data on California's congressional representation helps illustrate the transformation of the California delegation; the numbers suggest how the growth in concern for environmental issues impacted national politics (see Table 6.3). California was an afterthought in many national campaigns at the dawn of the twentieth century. In 1910, all eight of its House members were Republicans. By 1950, the size of the state's congressional delegation had nearly tripled, and the state's twenty House members were equally divided between Republicans and Democrats. By 2000, the House delegation had more than doubled again to fifty-two California members, with Democrats holding thirty seats. By January 2020, only seven Republicans remained among the fifty-three members of California's House delegation. Californians Pelosi of San Francisco and Republican Kevin McCarthy of Bakersfield were the leaders of their respective House party caucuses. While the California delegation lost a seat after the 2020 census, the presiding officer of the Senate in 2021 was the Bay Area's Kamala Harris, vice president of the United States.

The victory for Point Reyes funding offered mixed results for the political careers of its champions. Taken together, they provide further evidence of the consequences of political choices. Success was not kind to them all.

Pete McCloskey, Ehrlichman's close friend from law school and his carpool pal, lost his ride. McCloskey broke with Nixon in the days just before the Point Reyes deal was cut. The Nixon-ordered invasion of Cambodia in May 1970 was the final straw, and McCloskey did what months earlier would have been unthinkable: he launched a campaign for president, running as a Republican against the popular incumbent Nixon. The Bay Area congressman lost badly and then in 1973 became the first Republican member of Congress to call for Nixon's impeachment in the aftermath of the Saturday Night Massacre, when Nixon fired the Watergate special prosecutor, and both the attorney general and his deputy then resigned. McCloskey played a key role in shaping environmental bills, including the 1972 Marine Mammal Protection Act and the 1973 Endangered Species Act, before running for Senate in 1992, when he lost to Pete Wilson in the primary. In 2007, he left the Republican Party and became a Democrat.

Table 6.3   Trends in California Congressional Delegation Composition

Year	Total	Democrats	Republicans
1910	8	0	8
1940	20	10	10
1970	38	22	16
2000	53	42	11
2020	53	45	8

Source: US Census Bureau and Ballotpedia. Delegation size and partisan balance reflect each year's totals prior to November elections and subsequent reapportionment.

McCloskey never received—or asked for—public credit for his essential role in saving Point Reyes from subdivisions. It is his type of behind-the-scenes assistance that practitioners claim can be missed if scholars rely solely on data analytics to measure legislative effectiveness.

George Murphy lost his Senate reelection bid despite clumsy efforts by Behr and others to suggest that Murphy's role in the Point Reyes campaign had yielded a Sierra Club endorsement. These partisan maneuvers by Behr to help Murphy infuriated SOS allies, but Murphy was defeated by a freshman House member from Southern California, John Tunney. Tunney's first engagement with Point Reyes would be to join fellow California Democrat Alan Cranston in a 1972 push to ban private autos from most of the PRNS. Tunney would become the last Southern California Democrat elected to the Senate until 2022.

David Brower and the Sierra Club parted ways in May 1969, even though the club membership had grown from seven thousand to more than seventy-five thousand under Brower's leadership.[25] Brower's forces at the newly founded Friends of the Earth took pride in taking the battle to their adversaries rather than just advocating for their preferred policies. Brower asserted that "politicians are like weathervanes. Our job is to make the wind blow."[26] A parallel effort, the LCV, was launched in 1970 to educate voters on environmental issues. It succeeded in teaming with the Dirty Dozen effort and defeated the anti-conservation chairman of the Public Works Committee, George Fallon, a Maryland Democrat.[27] From the idea of a single congressional staffer, Marion Edey, the LCV has grown to more than two million members today. It raised more than $23 million for environmental champions in the 2018 election cycle. The Sierra Club and Friends of the Earth were joined in Washington by a new type of environmental lobby, a group designed primarily to litigate. The Natural

Table 6.4 Membership Trends in Selected Environmental NGOs, 1970–2000

Organization	1970	1980	1990	2000
Sierra Club	113,000	182,000	630,000	642,000
National Audubon Society	82,000	400,000	600,000	550,000
Parks Conservation	5,000	32,000	290,000	450,000
Wilderness Society	54,000	45,000	350,000	200,000
The Nature Conservancy	22,000	80,000	511,000	1,029,000
Environmental Defense Fund	11,000	46,000	200,000	300,000
NRDC	N/A	40,000	170,000	400,000

Source: Christopher J. Bosso, "Rethinking the Concept of Membership in Nature Advocacy Organizations," *Policy Studies Journal* 31, no. 3 (2003): 397–411.

Resources Defense Council (NRDC) grew out of the New York state fight over the use of the Hudson River for hydroelectric power. Its tactics mirrored those of the anti-Marincello lawyers and the Sierra Club lawsuits over Mineral King. The addition of veteran litigators saw the NRDC grow from a half-dozen part-time lawyers in 1970 to an annual budget of more than $185 million in 2020 and a staff of 750.[28] The Sierra Club created its own Legal Defense Fund, now called Earth Justice, which reported income of over $111 million in 2019 and employed 137 attorneys in 634 legal battles.

Richard Nixon won his 1972 reelection bid in a forty-nine-state landslide. Until Election Day, he continued to sign a stream of bills authored by Capitol Hill Democrats elevating environmental issues. Nixon had in his first term approved the National Environmental Policy Act (NEPA) measure requiring an Environmental Impact Statement (EIS) before major construction projects. His team was in place when the administrative infrastructure for federal environmental protection laws was created by NEPA, including establishment of the Council on Environmental Quality and the Environmental Protection Agency (EPA), proposals that had been pushed for years by his Senate rivals Muskie of Maine and Henry ("Scoop") Jackson of Washington state. As McCloskey recalled years later, Nixon had long "perceived that he would be opposed by either Jackson or Muskie . . . the two environmental champions. When [President Nixon] was re-elected he didn't need to worry about that. . . . Suddenly he was no help at all [on environmental issues] . . . it was almost as if everything before had been opportunistic."[29]

Nixon continued to delay spending funds for some Democratic initiatives. This led to passage of the Budget Impoundment and Control Act of

1973 and, over Nixon's veto, the War Powers Resolution in 1974. In conversations with staff and with industry officials, Nixon would talk tough about environmentalists being elitists who supposedly wanted to return to a primitive era, and he continued "to have an instinctive distrust" of the issue of environmental regulation.[30] "The environment is not a good political issue for us. . . . I have an uneasy feeling that perhaps we are doing too much. We're catering to the left in all of this," Nixon complained to his chief of staff, H. R. Haldeman.[31]

When the Organization of the Petroleum Exporting Countries (OPEC) oil embargo in 1973 severely disrupted the US economy, Nixon's instructions to his staff were to "prepare as soon as possible legislation that would remove all environmental roadblocks to energy production and supply by cancelling environmental inhibitions."[32] When the details of the Watergate break-in and attempted cover-up were revealed and the full extent of the criminal behavior that Nixon was imposing on his White House and Committee to Re-elect the President staff became clear, articles of impeachment were adopted in the House Judiciary Committee with substantial Republican backing. It fell to archconservative Senator Barry Goldwater to lead a delegation to the White House in August 1974 to secure Nixon's resignation.[33]

John Ehrlichman, one of the unsung heroes of the Point Reyes funding fight, went to prison. The laconic Seattle attorney, who had first been recruited to Nixon's orbit for the failed 1962 California gubernatorial run, was pilloried in the press. He was badly mauled by the Senate Watergate Committee and then convicted in federal court. His reward for loyal service to Nixon, and for breaking federal laws in carrying out that service, was conviction on charges of obstruction of justice and perjury. After serving eighteen months in prison, Ehrlichman moved to New Mexico, where he became a consultant, a novelist, and a supporter of selected environmental causes. McCloskey repaired their shattered friendship with an emotional prison visit to his friend. Ehrlichman agreed years later to a McCloskey plea that he sit down for an oral history interview about Point Reyes to be conducted by Clem Miller's former aide Duddleson. The two men met at Ehrlichman's Taos home on June 11, 1991, where Duddleson shared the paper trail he had uncovered in the files of the Nixon Library. They recorded hours of conversation as they reviewed the documentary evidence of Ehrlichman's crucial assistance in saving Point Reyes.[34]

Peter Behr was one of the few political leaders whose fortunes did not sour after the April 1970 bill secured the funds to complete the PRNS. He used his Point Reyes success to move smoothly from his Marin County Board of Supervisors seat to election as a Republican to the California State Senate. He was successful in advancing a host of bills on the environment in the state legislature. These included the landmark California Wild and Scenic Rivers Act of 1972. He moved to a home on Inverness Ridge in West Marin, but his home was subsequently destroyed in the 1995 fire that ripped through the Point Reyes Peninsula.[35]

Ronald Reagan was succeeded as governor in 1975 by Jerry Brown, son of Reagan's predecessor, Pat Brown. The younger Brown ran as an ardent environmentalist; he was also known as "Governor Moonbeam" due to his alternative lifestyle. Reagan campaigned for national office, narrowly losing a bitter 1976 GOP convention fight to the incumbent president, Gerald Ford, who then lost a close general election to Jimmy Carter. Yet Reagan won the presidency handily in 1980, ushering in an era of deregulation and rollback of environmental protections. As Carolyn Merchant's authoritative *American Environmental History* states, the Reagan administration "allowed industries to play a much greater role in regulating themselves than was the case in the 1970s. The EPA and OSHA suffered severe budget cuts and the CEQ became a minor player."[36] Reagan's picks for environmental leadership, Anne Gorsuch Burford at the EPA and James Watt at Interior, resulted in vitriolic pushback from Democrats in Congress. Watt used inflammatory anti-environmental rhetoric and promoted staff from his previous job at the conservative Mountain States Legal Foundation, bankrolled by Joseph Coors, a right-wing industrialist. Burford and Watt favored private land rights and extractive industries to such a degree that both became political liabilities for Reagan and were ultimately replaced. Environmentalists, as Hays notes, "were appalled by the victory of Ronald Reagan. . . . The Reagan environmental program involved drastic and radical action, under executive power and discretion, to make across-the-board changes in almost every environmental program and to turn them to the direction of their opponents."[37] The Reagan-era efforts to cut taxes and to shrink government also had an enduring impact. "History will confirm that Ronald Reagan's legacy created a massive fiscal debt," former secretary of the interior Stewart Udall charged, "restricting the options of his successor(s) and of the American people for positive action on behalf of their air, water, and land."[38]

Alan Cranston served four terms as US senator from California, rising to the number-two Senate post of majority whip. He led fights for additional wilderness acreage at Point Reyes, championed the landmark Alaska National Interest Lands Conservation Act and pushed for creating national parks from the Santa Monica Mountains to the Mojave Desert. His leadership on national environmental policy causes and his familiarity with environmental donors helped him to lead the Democratic Senate Campaign Committee, although his final term was clouded by an ethics scandal after he and several Senate colleagues pressed regulators for a decision on practices of savings and loan owners.

Phil Burton rose to lead the liberal wing of the House caucus, though his political career was subsequently haunted by his one-vote loss in a bitter 1976 contest for majority leader to Jim Wright of Texas, who later became speaker. Burton nursed his wounds and then used his status as leader of the progressive faction of the House Democrats to transform his perch on the Interior Committee into an environmental juggernaut. As his biographer John Jacobs notes, "[Burton] recognized the political advantages associated with parks and wilderness: he could turn environmentalism into an elaborate system of chits . . . his omnibus parks bill of 1978, the largest single park bill in history, tripled the acreage of park wilderness, tripled the miles of national trails, and doubled the miles of wild and scenic rivers."[39]

Burton's gargantuan "park-barrel bill" created an omnibus model while funding parks projects in 44 states and more than 140 different locations. The measure added 48,000 acres to the Redwood National Park north of Point Reyes.[40] After Burton died, his widow, Sala Burton, won a special election to replace him. She then tapped a local Democratic activist, Nancy Pelosi, to succeed her in the seat.

Nancy Pelosi arrived in Congress in 1987 and promptly secured a position on the Appropriations Committee. One of Pelosi's major legislative accomplishments before her rise to speaker was the 1996 measure establishing an innovative and highly successful Presidio Trust in San Francisco. She was heavily criticized for the move by a few environmental activists. Some local groups favored removing all vestiges of the military presence and "rewilding" the lands. The Presidio Trust has since managed the 1,500-acre complex, which includes some of the most valuable real estate in North America. These include parade grounds, officer housing, a golf course, wetlands, an old airport, and the stunning beaches west of the Golden Gate Headlands. The Save San Francisco Bay Association and Point Reyes National Seashore Foundation wins in the 1960s thus set up the GGNRA in the 1970s, with the grand prize of the Presidio coming to park advocates in 1993.

The volume of environmental protection measures moving in Washington continued after Richard Nixon's presidency through the Ford and Carter presidencies. These measures included the Endangered Species Act, the Marine Mammal Protection Act, the designation of more than 33,000 acres at Point Reyes as wilderness (later named for Phil Burton), and measures protecting the Tongass National Forest in Alaska and both the Mojave Desert and Santa Monica mountains in Southern California. These last three measures benefited especially from the leadership of Bay Area political leaders Burton and Cranston.[41] There followed legislated offshore drilling moratoria for a time on both the Atlantic and Pacific coasts. There was rapid expansion of the Pacific Ocean sanctuaries west of Point Reyes and Monterey. States from the Midwest and East Coast pressed their own seashores and lakeshore parks (see Table 6.5). Using the Point Reyes and Cape Cod precedents, ten more such NPS-managed parks were added nationwide in the thirteen years after the Point Reyes authorization bill was enacted.[42]

Through the Reagan-Bush years, environmental activists shifted to defense. The 1990s proved to be an era of relative caution.[43] In the Bay Area, the Presidio Trust was soon led by Pelosi's former field director, Craig Middleton. On his watch, a series of extraordinary public-private partnerships were created, allowing the Presidio to become economically

Table 6.5 New National Seashores and Lakeshores Created, 1961–1975

National Seashore	Enacted	Established	Federal Acreage
Cape Cod, MA	1961	1966	28,000
Point Reyes, CA	1962	1972	87,000
Padre Island, TX	1962	1968	130,000
Fire Island, NY	1964	1984	6,000
Assateague, MD & VA	1965	1965	19,000
Cape Lookout, NC	1966	1966	25,000
Pictured Rocks, MI	1966	1972	36,000
Indiana Dunes, IN	1966	1966	11,000
Apostle Islands, WI	1970	1970	42,000
Bear Dunes, MI	1970	1970	57,000
Gulf Islands, MS, AL, & FL	1971	1971	100,000
Cumberland Island, GA	1972	1972	20,000
Canaveral, FL	1975	1975	58,000

Source: National Park Service National Park Index, 1916–2016.

self-sufficient.[44] Today, the former army base is one of the great success stories of the military base closure process; it hosts several dozen nonprofit organizations and large employers, including George Lucas's film company. There is public access to miles of hiking trails and beaches. The generals' private golf course became one of the most popular public links in the city. In 2007, Pelosi became the first woman elected speaker in American history as she continued to tap in to the Bay Area environmental donor base to support colleagues in races around the country. She reclaimed the post in 2019 after the Democrats won back the House majority, aided by Democrats winning forty-six of the fifty-three seats in California's House delegation. San Francisco's Pelosi was then succeeded as speaker of the House by Southern Californian Kevin McCarthy after the Republicans won a majority of House seats in the 2022 midterm elections.

What Happened Next at the PRNS

There are few final victories in politics. Yet many conservationists would argue that when it comes to environmental protection battles, as GGNRA champion Amy Meyer asserts, "all gains are temporary—and all losses are permanent."[45] The Point Reyes case shows how the tides can sweep back and forth, with future outcomes uncertain. Those who serve the cause in public office are, at their best, stewards of the public interest. They are players in a drama bigger than any one person. In this story, they are the people who tried to move the ball forward to create a national seashore preserve at Point Reyes. The exact nature of the park on the peninsula is still subject to contentious disputes and litigation. Protests at the site continue to this day. Continued heavy use and widespread pollution of taxpayer-owned parklands by commercial enterprises have grown increasingly controversial and subject to challenge by some local environmental groups and state agencies, including the California Coastal Commission.

There remains a deep split within the Marin County environmental community about the wisdom of continued ranching on public parklands at Point Reyes. Some activists want to nourish and support agriculture in West Marin; they fear the forced closure of the entire Point Reyes Peninsula to grazing would destroy the economies of scale necessary to support farms on the east side of Tomales Bay. Some maintain that the north coast prairie would suffer and become overgrown without the grazing herds. Noting the repeated pledges of federal officials since 1958 that the ranches and parklands could coexist, they push for more effective NPS monitoring of public lands in agricultural use but insist (as Clem Miller did) that the ranches should be allowed to remain forever. Local congressman Jared Huffman (D–San Rafael) is the most visible advocate of this pro-ranch and pro-environment component of the electorate.

Lawsuits were filed again in 2012, seeking to overturn the Obama Department of the Interior decision not to extend another long-term lease for the Drakes Bay Oyster Company. The Drakes Estero waters where the company operated had been designated "potential wilderness" by public law in 1976. This was when Congress altered the assumptions underlying the 1962 act authorizing the national seashore. By pressing for wilderness designation and anticipating the expansion of the wilderness zone, Congress changed the rules of the competition. Katy Miller Johnson revealed the logic and aptly described the stakes:

> The foresight of Congress in 1962 in setting aside the entire peninsula is every day more evident. Today Limantour and Drakes Estero are the last remaining unpolluted estuaries on the West Coast, and the least altered by man. These estuaries, irreplaceable research areas, can only be protected from pollution by reserving from development the entire watershed that feeds them, all the way to the crest of Inverness Ridge—as the 53,000 acre Seashore will do.[46]

The fate of the commercial oyster farm in Drakes Estero divided local park champions for years, even after its removal was mandated by the Obama administration's interior secretary Kenneth Salazar in November 2012. The Salazar decision was unequivocal; commercial oyster operations could not continue in the Estero. Yet it "balanced" this position with a firm declaration that new long-term ranch leases would be granted by the NPS. Even with letters from former Congressman McCloskey and Senator Dianne Feinstein defending the oyster farm, its lease was not extended by the NPS in a move ultimately backed by the courts.[47] This intervention of usually pro-environment political leaders in NPS park stewardship decisions alarmed advocates of wilderness preservation. Critics believed that bowing to political pressure at Point Reyes would set a dangerous precedent, potentially impacting every national park and seashore, if the NPS were to accede to new federal commitments to practices that degraded parklands, waters, and potential wilderness areas owned by the public. As at Mineral King, and at Hetch Hetchy nearly a century earlier, California activists at Point Reyes were fighting not just a local battle but also for a broader cause to prevent what they saw as a dangerous precedent in the use of public parklands.

The saga of the oyster-farm fight is told candidly by reporter Summer Brennan in *The Oyster War: The True Story of a Small Farm, Big Politics, and the Future of Wilderness in America*. Brennan concedes that she began her research sympathetic to continued use of the Estero for oyster farming. After scores of interviews and months of research, she concluded that the oyster-farm operations had to be removed from the estuary because the law required it. In fact, the NPS field office's solicitor had been on record since 2004 that "the Park Service is mandated by the Wilderness Act, the Point Reyes Wilderness Act and its Management Practices to convert potential wilderness, i.e., the [oyster company] tract and the adjoining Estero to wilderness status as soon as the nonconforming use can be eliminated."[48]

This decision to eject the commercial oyster farm from Drakes Estero represented "the culmination of five years of fierce, polarizing battles between advocates for wilderness and for sustainable agriculture," as Laura Alice Watt notes, "a dispute that would embroil the local community for years to come."[49] Watt's review of the history of NPS management is unsparing in its criticism of the NPS at Point Reyes for not doing more to accommodate local ranching families and oyster farmers. She argues that the NPS opposes any working presence on its landscapes and that it violated scientific best practices in concluding that commercial oyster operations had to go. It is noteworthy in this respect that the Lunny family members who invested in Drakes Bay Oyster Company had not operated that site for more than a few years, although they had ranched nearby for generations. They chose less than a decade prior to the Salazar ruling to take a chance in investing in the rundown oyster operation that was beset by the environmental hazards it had created. When the new investors bought into the Estero, lease expiration and eviction already appeared likely, and they were so informed repeatedly by the NPS. Regardless, the question of whether the oyster farm should be allowed to remain bitterly divided people of goodwill in the environmental community in the Bay Area.

The investors in Drakes Bay were relentless in their appeal to local environmental leaders and organic farmers. They insisted that they would institute new practices that would enable the oysters to help "clean up" the Estero. Yet their divide-and-conquer tactics invited backing from sources aligned with the Koch brothers, libertarian forces backed by extractive industry donors who argued nationwide for greater exploitation of public lands for commercial purposes. Kevin Lunny later appeared in an Oval Office photo op with President Donald Trump. Just one measure of the depth of the divisions that the oyster war caused in Marin is the fact that the exquisite book celebrating Point Reyes's history, authored by widely respected historian John Hart, was withdrawn from publication by the University of California Press when academic reviewers—and even the photographer who contributed art—struggled to resolve differences over the virtues of competing narratives about the closure of the oyster farm in Drakes Estero.

Another critical take on the conflicts between the NPS and the owners of the remaining ranches is provided in the provocative 2015 study by New York historian Jacqueline Mullen. She argues that the NPS team had manipulated the appearance of local support going back to the 1950s through collaborations between George Collins and the San Francisco–based Sierra Club while opposing any plans that would secure a viable future for ranchers who worked the land: "To cripple a dairy industry in order to create another 'playground' for San Franciscans disgusted Marin ranchers. To them, and to Westerners in other states, the Sierra Club represented a frivolous pastime by wealthy urbanites to create playgrounds for themselves, with no thought to the harm they cause local industries along the way."[50] Mullen notes that dairy farms were already moving out of valuable Marin land throughout the post–World War II era for reasons that had nothing to do with the proposed park at Point Reyes. Escalating land prices and real estate taxes made agricultural uses ever less practical in suburban Marin County. Yet she insists that the NPS gave the ranchers at Point Reyes the back of the hand, allegedly treating them in a condescending fashion, as PRNS rangers were allegedly eager to see the ranches close. Mullen asserts that NPS practices were a prime cause of the danger of housing subdivisions coming to Point Reyes.

The threat of subdivision, however, was *not* created by the NPS, and the park rangers should not be caricatured as villains. Plans embraced by the Board of Supervisors assumed that West Marin, home to barely one thousand citizens in the 1960s, would grow to a population of sixty-six thousand by the end of the century. The threat of subdivision was not *caused* by the NPS. Subdivision for homes on the Point Reyes Peninsula began before the seashore park proposal moved in Congress with the 1962 measure. Even the Shafters had proposed major subdivision moves—decades before the NPS was created. These proposals first surfaced in 1879; they ultimately included the successful 1890 efforts on the Point Reyes Peninsula to create the town of Inverness on scores of subdivided lots. These led to an ambitious 1905 plan to subdivide Inverness Ridge into thousands of lots for private homes, a scheme that was shelved after the 1906 earthquake brought destruction and hardship to the Bay Area, especially in West Marin towns that were near the earthquake's epicenter just offshore.

The Park Service Becomes a Punching Bag

A fight similar to that waged over the Drakes Bay oyster farm has raged over the growth of the tule elk herd.[51] Tule elk herds throughout the state had been decimated by hunting in the nineteenth century. Yet some survived in scattered locations, including a San Joaquin Valley ranch. A herd was reintroduced to the Point Reyes peninsula in the 1980s at the explicit direction of the US Congress. Soon the herd population behind a fence near Tomales Point at the northern end of the peninsula had grown to several hundred. Rangers then established a second, unfenced herd adjacent to the pastoral zone; soon thereafter, Point Reyes dairy operators complained about damage from the elk.

Lawsuits and on-site protests continue to the present day. Some of the more extreme animal activists allege that any containment of the elks' free range makes the place "Point Reyes Elk Penitentiary" and NPS employees inhumane jailers. The NPS management practice of limiting access for elk to water and forage amidst the severe drought of 2018–2022 was caricatured as unduly harsh and, it was argued, inconsistent with the public interest. A leading NPS critic, Susan Ives of the Marin-based Resource Renewal Institute (RRI), writes, "That the Seashore's limited staff and budget are deployed to maintain private ranching defiles the National Park Service's mission: 'to conserve the scenery and the natural and historic objects and the wildlife therein . . . as will leave them unimpaired for the enjoyment of future generations.'"[52]

A bigger fight remains at this writing over the basic public policy question the NPS has wrestled with for years: *How long can the ranches stay?*

The California Coastal Commission in the spring of 2022 challenged the NPS draft plan for continued operations by the two dozen remaining ranches still operating under lease on public lands. The same NPS proposal drew more than 6,500 public comments, with more than 95 percent of them opposed to continued NPS accommodations for the ranches. The deeply divided commission reversed itself in September 2022 with a 5–4 vote accepting revised NPS plans. The decision came within days of new water testing data from Point Reyes being released; these tests indicated extremely high levels of water pollution caused by the ranches in such public waters as Abbott's Lagoon and Drakes Estero. NPS concessions subsequently made to commission critics included new pledges for vigorous testing of water pollution emanating from ranches, greater transparency, and a pledge to sunset leases on any ranches that proved noncompliant.

The heart of the challenge remains the fact that the NPS staff is caught between warring public factions and public policy priorities that have changed time and again. Those who favor the "rewilding of the land" clash with those who insist that dairy and beef cattle operations are part of the special "cultural heritage" of the parklands and can remain on new long-term leases "forever." The NPS teams administering Point Reyes have sometimes exacerbated the problem by neglecting their duties as stewards of public lands and waters. Assertive environmental organizations, such as the RRI—originally founded by local environmental hero Huey Johnson—have repeatedly revealed to judges and reporters facts about chronic water pollution problems emanating from the ranches. These include the apparent lack of septic tanks for worker housing at some ranches, nonconforming land uses that violate lease terms, negligence in scrapyard dumps on leased land, and the failure for many years to adjust the prices that taxpayers charge the ranches for leasing public lands. These are issues that NPS professionals have struggled to catch and remedy in a timely fashion. The Park Service rangers are the taxpayers' property managers and the ranchers' landlord; the public interest requires greater vigilance and transparency, a direction the new PRNS leadership has committed to following.

Criticism of the NPS in West Marin is led by activists eager to return more of the Point Reyes Peninsula to a wilder state. These residents insist that they are pursuing the legislative intent of the park's founders. The legislative record of the 1950s and 1960s does not support this assertion; creating wilderness was not the primary objective of the 1962 law—public access to the shoreline and creation of more recreational opportunities were, along with the goal of blocking new freeways and housing developments on the pasturelands and forested hills. By 1976, federal objectives, as expressed by new wilderness and potential wilderness designations, changed. Over time, the compatibility of the pastoral zone with escalating public demands for more open spaces ensured confrontations. These are confrontations that a handful of public servants charged with maintaining the entire peninsula have been obliged to referee. Different views of public policy priorities have divided local leaders, community members, and civic activists ever since.

There is even divided opinion among scientists and scholars regarding whether "rewilding" is genuinely in the public interest, especially on lands where the human footprint has been substantial for more than two hundred years. This debate has been fueled by provocative scholarship advanced by Wisconsin professor William Cronon and colleagues in *Uncommon Ground: Rethinking the Human Place in Nature*. Despite his solid credentials as a scholar and environmental advocate, Cronon and his coauthors were pilloried by activists for his exposition of the human concept of nature, which notes that rewilding proponents often overlook inconvenient facts. These include the role humans have played in shaping "natural" parks from Yosemite and Niagara Falls to New York's Central Park as well as the fact that it is often wealthy city dwellers and suburbanites who insist that the NPS must restore public lands to a natural state:

> Human beings have been manipulating ecosystems for as long as we have records of their passage . . . "nature" is not nearly so natural as it seems. Instead it is a profoundly human construction. . . . The dream of an unworked natural landscape is very much a fantasy of people who have never themselves had to work the land to make a living—urban folk for whom food comes from a supermarket or a restaurant instead of a field.[53]

Cronon notes that the push for national parks and the back-to-nature movement first began in the early 1900s, precisely when the advance of industrialization and the closing of the American frontier increased the romantic appeal of the natural world.

Scholars opposed to rewilding, such as David Lowenthal, maintain that because Point Reyes has long been "a peopled landscape," the NPS should not accede to environmental activists' demands: "Underlying all negotiations for public management is the drumbeat of progressive rewilding."[54] They argue that if all the five thousand dairy cows and beef cattle were removed from Point Reyes, the grasslands would soon become overgrown with brush and invasive species, echoing a warning issued decades ago by the ranchers' lobbyist Bryan McCarthy, one to which some local environmentalists subscribe. Some argue that to preserve the parklands' sweeping vistas, cows are essential for range management on the northern coastal prairie grasslands. They also maintain that Drakes Estero has such strong tidal flows that pollution of the Drakes Bay waters by ranches is washed away with the tides. Finally, critics who maintain that the NPS is too sympathetic to environmental activists argue that rewilding of the entire peninsula is not appropriate for a national seashore that was established with the commitment that the ranches could stay so long as they conformed to agricultural best practices and did not harm the public lands and waters.

"The presence of so many obviously working people," Watt maintains, "sits uneasily with a national parks ideology that has traditionally emphasized empty landscapes, a wilderness aesthetic, and recreation."[55] Watt champions the "preserved landscape," suggesting an ecological stasis that defies the course of human history, where land use patterns change from generation to generation. She concurs in criticism of the NPS handling of the original Point Reyes purchases and then piles on, asserting that the "major role NPS played at Point Reyes, both in pushing to establish the park in the first place, and in driving the threat of development, thereby created its own justification for acquiring the ranches."[56]

Few versions of Point Reyes's history grant the NPS a positive role. This seems unfair and there is no excuse for the vitriol and name calling directed in online fora against NPS staffers who work each day in West Marin. It was NPS staffers Knight and Wirth who first proposed a government purchase of parkland on Point Reyes in the 1930s. It was NPS staffer George Collins who revived the idea in the 1950s under the leadership of then director Wirth. The NPS embraced and supported congressional proposals for new seashore parks in the late 1950s.

The NPS went about securing some lands at Point Reyes in the 1960s with only a fraction of the federal funds needed. The NPS has respected the ranching families while administering ever larger expanses of wilderness and near wilderness as Congress has repeatedly intervened and changed the rules of the game. Park Service professionals have worked under intense pressure to mediate between cattle and elk, between wilderness hikers and townspeople, between oyster farmers and kayakers, and between disparate factions of the environmental community, where activists regularly assail fellow activists in the local press. These written assaults and counterassaults mix passionate pleas to accept one version of nature with overt virtue signaling and criticism of neighbors who have reached different conclusions about how to secure the public interest.

The NPS has made serious errors as well, from Hartzog's tone-deaf 1969 plan to cannibalize parklands in a fire sale to the failure in subsequent decades to monitor water quality and track pollution sources. Its basic science and land management practices have been flawed, at times lacking transparency and public accountability. The draft NPS plan to once again extend long-term leases to ranchers—fifty to sixty years after their descendants were paid large sums by taxpayers—is alleged by critics to be at odds with basic national park principles that are embodied in the original act establishing the NPS.

The NPS policy has in the past appeared to be one of benign neglect towards ranch property maintenance. The commitment new NPS leaders have made to greater transparency after years of resisting Freedom of Information Act requests appears likely to force policy changes. For example, groups such as the RRI are pressing fundamental questions, such as *Why has the Park Service continued to charge tenants far below market rates for grazing? Why does the overstretched NPS leadership apparently spend more than $1.3 million each year to "administer" these ranch lands while collecting less than $500,000 per year in rent from the ranchers?*

The NPS is a federal bureaucracy buried within a larger bureaucracy, the Department of the Interior. It is, by nature, slow to adapt. Its career service leaders tend to think long term while practicing conflict avoidance with politicians and the local press. At Point Reyes, the NPS gets little credit for how many roads and decaying ranch structures it has removed as well as cleaning up the Estero. Despite all their protestations of environmental sensitivity, the owners of Drakes Bay Oyster Company left vast amounts of junk in the Estero when evicted. It cost taxpayers several million dollars to clean up the tenants' mess.

NPS officials have few chances to defend their work when its leaders appear before Congress to ask for funding or before senior executive branch staff to ask for backing of NPS proposals. NPS staff are in most cases modestly paid civil servants who have dedicated their careers to environmental stewardship. Yet often they have become inviting punching bags for those engaged in local policy disputes or national funding contests. A more understanding assessment is found in Watt's summary of the experience of integrating Cape Cod, Point Reyes, and a dozen more new national seashores into the NPS: "The late 1960s and early 1970s represent an era of transition, where writers of park legislation experimented somewhat with acquisition strategies, including private use zones, or encouraging less-than-fee acquisition methods. The NPS, however, does not appear to have been entirely ready for these new approaches."[57] Watt's point is underscored by the fact that the NPS at the same time was caught between changing public preferences. In the 1950s, the NPS was driven to expand park access for the growing suburbs; this meant more cars, more access roads, more parking lots and marinas, and the development of more recreation opportunities. In the 1960s, the new environmental policy wave pushed instead for more wilderness protection and restoration of lands damaged by extractive industries and agricultural practices. The fight for Point Reyes proved to be a watershed battle that marked this difficult transition.

From Wirth to Udall and from Whitaker to Hartzog, the memoirs of executive branch policymakers from this era are honest about the difficult balancing task the NPS was asked to perform. Through eras of changing cultural values and political norms, the NPS took criticism from both sides while delivering a national seashore that is today far healthier than it was after herds of beef cattle, dairy cows, and hunting clubs first came to the peninsula in the latter half of the nineteenth century. There have been substantial improvements under NPS management over the past half century in how manure, waste, and buffer zones are handled as NPS officials have gone about removing old roads and ranch structures to rewild parts of the federal lands.

The Costs of Victory: To Govern Is to Choose

A new pro-environment majority led by Republican Gary Giacomini was in place on the Marin County Board of Supervisors by 1973. The board reclassified most of the private land in West Marin with an A-60 zoning designation, which bars any subdivision below one house for every sixty acres. When lawyers for the developers met with Giacomini, they were surprised to find that they could not induce him to block the measure. The Giacomini family of West Marin ranchers included several who were angry with Gary for years because they believed he had harmed them financially with his A-60 vote. There would no longer be a realistic possibility of housing subdivisions in West Marin.[58]

In the wake of the battle over Point Reyes, California lawmakers moved parallel to and soon blazed a trail ahead of new federal initiatives on environmental protection. Midway through Reagan's second gubernatorial term in 1972, California voters supported an initiative creating a California Coastal Commission by a 3–1 margin. The powerful commission has its roots in a West Marin fight over access to Tomales Bay. Today, it wields authority over any development impacting the state's 1,200 miles of coast-line and has taken a tough line against most coastal construction. Watt offers a different take on the role played by PRNS management in these events, the paradox that preservation efforts have sought to erase human impact: the "continuing story of landscape change at PRNS, where preservation management [by the NPS] has devalued and eroded the working landscape in favor of a more wilderness-like vision of the future."[59]

Republicans have been hard-pressed to win the votes of environmental activists in the four decades since 1981. President Reagan's team of environmental policymakers, led by Secretary Watt, also sparked an explosion of membership for environmental groups. The Sierra Club's membership soared to 500,000. Even the relatively sedate National Audubon Society soon had a $38 million annual budget. Other leading conservation groups rocketed upward in size, clout, and land purchasing power in the 1980s.[60] The private land rights backlash of the Reagan years took as its target perceived overregulation of private lands by federal bureaucrats. Yet this "sagebrush rebellion" sparked its own reaction of consumer and voter response. Since the early 1980s, the national Democratic and Republican Parties have had few crossover voters on environmental policy legislation.

The environmental movement begun at Point Reyes launched another important phenomenon: the trend towards more robust state regulation. Green politics fueled in the Bay Area during the 1960s led directly to the creation of a system of laws in Sacramento that became models for the forty-nine other states as well as some foreign countries. One example from recent years illustrates this point. When President Donald Trump tried in March 2020 to roll back national Corporate Average Fuel Economy (CAFE) standards for auto emissions, many domestic and foreign auto manufacturers refused to go along. With California regulators maintaining far stricter standards, the automakers chose to hold the line. They resisted the lower Trump administration standards because they could not afford to turn their backs on selling in the California market. As the sixth-largest economy in the world, California retains the ability to influence global environmental practices.

Berkeley business professor David Vogel has written extensively about the impact that California has had through the state's creation of the regulatory infrastructure that other states and nations have adopted as their own model: "California's attractive geography gave it the potential to be a desirable state in which to live, invest, work, and vacation. But without effective government regulation, that potential would have been squandered. . . . No other state has enacted so many innovative, comprehensive, and stringent environmental regulations over such a long period of time."[61] Vogel's conclusion is that one of California's most valued exports is the model for a regulatory infrastructure that balances the need for growth with the demand for protecting the quality of public goods—the land, the water, and the air. His thesis underscores that it was not just a high degree of citizen mobilization that led to such results. Business community support for conservation measures also provided a crucial partnership at key junctures.

The Save San Francisco Bay Association began with a petition drive focused on legislators in Sacramento. It noted in 1962 that only 6 miles of the bay's shoreline from San Jose to the Carquinez Straits offered public access to the water. By 2000, the public access had grown to more than 300 miles. Today, the filling in of San Francisco Bay that so alarmed Berkeley activists in the early 1960s has been reversed. Some tidelands are now being restored, and the footprint of the bay is growing on the margins. The San Francisco Bay is once again relatively clean and swimmable. The ultimate yield of the Save San Francisco Bay efforts in the 1960s was a moratorium on all bay fill activities and a regionwide alliance via an intergovernmental compact produced by the Bay Conservation and Development Commission (BCDC). Together with the California Coastal Commission, this government body has substantial powers over any proposed developments destined to impact the region's bays and coastlines.

The Price of NIMBY (Not in My Backyard) Politics

Most of the cheery stories about Point Reyes end with the 1962 victory; many do not even cover the second crucial 1969 battle to secure funding. Others feature the petition drive as an example of grassroots activism untainted by Washington insider dealings. Collections of dreamy photographs of cliffs, forests, and fields empty of evidence of human habitation often follow. What of the claims of park opponents, however, that locking up lands in the hills of West Marin would exacerbate the region's affordable housing crisis that has persisted for multiple generations?

These critics have a point. Marin is now one of the most expensive counties in the country in which to live. The average price of a single-family home in the county passed $2 million in 2022. Fearing higher density and crowding—after first supporting rapid transit via a transbay tunnel or a second deck on the Golden Gate Bridge--Marin politicians and local voters have kept Bay Area Rapid Transit (BART) lines out of the county. Decades of agonizing traffic jams have ensued. Thousands of commuters to San Francisco jobs who could not find affordable housing in Marin moved farther north. Those residing in Sonoma and Napa Counties now face brutal two-hour commutes through Marin to get to San Francisco. NIMBY politics in Marin have become, as journalist Jessica Lage notes, "particularly fierce" given the entitlement to adjacent open spaces that many Marin homeowners feel.

Marin County officials were once again in 2022 castigated by regional authorities for failing to meet the affordable housing targets mandated by new state laws. Marin County is an integral part of a highly diverse metropolitan area of some seven million people. Yet Marin officials today report a Black population of less than 3 percent among the county's 260,000 residents. During the COVID-19 pandemic, three closely followed news stories covered in Marin were the closure of the only West Marin public golf course (to create more open space, not more affordable housing), the renaming of Drake High School and its "Pirate" nickname (after the realization that Drake had previously served as an officer and later, in Mexico, as a captain in a flotilla of slave traders), and the defacing of a Mission San Rafael statue of the man now blamed by many for the decimation of the Coast Miwok, Father Junípero Serra.

Marin officials continue to move slowly in encouraging affordable housing, while the state of California, with 12 percent of the nation's population, has more than 25 percent of the nation's homeless.[62] In late 2022, local headlines were dominated for days by not only the fight over the future of ranch leases at Point Reyes but also persistent efforts to eject the large homeless encampment from under the 101 Freeway not far from the county seat and Mission San Rafael. As Jessica Lage notes, "Profound socio-economic changes . . . have left in rural Marin gaping income inequality and severe housing shortages."[63]

The San Francisco Bay Area, including especially Marin's county seat of San Rafael, has had long and difficult struggles with its large homeless populations. The opponents of building more affordable housing and permitting greater density in Marin have often prevailed, yet on housing policy, there is cause for introspection. As *New York Times* columnist Ezra Klein notes, the landmark California Environmental Quality Act, forced upon Governor Reagan by activists in the 1960s, "has perversely become a weapon against projects that would better the environment. . . . The most popular targets of CEQA lawsuits are multifamily housing projects." As Klein explains, "industrial, mining, and energy projects accounted for fewer than a quarter of the [CEQA] lawsuits in 2018." [64] Housing shortages continue to be a primary driver of poverty in the Golden State, especially in West Marin, where there are enormous means gaps between wealthy owners of second homes and the blue-collar workers who service the tourists and the ranches.

As climate change impacts accelerated over the past decade, a once-in-a-thousand-years drought set in from 2018 to 2022. The record heat led to longer wildfire seasons that reached deeper into California suburbs, in large measure because the suburbs have extended ever deeper into rural hills and forests. As Miriam Pawel, the biographer of Governor Brown and Cesar Chavez, writes, fires and drought have "sapped the collective sense of zealous optimism that long characterized the state's seductive appeal . . . the need for millions of housing units collides with natural limits. Resistance to increased urban and suburban density has meant more and more construction in the fire prone areas known as the 'wildland urban interface' now home to about a quarter of the population." [65]

The nation's largest state moved to diversify its economy after decades on a war footing as Fortress California. Key to this transformation has been the creation of intellectual capital from the Berkeley and Lawrence Livermore research laboratories, Stanford's innovative engineering and business schools, and the tech revolutionaries in nearby Silicon Valley. These people, of course, choose to work and live in the Bay Area in part because of the quality of life afforded by the stunning parks of Point Reyes and the GGNRA, parks close to suburban homes. These choices, however, were not cost-free.

Marin County groups continue to build out the buffer of open lands. An unusual collaboration between conservationists and ranchers has each year secured more lands adjacent to Marin open spaces, added to conservation set-asides via the Marin Agricultural Land Trust (MALT). MALT was founded in 1980 by a dairy rancher, Ellen Straus, and a biologist, Phyllis Faber, as the first US land trust devoted to the preservation of farmland. These agricultural preserves now total more than 50,000 additional acres.

The Marin model used by MALT has been replicated in many other states. These MALT lands in Marin serve as another layer of protection for the fragile Point Reyes ecosystems and the greenbelt created by the park complex. MALT has attracted numerous critics as well, and the organization has faced pushback for the way some board supporters' transactions have been financed with taxpayer funds. The ethics issue threatens to tarnish the land trust model and discourage its adoption elsewhere if not successfully addressed. MALT has subsequently altered its approach, brought in a new leadership team from the environmental NGO community, and pledged to increase transparency and enact greater safeguards against self-dealing.

The comprehensive study of the history of Point Reyes's management conducted in 2007 by historian Paul Sadin is blunt about how grassroots activists changed national politics. The conclusion is tucked into an exhaustive administrative record:

> Repercussions of the political and legislative battles for PR were felt far beyond the newly secure boundaries of PRNS. The push to fund land acquisition for PR had the immediate consequence of unlocking money in the LWCF for other NPS sites. The SOS endeavor also demonstrated the kind of political power the growing environmental movement could wield. The implications included an awareness and appreciation for environmentalism—as a political force—in the Nixon White House. It helped convince the president and other elected officials that they could make political hay if they positioned themselves in the environmental camp.[66]

Duddleson was more succinct on this point, noting that the SOS campaign was "a citizen-action enterprise that succeeded beyond the dreams of those who set it in motion."[67] Mullen concludes her research on Point Reyes by deploring the ejection of the oyster farm from Drakes Estero and castigating NPS staff for a move that divided the local community. The heart of her argument, however, remains her grievance with Collins and other NPS officials who allegedly favored conservationists' agenda over that of the ranchers. She ignores the fact that the Sierra Club was distracted and otherwise engaged and thus was not a significant factor in the crucial SOS campaign that Behr and Johnson guided in 1969–1970. Mullen relies heavily on the fact that George Collins was still on the NPS payroll in 1959, when he worked closely with Congressman Clem Miller and local conservation groups to create the appearance of grassroots support for a national seashore proposal that had originated with NPS staff:

The steadily top-down manner in which the Park Service promoted Point Reyes exposed the growing power of conservation groups like the Sierra Club in national politics of the 1960s. Point Reyes National Seashore did not pass due to grassroots efforts . . . the Park Service tapped into the political strength of the Sierra Club in the Bay Area and nationally, who used their wilderness era coalitions to orchestrate local support and quell opposition.[68]

The fight over public lands policies for Point Reyes continues to simmer. Environmentally sensitive local activists continue to hold divided views over the best way forward. There is no common vision for the park's future that all factions embrace. Some smaller groups focused on individual species, such as the tule elk or turtle restoration, have joined with local scientists to hammer the NPS for failing to monitor water quality at the publicly owned ranches and the bodies of water downstream. Nonetheless, many of the organic farmers east of the park and local consumers supported the Lunny bid to clean up and run the oyster farm in Drakes Bay; some view maintenance of ranching at Point Reyes as crucial to maintaining support for West Marin farms in general.

Several respected environmental groups are suing the NPS, alleging mismanagement of the ranch leases; park activists are now joined by animal welfare organizations dedicated to the survival of the herd of tule elk. Supporters of rewilding more of the peninsula and proponents of finally ending the ranch leases still lean heavily on the original NPS act and the Point Reyes legislation. They argue that it is fundamentally incompatible—as rancher Boyd Stewart testified in 1970—to have five thousand cows on top of a fragile park watershed. Some activists have pressed to end the ranch leases, as Stewart and the ranchers anticipated in their key 1970 Senate testimony: "The ranchers in that area realize that dairying is not going to continue indefinitely . . . they realize they aren't going to dairy indefinitely in Marin County." Yet activists are also careful not to misrepresent what Clem and Katy Miller said.

Congressman Miller declared during his 1962 reelection campaign that he believed the dairies could stay "forever." Every legislator involved in the 1962 seashore campaign—from Aspinall and Bible to Engle and Kuchel— insisted that ranching rights should be retained where possible. Miller said so again in the draft of his last newsletter to constituents in October 1962 explaining the impact of his landmark bill. These positions, however, were based on the assumption that limited ranching would not undermine the central mission of NPS professionals: to conserve and protect for future generations all parklands and waters. The pledge that the ranches could remain was always contingent upon their not harming the lands and waters of the park and thereby undermining the basic principle governing all national parks and seashores. The incongruity of the two principles lends an air of inevitability to many debates over the future of PRNS. National parks do not host substantial commercial enterprises (unless they are infrastructure to host and transport visitors). The leaseback arrangements on publicly owned parklands at Point Reyes are decidedly commercial. Congress has clearly favored the restoration of potential wilderness within PRNS to a more natural state while setting rather arbitrary boundaries for where wilderness can prosper. Future prospects for investing in more extensive farming operations are thus cloudy.

Public policy priorities have changed dramatically since the national seashore was authorized in 1962 with an initial focus on facilitating outdoor recreation while blocking ongoing housing developments. The NPS mission began to change with the passage in 1964 of the Wilderness Act. The NPS was directed by Congress and the executive branch under President Johnson to shift from a recreation mission to a conservation and preservation mission. Congress fundamentally altered its approach in less than a decade, between 1962 and 1969, after Clem Miller's death. It insisted in just a few years on federal ownership of the entire peninsula and then designated one-third of its acreage as wilderness in 1976, with other major parcels as "potential wilderness." Congress in its wisdom chose to move the goal posts and alter public priorities as the environmental costs of post–World War II developments and ever-expanding suburban sprawl became apparent.

Critics of the NPS note that it has been more than sixty years since the seashore was created. It has been more than fifty years since the ranch families and their heirs were paid generous and often inflated market prices by taxpayers. The sums paid for public title to these lands are equivalent in today's dollars to more than $300 million. Substantial public policy arguments have been advanced to curtail future commercial leases on some of the most fragile parklands. The facts have changed, as has the science.

The archival record is replete with indications that park champions in Congress in the 1960s would not today back continuous use of the public lands by ranches if the cows degraded the seashore's public lands and waters.

The first NPS study conducted by Wirth and Knight in the 1930s assumed that all the ranchers would be ejected. Collins in the 1950s assumed that the ranchers would fade out over one generation through "attrition." Even the ranchers' passionate champion, lobbyist Bryan McCarthy, conceded that with the passing of a single generation, interest in maintaining the ranches would likely "dissipate." Yet today, many environmental activists still believe commercial agriculture and wilderness expansion can coexist within PRNS boundaries.

Here the Mineral King conclusion is especially instructive. In the 1940s, even the Sierra Club backed developing the remote Sierra Nevada valley to afford greater access for winter skiing and year-round outdoor recreation. New information and new science altered its thinking. Subsequent litigation highlighted the dangerous precedent that would be created if federal policymakers approved bisecting adjacent Sequoia National Park with a new 25-mile section of highway exclusively for the use of developers and investors in a neighboring ski resort. As the definitive study of the epic fight between Disney and the environmental activists concluded,

> The changes reflected in the dispute over Mineral King extended well beyond the legal question of standing. The dispute arose when new information and ideas about the environment began to alter government decision-making. Among others, these forces included increased scientific understanding of how environmental effects occur, expanded knowledge about the long-term health effects of pollution, and emergence of a large citizen movement dedicated to protecting the environment. The use of the law as a tool for environmental protection intersected with these developments and magnified their effect.[69]

Critics of the NPS argue that another generation of status quo ranch leases in the watershed of designated and potential wilderness areas at Point Reyes may be fundamentally incompatible with US laws, as NPS counsel Ralph Mihan concluded in the oyster-farm case. They point to the basic mission of the NPS: to preserve and protect the lands and waters it stewards. As the science of what five thousand cows do to the public lands and waters becomes clearer, the NPS is struggling to meet its obligation to collect and share more reliable data with the public owners of these lands.

Tests conducted in the summer of 2022 revealed extremely high pollution levels at multiple points in the public park waters.[70] Environmental groups wielded the new studies as an argument for the California Coastal Commission, if not the courts, to reject continued ranch leases. Their framing of the issue is direct: "The degree of pollution is astounding, especially considering it is occurring on the California coast and in a National Park," says Scott Webb, policy director of the Marin-based Turtle Island Restoration Network; "we need to stand up to private industry that continues to profit off destroying public land." As the Center for Biological Diversity/ RRI report notes, this 2022 study was the first to cover all the dairies with a large sample size and revealed that eight popular destinations in the Drakes Bay, Drakes Estero, Kehoe, and Abbotts watersheds contained bacteria concentrations exceeding state standards. Some concentrations of fecal coliform bacteria were reported to be 174 times the health-based standards.[71]

Each day under resourced NPS professionals are called upon to weigh the interests of the two dozen ranch leaseholders—and those of some of their allies in the farming communities east of PRNS—against the interests of more than two million annual visitors to the PRNS. One likely outcome of this difficult balancing act is more compromise. The short-term outlook is for leases of shorter duration to be offered with more vigorous accountability and respect for the Coast Miwok legacy. Pressures will grow to protect the Drakes Estero and Tomales Bay watersheds and to clean up places like Abbott's Lagoon, remove many of the dairies while sunsetting leases of any noncompliant ranches. Court-ordered mediation efforts continue at this writing. The court has pressed both the ranchers and the most persistent environmentalists into a facilitated dialogue with unclear prospects.

The multiyear drought from 2017 through 2022 caused water tables on the Point Reyes Peninsula to plummet. Ranchers were forced to truck in ever more water and feed. A few more beef and dairy ranches left the peninsula, including the largest and oldest operation, run by the McClure family. The critical shortage of affordable housing for the workers in West Marin who serve the tourists and work the ranches grew so acute that in 2022, the Marin County Board of Supervisors enacted a two-year moratorium on any new short-term rental licenses in West Marin. Thus does the debate over public lands and park policies in Marin County continue. Neighbors of goodwill on all sides of this dispute have common goals: to protect the lands and waters for future generations while affording those who work in West Marin opportunities both to make a living and to preserve their common inheritance on the peninsula.

Limantour Beach and Drakes Bay. Author's collection.

CHAPTER SEVEN

Lessons Learned: Point Reyes and Future Policy Challenges

Most accounts of Point Reyes carry a similar refrain. It seems a miracle that there is this much open space—including wilderness trails, deep forests, and mile after mile of pure white sand beaches—so close to a major metropolitan area. This did not happen just because Marin County citizens loved nature. The creation of the greenbelt from Point Reyes through Mount Tamalpais, Muir Woods, and the Golden Gate headlands "is an act of social engineering," Richard Walker concludes. "So, let's clear our eyes about the blessings of nature, and see them through the prescription glasses of human action."[1]

Given the suburban sprawl that impacted so many California coastal communities, study of this anomaly that defines the San Francisco Bay Area proves especially instructive. Analyzing how it was achieved helps us understand how interest groups, coalitions, and legislative maneuvers can produce substantial results. It also helps us see the significant role played by luck and how good luck benefits from careful preparation.

Events could have gone another way. Success was achieved against considerable odds. Two ordinary citizens, Clem Miller and Katy Miller Johnson, made extraordinary efforts. Many others helped to lead. Consider what had to go right for the Point Reyes National Seashore (PRNS) and the Golden Gate National Recreation Area (GGNRA) to be created and then to be expanded.

The Abundance of What-Ifs

The archival record reveals a complex series of events that shaped the effort to preserve Point Reyes. Absent almost any one of these events, and the political dynamics and land use options they created, the Point Reyes seashore today would be lined with private developments. Its wetlands likely would have been dammed to create a powerboat marina, with much of the sand dunes paved over for parking lots and the ridgetops harvested for timber to create ocean views for thousands of private homes.

Individual initiative and grassroots lobbying prevented such an outcome. Consider just a few of the what-ifs from this political history, and the consequences of public policy choices become clear.

If the ham-handed administration of the region by Spain and then Mexico had encouraged immigration, Marin County would have had more settlements much sooner.

If the post–gold rush litigation over Point Reyes land had not resulted in one family of Vermont lawyers, the Shafters, owning all the land on the peninsula and committing most of it to dairies, more subdivisions would have arrived earlier.

If the back-to-nature outdoor recreation movement from 1870 to 1930 had not saved Muir Woods and created parklands on Mount Tamalpais, there would not have been a buffer shielding Point Reyes from suburban sprawl.

If the 1941 Japanese attack on Pearl Harbor had not mobilized the US military to occupy the Marin Headlands, the seacoast would have succumbed to development years earlier.

If the Democratic wave of 1958 had not begun the transformation of California from red to blue—leading to the election of Democrats Clem Miller and Clair Engle—local support might not have been strong enough for the federal initiative to create the national seashore at Point Reyes.

If Nixon had beaten Kennedy in the close 1960 presidential contest, the White House push for Cape Cod—which required a West Coast partner such as Point Reyes to provide regional balance—would not have occurred.

If a Berkeley group had not launched a 1961 campaign to protect the San Francisco Bay, Point Reyes supporters would not have had a ready local platform and grassroots model upon which to build their winning coalition.

If television coverage of the Santa Barbara oil spill had not sparked environmental activism, culminating in the massive turnout for the first Earth Day, there would not have been such strong national support for buying coastal parklands.

If the Point Reyes preservation battles had not been won in 1962 and

Drake's Bay
Estates For Sale
sign. Courtesy
of the Point
Reyes National
Seashore
Archives.

then *again* in 1970, it is unlikely that the GGNRA lands would have been secured.

Lessons learned from studying how policy advocates navigated these what-if scenarios can prove helpful to policymakers addressing future environmental policy challenges, such those presented by human-accelerated climate change. These lessons on timing and issue framing are baked into this case study. For example, note how park advocates pursued both immediate action items *and* the legislative long game. Observe how they built their case in Washington piece by piece while simultaneously building local coalitions. Recognize how advocates were able to generate grassroots support while remaining prepared to seize the moment when their champions could lobby the president directly in the Oval Office. Notice how park advocates reframed their arguments to court and win support from business interests. See how advocates evolved from first using federal champions and then creating local grassroots support to then using hybrid strategies supplemented by litigation.

How did David best Goliath? How did a nascent grassroots effort pull off this unlikely victory?

The bargaining to win these gains involved overt vote trades, regional alliances, and electioneering. It involved calculation by vote counters in Congress that it was best to accept "half a loaf," to enact an underfunded compromise bill as a legislative beachhead on the eve of the 1962 mid-term elections. They adopted a park outline that was an untenable mix of public and private tracts with insufficient funding to fill in the checker-board. Grassroots efforts were augmented by insider bank shots of grass-tops lobbying, pressing voter concerns directly from local leaders to federal decisionmakers.

It was not shifting politics alone that saved Point Reyes and blocked Marincello. It was not citizen action and petition drives alone that won these results. Larger economic forces were at work both in the Marin Head-lands and at Point Reyes. Soaring land values near one of the fastest-grow-ing metropolitan areas in the country meant Marin County's days as an agricultural region were numbered. It was skyrocketing land values—and the attendant tax increases—that forced many of the ranchers to agree to sell to the National Park Service (NPS). It was a recession and the threat of a growing consumer boycott that led Gulf to abandon its Marincello investment. The timing of these campaigns mattered. The legislative his-tory of the San Francisco Bay Area parks is also replete with examples of advocates taking advantage of election-eve opportunities and shifting interest-group politics to achieve what proved to be enduring victories.

Historical Applications for Policymakers

The history of the battle to preserve the PRNS is a story with many heroes but few villains.[2] The zeal of conservation advocates should not obscure the legitimacy of the differing perspectives of park opponents. Ranchers such as Zena Mendoza Cabral, who wanted only to pass lands her family had worked for generations on to her children, gave compelling congressional testimony against the park, which they believed would force them to forfeit their rights. As Cabral stated, Point Reyes "is where my children were born and my grandchildren raised. . . . Now I am faced with the possibility of losing everything . . . every inch of my land is supposed to disappear."[3] Other ranchers' voices, from the Stewarts' to the McClures', echoed the sentiment. It was only by dividing the opposition that local activists were able in 1962 to persuade the Marin Board of the Supervisors to support the federal initiative to create a national seashore. Similar divide-and-conquer tactics worked in 1969 to win the *support* of many ranchers that was needed to secure full federal funding to complete the park.

Home builders in West Marin are often vilified by environmental activists. It should be clear, however, that the developers were *responding* to pressing consumer demands in Marin and throughout the Bay Area. The same is true of the beef and dairy ranches—and even the "butter empire" the Shafters created—as these were responses to soaring consumer demand, action taken by farsighted business adventurers who risked their capital. Voters, taxpayers, and new California residents had urgent needs for more housing and transportation infrastructure; they still do today. It is understandable that many investors in the 1950s and 1960s resisted the public lands proposals of federal bureaucrats and local activists. Outdoor recreation advocates intent on building marinas and golf courses on the Point Reyes Peninsula believed freeways were essential to make the new park more accessible. However wrongheaded these initiatives may seem in hindsight, they sought to advance the interests of millions of diverse city dwellers, not just those of Marin residents and wilderness hikers.

In the years since the national seashore was created at Point Reyes, Marin officials have sharply limited construction of housing. The proximity of Point Reyes, Muir Woods, and Mount Tamalpais parklands has helped make homes in Marin among the most valuable in the nation. These values reflect the fact that Marin residents are privileged to live so close to vast open spaces. Here, so-called green politics have manifestly been an alliance that has advanced the interests of both environmentalists and wealthy homeowners.

In the end, it took not just the one act of Congress authorizing the PRNS in 1962 or the second major effort, in 1969 and 1970, to secure funding.[4] Instead, success also benefited from a raft of legislation pushed by the political transformation that vaulted the environmental cause to the top of the national agenda for a time. Efforts to secure the peninsula against commercial development were built upon in the 1970s by carving out the boundaries of the Burton Wilderness Area within the PRNS. The legacy included the 1981 creation offshore from Point Reyes of the Gulf of Farallones National Marine Sanctuary of nearly 1,000 square miles as well as the nearly 400-square-mile Cordell Bank National Marine Sanctuary in 1989. It was the combination of all these measures that fully secured public access to a protected seashore at Point Reyes while helping to restore the natural habitats of tule elk, harbor seals, and other vulnerable native species.[5]

These were rarely partisan campaigns. The two national parties were undergoing dramatic realignment in the 1960s and 1970s. This was an era when Democrats were playing catch-up on the "ecology" issue, but Republicans soon were on the defensive. As Samuel Hays notes, "the Washington-based environmental movement of the 1970s emphasized practical gains rather than affirmation of ideologies."[6] Through the course of several generations, the leadership baton in this bipartisan relay was frequently passed. It moved from local Republican activists to Democrats in Congress, from Republican members of California's congressional delegation to the Nixon White House. Leadership in this effort went from Department of the Interior planners to the self-styled group of "little old ladies in tennis shoes" who promoted Bay Area conservation in the early 1960s.[7]

Leadership passed to Democratic President Kennedy and Congressman Miller in 1961. Then it was shared by a series of Republican leaders, such as Peter Behr and Pete McCloskey. Then the point position shifted back to California Democrats and then to the Nixon White House, where Congressman McCloskey lobbied John Ehrlichman. In subsequent years, funds for expansion of the PRNS and the GGNRA were secured through efforts led exclusively by Democrats Nancy Pelosi, Dianne Feinstein, and Barbara Boxer.

Starting in 1993, *both* California Senate seats were held by Northern California Democratic women for the next twenty-eight years. This fact is in some measure attributable to the extraordinary power and resources of Bay Area environmental activists, backed by Democratic donors from Silicon Valley to Berkeley and Pacific Heights. By the turn of the new century, GOP leaders in Washington were counseled to avoid taking on parks funding and public lands protection measures, which George W. Bush pollster Frank Luntz noted in 2003 had become "the most popular federal programs today . . . [including] conservation of public lands and waters through parks and open spaces."[8]

An Environmental Case Study Reveals National Precedents

From our contemporary perspective, the twentieth-century debates over California parks seem remarkably *civil*—bargaining among neighbors to protect the competing interests of park visitors and the ranchers. Beginning in 1963, developers' stakes and hunting lodges, rodeo rings, paved roads, and concrete infrastructure for large housing blocs atop Limantour Beach were removed. Logging operations at Point Reyes were shut down. The eighteen tract homes that had already been constructed at Drake's Bay Estates were hauled away on flatbed trucks, with just a few retained

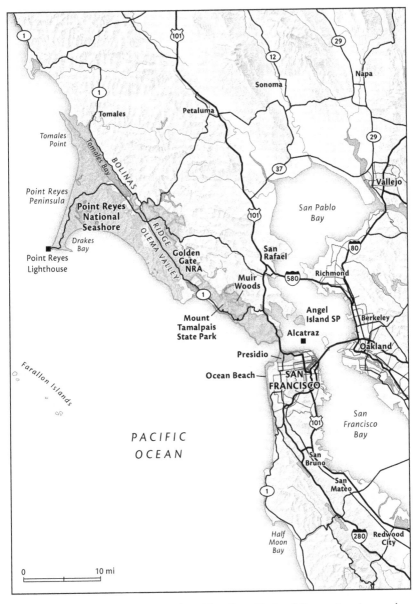

Point Reyes National Seashore and Golden Gate National Recreation Area today.
Courtesy of Erin Greb Cartography.

for NPS use and one being repurposed as the first, temporary Bear Valley National Seashore Information Center in the mid-1960s.[9] A portion of the large asphalt parking lot at Drakes Bay was finally removed in 2021, restoring more natural wetlands for the abundant migratory birds and sea life that pass daily through the seashore's lands and waterways.[10]

Applying lessons learned from the Point Reyes story yields several helpful insights for public policymakers. The fights over Point Reyes illustrate at least three key themes that can readily be applied to current policy challenges such as energy and climate adaptation.

1. Legislative Victories Are Difficult to Sustain. There are rarely final victories in modern American political history. Granting women suffrage in the 1920s did not secure equal rights for women, nor did the Supreme Court ruling in the 1973 *Roe v. Wade* case ensure that access for women to reproductive health would not subsequently be curtailed. Adoption of the Civil Rights Act in 1965 did not end racial discrimination. In analogous fashion, but on a far more modest scale, passage of the 1962 authorizing legislation did not secure a park at Point Reyes. Advocates in each battle had to build their case methodically if they were to prevail over the long term. Strategists need to know when it may be best to embrace incremental strategies, to accept a legislative deal to secure part of their goal, as Miller and Engle did with their 1962 compromise. Legislators and NGO leaders need to devise fallback options for how to use an initially modest victory to build the case for securing the remainder of their objectives in a sustained follow-up campaign. The Point Reyes story underscores the benefits of incrementalism and of preparing the next generation of allies to carry on the issue in the future, after the original authors have passed from the scene. Having the infrastructure in place to renew grassroots organizations and to help new champions emerge is one crucial way to sustain a policymaking victory.

2. Timing for New Initiatives Is Crucial. Legislators and NGO leaders often work for years with minimal results before finally achieving a policymaking breakthrough. Progress in realizing a vision backed by activists can take decades. Public policy advocates benefit from having clear benchmark goals for both the short and long term. They need to prepare for an extended battle but also to recognize the moment when their political stars have aligned. They must know when to sail with the prevailing political winds when a promising opportunity arrives. In the case of Point Reyes, this meant waiting four years to see action on the original 1958 seashore study and then essentially hitching a ride on President Kennedy's Cape Cod bandwagon. Then it meant waiting for another seven years—until after the 1969 Santa Barbara oil spill made environmental protection and coastline preservation a front-page story—before pressing for full funding to complete Point Reyes land acquisition. Although the science of climate policy creates great urgency, activists in both NGO and corporate boardrooms may accomplish more by balancing short-term demands with robust plans for the long game. For example, after the failure of the 2010 effort by Congress to enact cap-and-trade legislation, champions waited more than a decade before successfully passing a significant set of climate policy proposals. These finally were enacted in a catch-all Democratic measure pushed by the Biden administration, the Inflation Reduction Act, that Congress moved via the budget reconciliation process in August 2022.

3. Coalitions Are Essential. The fruits of policymakers' labors often are harvested after their champions have departed the scene. This fact upholds the belief held by many religious faiths that it is a noble act to plant seeds for trees that won't flourish until the next generation. Kent did not live to see a national park atop Tamalpais. Wirth waited three decades before his vision for Point Reyes inched forward. Clem Miller never got to see the opening of the PRNS. Phil Burton did not live to see much of the San Francisco Presidio and Marin Headlands restored as parklands. The campaigns they led, however, were advanced after their deaths by such individuals as Katy Miller Johnson, Huey Johnson, Bill Duddleson, Amy Meyer, and Nancy Pelosi. Each used the political infrastructure Miller, Cranston, and Burton had systematically built. They formed alliances and attracted political allies. These coalitions endured through numerous setbacks until they prevailed. The most effective NGO groups today must make similar investments in building sustainable organizations to advance their issues over multiple generations. This is equally true of groups such as the conservative Heritage Foundation or Federalist Society and the liberal Center for American Progress. Each has created virtual farm teams to develop ideas and to train future activists, lawmakers, and judges.

The political history of the Northern California parks offers a rich case study for a body of academic literature on NGO leadership that is still in its infancy. There are several good sources that can help identify and apply the lessons learned by activists pressing causes such as the park at Point Reyes. One useful guide encouraging NGO leaders to adopt best practices from the business world originated in a University of Virginia workshop on NGO leadership and management guided by the longtime dean of the Darden School of Business, Robert Bruner.[11] Another checklist that is on point grows from the tribute John Hart wrote based on interviews with California activists from the Point Reyes and GGNRA campaigns. It offers an accessible to-do list from environmental campaign veterans, abbreviated as follows:

Start with a specific local challenge.
Go to the meeting. Show up and be heard.
Do your homework. Know the facts. Use them.
Be persistent. Trench warfare is the norm.
Earn trust. Never exaggerate or twist facts.
Don't burn bridges, build them.[12]

Hart's list is drawn directly from the experience of early environmental policy leaders in Northern California. It highlights the importance of both creating alliances and winning converts. The ability of one side of a political argument to swing an influential voice from the opposition is often the crucial factor that alters the political dynamic. Boyd Stewart and the ranchers of Point Reyes were key to support for the full funding of PRNS land acquisitions. Converting votes on the Marin County Board of Supervisors and the unprecedented recall and replacement of a county supervisor in 1961 were essential to overcome the initial opposition to Point Reyes becoming a national seashore and to convince Chairmen Aspinall and Bible to move the PRNS authorizing legislation.

Collaborations between corporate partners and nonprofits have played a significant role in addressing other issues in the United States, from childhood hunger to efforts by fast-food corporations to reduce consumer waste. Vogel's definitive history of California's green politics notes how environmentalists benefit from coalitions with business group breakaways or converts to the cause. In such coalition partnerships, today's adversary may become tomorrow's ally.

This phenomenon was clearly manifested in the Point Reyes story. Consider how McCloskey and Ehrlichman were able to move Nixon to act on environmental agenda items. It was not an easy sell: President Nixon was by no means a "birds and bees" champion, as Ehrlichman wryly noted. Proponents of the PRNS needed to convince some of the ranchers that their interests would be protected. Only after the opposition was split could the national seashore proposal win support for completion. Groups active in climate policy have applied similar lessons to enlist large corporations in coalitions to back specific environmental measures. The first attempt in 2010 to pass legislation capping carbon emissions in the United States while facilitating the trading of emissions allowances, the so-called Waxman-Markey cap-and-trade bill, was backed not only by environmental groups launched in the 1960s but also by large utilities and energy companies, including Duke Power and Shell. Business allies sought market certainty and a clear definition of marketplace rules.

What did the PRNS champions conclude were the key lessons learned? Recruited to return to Washington and testify nearly two decades after her lobbying campaign, Katy Miller Johnson told the House Interior Committee in April 1987 that the unlocking of the Land and Water Conservation Fund (LWCF) proved key, for when it was replenished for Point Reyes in the Nixon-Aspinall-Saylor deal, "lo and behold the Land and Water Conservation Fund was unlocked for the rest of the nation." Johnson summarized the experience for the committee chairman, George Miller (no relation), a Democrat from the East Bay: "Mr. Chairman, there are two lessons from that story which are relevant to today's budget crunch on parks: first, that officials in government underestimate how much the people care about their parks, and second, that priorities can be quickly rearranged by government—money can miraculously materialize to support parks."[13]

Katy Miller Johnson's takeaway also included her recognition that Saylor had dug in his heels when offered a Point Reyes–only deal in 1969 but chose to hold out for hundreds of millions more from the LWCF; she insisted that this showed "how important it was just to stick to a position under some circumstances, how important it is to know when not to compromise."[14] Local environmental activists are lionized in most retellings of this challenge: "[These] leaders have a habit of taking on seemingly hopeless campaigns—and winning," as John Hart notes.[15] These accomplishments in the face of great odds are repeatedly cited by activists as a source of inspiration. "Other places heard about what happened here," Harold Gilliam said of the Point Reyes battles, "and began to realize that victory was possible after all, in spite of the fact that the big interests and big money were on the other side."[16]

Amy Meyer, the brilliant citizen-activist who was the driving force behind the creation and growth of the GGNRA adjacent to Point Reyes, reflected on the success of the two parks a half century later in an interview.

She stressed the importance of starting small with a specific goal and then growing from that beginning. She likened her hopes for the nascent parks to growing a crystal: "When you have a crystal and you put it in proper solution, the crystal gradually grows. That's what we had. What happened passed my hopes or knowledge each step of the way. The idea that people are engaged, want to contribute, and want to get involved in something that is bigger than themselves is running through this park like a trail."[17]

Clem Miller gets the last word on this point. He was aware of the challenges of taking on developers in the name of conservation, of using taxpayer dollars to purchase and protect lands against development. He repeatedly cautioned his supporters to be cognizant of the difficulty of asking members of Congress to vote for bills that spent taxpayer dollars when the politically smart move might be to oppose such spending, noting in a 1961 address that "the conservation bill is the easiest one to vote against—the one that will build up a Member's 'economy' record."[18] While spreading his wings and beginning to give speeches beyond his California district, likely as part of an exploratory effort for a possible US Senate run, Miller counseled the California Wildlife Federation not to be too righteous in its lobbying efforts: "It is an unfortunate fact that a whole lot of conservationists exhibit the qualities most calculated to get a congressman sore."[19]

Feasibility: Point Reyes and the Overton Window

Generalizing useful lessons from the specific case study of Point Reyes requires caution. Many external factors were involved in the Point Reyes success. These included the rise of the antiwar and civil rights movements as well as the growing voter consciousness of the environment sparked by the Santa Barbara disaster. Insights into political feasibility drawn from the Point Reyes case can nevertheless prove useful. At each step of the fight for creation of the PRNS, advocates did best when they had sound political intelligence. Policy entrepreneurs were required to make an unsentimental assessment of what was politically doable at a given point in time to understand the context of the times.

Political scientist Joseph Overton offers a concept that can be helpful here, an idea called the Overton window.[20] This is a measure of the political bandwidth available for a successful policy proposal. The concept offers a reality check of what is feasible versus what is beyond the ability of the current political opening to accommodate. If your proposal resides inside the Overton window, you are pushing policies that may prove acceptable to mainstream voters at that point in time. You have a chance of getting this proposal adopted and making it stick through public law or regulation. Think of the Overton window principle like the Goldilocks test. Overton helps assess whether some proposed policies may prove too hot or too cold for the contemporary political discourse. This test can prove a crucial aid in determining what is achievable.

Public policy examples of the Overton window concept abound. For example, the legalization of marijuana was not doable in 1970, nor was federal support for gay marriage rights. Grassroots lobbying and successful litigation moved the window substantially on both these issues. Interest groups shifted the window by sustained lobbying campaigns. Today a majority of American voters embrace these positions. As a result of interest-group activism and new legal precedents, the public discourse has changed. So, too, have voter attitudes.

The importance of Overton's concept is on display in this reassessment of the Point Reyes battle. From 1958 through 1962, Engle and Miller had to repeatedly reassess what was doable. They had to be realistic about the political context of their times. Miller was an idealist, but one whose decisions were informed by the careful calculus of a savvy politician, albeit a relative legislative novice.

If Miller had proposed in 1959 that the Point Reyes Peninsula be declared a protected wilderness, that the ranches and the oyster farm be ejected, that tule elk be reintroduced and given free range, and that US taxpayers spend more than $50 million to buy land, his idea would have gone nowhere. He would not have gotten even a committee hearing from Chairman Aspinall. When Miller decided in 1962 to accept a smaller park with large private holdings incorporated, he was compromising based on careful calculation. He proceeded with the added intelligence gained by his extraordinary effort to speak directly to all 434 of his House colleagues to gauge their support for his bill.

Political calculations played a similar role in parallel environmental protection efforts that energized Point Reyes activists. Consider the Save San Francisco Bay (Save the Bay) campaign initiated by a grassroots group in 1961. If the three Berkeley women who launched the effort to block their city from filling in tidelands had insisted at the outset on a series of maximum demands, they would have failed. Yet their modest start of a letter-writing campaign opposing the Berkeley city proposal to fill just 4,000 more acres led within years to a moratorium on any more Bay fill and ultimately to a regional program of tidelands restoration. Because of their work, the San Francisco Bay is larger today than it was in 1961.

The same calculation of benefits was in evidence in the fights over Mineral King, Redwood National Park, and the GGNRA. In the latter case, consider what would have happened if proponents in 1972 had insisted that the government commit to spending close to $100 million to buy lands for more parks in San Francisco and Marin and to turn over the Sixth Army's headquarters at the Presidio to the NPS. There was no way President Nixon would have endorsed such a plan. The GGNRA has grown piece by piece over the course of several generations.

Viewed through the efforts of early environmental activists, it is easier now to see that much of the progress on environmental policy issues for liberals and conservatives alike has been incremental. The experience of California parks champions demonstrates that building campaign infrastructure, expanding organizational capacity, growing association membership, creating coalitions, and educating voters are all key elements necessary for long-term success. They create a platform for growth. Look once more at the origin stories of the large environmental groups. It is from humble beginnings such as the Mount Tamalpais hiking clubs that groups such as the Sierra Club, Earth Justice, and the League of Conservation Voters grew into national organizations. The environmental movement also gave rise to new industries, not just in renewable energy and pollution control but also in outdoor recreation fueled by the backpacking boom, with roots in baby boomers' car camping in national parks in the post–World War II era.[21]

Timing: Point Reyes and the Moment of Opportunity

The numerous associations created by Caroline Livermore provided local models for the Save San Francisco Bay group, the Save Our Seashore (SOS) campaign, and the PRNS Foundation. These types of organizations have a long history in the United States. From the Sons of Liberty and other organizations pushing for American independence from Great Britain, interest groups evolved in the new nation. Alexis de Tocqueville saw this clearly in the early nineteenth century. In his classic *Democracy in America*, he wrote of the remarkable proclivity of Americans to form their own neighborhood-based groups to advance their agenda. His observations clearly anticipated the power of local organizations such as SOS as they squared off against the developers. Such citizen groups have proved to be gap-fillers throughout our nation's history. NGOs fill in where gaps exist between local concerns and federal objectives. Nongovernmental associations flourish when neither the government nor the private sector is meeting the needs of a vocal group of citizens.

There is an additional lesson from the Point Reyes experience that is a useful takeaway here. This idea supplements the Overton window concept by emphasizing that groups can work on issues for decades and see only limited progress. Think of Knight and Wirth's pre–World War II proposal for a park at Point Reyes, one that would have cost less than 5 percent of what land purchases required a generation later. When the opportunity for action does finally arise—because of years of work by interest groups or due to a sudden change in external factors—the Overton window shifts. What was unthinkable for decades suddenly becomes possible, but only if NGO leaders and legislative allies can move with agility. This means that policy advocates need to know where they are in the political life of the nation. They must be clear-eyed in their realistic appraisal and then must recognize when it is time to advance with no thought of retreat.

Examples of this phenomenon are plentiful. From gun safety to criminal justice reform, some leaders have been able to seize the day when dynamics change. Leaders cannot do this, however, if the organizational infrastructure is not in place. They must first ensure that the foundational homework has been done. Consider how President Barack Obama early in his tenure used the need for economic stimulus to load up legislative proposals with a wish list of shovel-ready construction projects that would both stimulate the economy and advance his environmental policy agenda. These ranged from the extension of the Metro to Dulles Airport in Virginia to controversial federal subsidies for producers of solar energy equipment.

Idealism tempered by realistic calculation proved essential for groups working to create a national seashore at Point Reyes. Conservation champions began with an ambitious vision in Marin. This originated with Kent's 1905 dream of a Tamalpais National Park in Marin County. The vision grew with the 1935 NPS study of a possible national park at Point Reyes. When Miller arrived in Washington as a freshman congressman in 1959, he continued to make incremental progress. His first move with Senator Engle after $15,000 in federal funds were appropriated for a feasibility study was to propose a small shoreline park at Point Reyes. Once Miller had established that legislative foundation, he expanded his efforts, pressing for the creation of grassroots support groups and pushing for an ever larger national seashore.

The Save San Francisco Bay campaign had similarly modest origins. When the early 1960s grassroots efforts to halt the filling of the bay began, its target was just the Berkeley City Council. The campaign snowballed, however, leading to the creation of the Bay Conservation and Development Commission and the California Coastal Commission as well as major changes in how the nation's most populous state regulates public lands and waters.

Consider how efforts with such modest origins have impacted future generations. It is a substantial legacy. The GGNRA and Point Reyes have become the second-most-visited sites in the entire national park system. In 2019, the last pre-pandemic year for which data is available, 327 million people visited lands administered by the NPS; the parks saw increasing numbers of visitors at several intervals during the COVID-19 pandemic. There nevertheless remained in 2022 a backlog of some $12 billion in deferred national park maintenance, despite Biden administration proposals to hire more rangers and dedicate more federal resources to parks.[22]

The takeaway lessons from Point Reyes for practitioners are clear. Know what is doable in the short term by soberly assessing the bandwidth of the Overton window. Work to change the political dynamics. Promote both grassroots activism and grasstops lobbying targeting key federal decision-makers. Prepare to act swiftly when NGO efforts and surprise developments create a new dynamic. As Rahm Emmanuel, President Obama's first White House chief of staff, liked to declare, "Never waste a good crisis." Groups cannot exploit a wave of public opinion, however, unless they have prepared both crisis *and* opportunity plans while systematically building their organization's capacity to act.

At Point Reyes, the simple fact that President Kennedy was pushing his Cape Cod bill and needed a West Coast proposal to partner it with so as not to appear parochial was a lucky boost. The park might never have realized its potential if a similar moment-in-time phenomenon had not occurred in 1969. After the Santa Barbara disaster, White House aides Ehrlichman and Whitaker convinced Nixon that he needed to get out ahead on the environment issues to blunt the support for Democratic Senator Muskie heading towards the 1972 presidential race and to help Republican Senator Murphy's reelection in 1970.

Chairman Aspinall and Congressman Saylor took advantage of this confluence of events by raising the political ante on President Nixon. Phil

Burton a few years later seized upon their precedent to allocate park resources like traditional pork-barrel funds; his 1978 parks bill was exponentially larger than any measure Aspinall and Saylor had ever moved. These developments were all manifestations of the corollary to Overton: successful politicians use inflection points to press advantages when the moment in time arrives and then push forward to seize the opportunities presented and to exploit them to help advance a legislative agenda.

Cycles in American Politics and the Point Reyes Campaign

There is one more analytic construct illustrated by the Point Reyes experience to be weighed before concluding: the idea first advanced by Arthur Schlesinger, Jr., that the political life of the American people moves in discernible cycles.[23] Schlesinger notes that for much of the twentieth century, the cycles of American politics swung like a pendulum. The progressivism and selective government activism of Teddy Roosevelt and Woodrow Wilson led to the conservative "return to normalcy" that embraced a stable status quo under Presidents Harding and Coolidge. When President Hoover's laissez-faire approach to market regulation proved inadequate in the wake of the stock market crash and resulting economic depression, a generation of big-government programs poured forth under FDR and Truman. After World War II and Korea, Presidents Eisenhower and Kennedy were too slow for many voters to move on civil rights for Black Americans; it then fell to President Johnson of Texas to pass sweeping civil rights measures. After LBJ's era of big government Great Society programs, the countervailing reaction led to the conservative presidencies of Nixon, Ford, Reagan, and George H. W. Bush.[24]

Schlesinger's cycles offer a valuable analytical tool to help reflect upon lessons from Point Reyes. Think about the challenges confronting public policymakers in the California of the 1950s. Look at the growth of population in the state. Look at the differences in how Orange County and Marin County responded. After years of exponential population growth in California, the political cycle turned against the filling in of tidelands and the construction of housing blocs on coastal headlands.

McCloskey's recollection of being accosted in the House cloakroom by Republican colleagues angry about the Dirty Dozen campaign is especially revealing on this point. For years after the first Earth Day, neither major political party resisted the legislative push for new environmental protection measures. Throughout the 1970s, there was limited opposition among even the most conservative legislators to the environmental policy measures proliferating in both Washington and Sacramento.

Schlesinger's cycles illustrate the fact that excess usually begets reform. In American political history, the pendulum rarely swings too far before a course correction ensues. The zeal of righteous environmental activists, which peaked in the 1970s, met with a predictable counter-reaction under President Reagan in 1981. While environmental champions were passing laws, other interest groups opposed to their goals were gathering resources under the banner of the so-called sagebrush rebellion. These groups ardently defended private property rights, especially in the states west of the Mississippi River, where the federal government has for generations controlled a large percentage of lands. In the wake of the 1970s, American voters twice sent Ronald Reagan to the Oval Office with a broad mandate to champion individual liberty, private property rights, and small government.

Reagan, the former Democrat, fashioned himself as a rugged individualist. The longtime resident of Hollywood often appeared in a cowboy hat during his presidency while spending time horseback riding, entertaining, or clearing brush in the mountains near Santa Barbara. He advanced a view of the relationship of citizens to the land that was strikingly different from the public position taken by Nixon after the Santa Barbara disaster—which occurred just a few miles south of what would become Reagan's western White House ranch.

It is no coincidence that every Republican elected president since Calvin Coolidge—except for the two nonpoliticians Eisenhower and Trump—had their political base in California or Texas. These are states where the relationship between private property rights and the federal government has been fraught since each achieved statehood before the Civil War. The triumphalist literature that celebrates the rise of the environmental movement often fails to provide a sober assessment of the political reaction sparked by federal regulations. Just as Lyndon Johnson "lost" the South for Democrats with his championship of civil rights, so, too, have Democrats pushing environmental protection exacerbated the urban-rural divide in the Mountain West. This has contributed to the loss of support for Democrats among rural voters in much of the "flyover" country between midwestern cities and the Pacific Coast, coloring hundreds of predominantly rural counties bright red on political maps—although some states in the region, such as Colorado and Arizona, have grown politically competitive as their city and suburban populations have swelled with Democratic voters.

Point Reyes and Marin County History in Context

Marin used to be called a "cow county." The county seat of San Rafael was a ranch supply town. It was once considered so typical of Middle America that local filmmaker George Lucas used San Rafael's main drag of Fourth Street for scenes in his classic movie *American Graffiti*. By the 1960s, however, as the county population grew and home values skyrocketed, journalists began to caricature "Marvelous Marin" as a place where everybody supposedly had a backyard hot tub and drove a European import.

If there was a global headquarters for proponents of the NIMBY outlook, cynics suggest, surely it would be in exclusive Marin County villages such as Belvedere or Ross. These are towns where some houses built in the 1950s for less than $10,000 on choice lots formed out of landfill along the Belvedere Lagoon were sold in 2022 for more than $10 million. Yet the public housing hastily constructed in Marin City during World War II for some of Marin County's first Black citizens remains isolated eighty years later, backed into a canyon and cut off from bay access by a ten-lane freeway. Marin City still suffers from substandard schools and decaying public housing blocs.

The charge of elitism has dogged the environmental movement since the days of the railroad barons backing national parks. It took a century for the Sierra Club to address the racism of some of its founders, including the exalted John Muir. San Francisco progressives in the first half of the twentieth century embraced some virulent racists, including Mayor James Phelan and his Senate campaign to "Keep California White." Parks champion William Kent left an extraordinary legacy; he is celebrated as a generous leader who helped shape modern Marin. Yet parallel to his championship of parks, Kent firmly embraced and advanced racist anti-Asian, anti-immigrant policies that were central elements in his legislative agenda in Congress.

Citizens involved in early parks legislation and companies hiring immigrant crews to build the roads and lay the train tracks up Mount Tamalpais and over White's Hill to Point Reyes often looked the other way regarding overtly racist acts in the Bay Area.[25] These include the Chinese exclusion acts, the detention of Japanese American farmers from West Marin, and the repeated use of Marin's bucolic Angel Island as an internment camp for Asian immigrants.

This legacy offers some insight into why exclusive Marin has benefited so greatly from the parks. Marin County residents blocked the proposed four-lane freeways to Point Reyes, yet the freeway plan would have made the remote park more accessible to urban residents. Still today, West Marin residents resist more public signage that might help auto drivers find the national seashore at the end of narrow, winding roads. For decades, guerrilla activists in the town of Bolinas have systematically removed every effort by the county public works department to erect road signs to help visitors find the town at the southern end of the national seashore. The nearest highway, US 101, still has zero signs directing visitors to the PRNS. Many Marin residents love their proximity to nature yet welcome various local efforts to limit access.

City dwellers have not been able to live closer to the open public lands in part because there has for decades been so little affordable housing in Marin. Public parks and water district lands have blocked 50 percent of the county from any housing development, and the BART subway and rail system remains excluded. Higher housing density in Marin could enable more citizens to live in closer proximity to wilderness. Instead, the East Bay still has concentrations of poorer, more ethnically diverse communities adjacent to oil refineries and shipyards. The resulting pollution has had an especially harmful impact on the health of residents in places such as Richmond and Vallejo, communities disproportionately inhabited by people of color.

Critics of environmental activism aimed at rewilding Point Reyes cite the need to protect the cultural heritage of parklands and to respect the traditions of the local population. This argument can be taken only so far. At Point Reyes, the Shafters were not natives of Marin or California. They were Vermont dairymen and politicians and then transplanted San Francisco lawyers and fortune seekers. They were city investors who gained most of their West Marin lands in lieu of legal fees and then repeatedly sought to develop the lands for commercial gain by proposing housing subdivisions and new resort towns on peninsula lands. They were business owners who, for two generations, reaped profits from hunting clubs and tenant farmers from whose lands virtually all traces of scores of Miwok villages and their cultural heritage were erased. At some point, reverence for one particular land use—grazing cows on public parklands—needs to embrace and respect the Coast Miwok, whose cultural heritage from centuries of living on these lands warrants preservation, too.

Most of the Shafter tenants were first-generation European immigrants who were hard workers; they fished, grazed cattle, and ran the dairies. They were not natives, yet their success is a quintessentially American story. They came to form the backbone of the Point Reyes community in the first half of the twentieth century; families who fished and staffed the dairies had an outsize impact on local politics, construction, and sports, with names such as Alioto, Mendoza, DiMaggio, Kehoe, and Giacomini.[26]

The summer of 2021 brought news that the owners of the longest-running and largest independent dairy at Point Reyes, the McClure ranch near the seashore's north end, were selling their dairy cows and shutting down their dairy operations on parklands.[27] The McClures had held on for five generations. They believed that public policy choices on land and water use, combined with the prolonged multi-year drought, had forced the family out of a business they had maintained for decades. It wasn't just the sinking water tables throughout the region; the McClures were also undermined by an oversupply in the organic dairy business as a growing number of competitors made their costs noncompetitive.

Point Reyes and Climate Policy

Park visits remained in high demand as the COVID-19 pandemic that began in the early months of 2020 lingered. The disruption of Bay Area commuting patterns during the pandemic, as many people worked from home, also changed the thinking of many about certain public policy choices. March 2020 marked the first time in human history that all global citizens endured a long crisis *together*, in real time, while being able to share their experience daily via social media with others among the eight billion people impacted. It is unclear how this shared experience of a global public health crisis will impact efforts to address climate change. Climate change policy activists will need to use some of the same tactics employed by national park advocates to increase their chances for progress. It is one thing for citizens to witness more superstorms, once-in-a-thousand-year droughts, epic floods, and catastrophic wildfires sweeping into suburbs. It is another to translate awareness of these specific manifestations of accelerating climate change into a consensus on legislative action to address a global challenge that will require multilateral collaboration.

The Point Reyes experience offers some lessons that are more portable to our current era than others. What has not changed is the fact that legislative progress often requires action on multiple fronts, so-called over-under strategies where policy advocates press committee leaders in Congress and White House officials while also fueling grassroots activism to highlight evidence of voter concern. Climate policy advocates face challenges with some distinct similarities. It is insufficient to set global targets, as was done at Paris and Copenhagen, if enough progress is not made in individual national capitals, such as Brasília, where the fight to curb deforestation in the Amazon continues. It is insufficient to phase out use of internal combustion engines that motor along the Great Highway along the open Pacific shoreline in San Francisco if India and China are still building dozens of new coal-fired plants. Climate activists must press their case on multiple fronts with flexible strategies, "thinking globally while acting locally" once again.

Environmental policy work succeeds when it is done with more partnership and less partisanship. Emphasis needs to be placed on creating a common factual basis for proceeding as well as respecting the short-term needs of citizens for jobs, transportation, and housing. The apparent elitism of First World policy advocates lecturing those who have far lower economic means, and who have historically contributed far less to heating the planet, must be checked by sober realism. Many of those most pointedly lecturing coal miners and highway builders about pollution regularly burn jet fuel traveling about the globe for adventure vacations or to visit second homes—homes often built on the edges of the wildland-urban interface in places such as Inverness, Lake Tahoe, Aspen, and Cape Cod.

The Point Reyes story illustrates the benefits of bipartisan collaboration and innovative public-private partnerships. Here, the history of the environmental movement in the American West and Washington is especially important. Yosemite, Yellowstone, and Glacier parks each got a major push from the railroad companies that planned to profit from tourists. The first parks in Marin County were created from private donations by benefactors interested in the common good but who also stood to gain financially. Similarly, many of the changes in Americans' environmental practices that have had the largest impacts have been achieved not through legislation but through coercion of corporate leaders by consumer groups. Climate policy initiatives will benefit from pressing producers to adopt more sustainable policies under threat of consumer backlash, similar to how fast-food companies were pressed by consumers and stockholders to reduce their environmental footprint. These initiatives advance more swiftly where grassroots activists have been able to forge coalitions with business interests. Such coalitions may do more to change Americans' carbon footprint than restrictive bills passed into law with razor-thin margins or executive orders subject to reversal each time the political pendulum swings.

Alliances between green activists and business interests aided the Point Reyes success. Miller brilliantly reframed his original pitch, going on local TV to note the beneficial impact that parks would have on Marin property values. In shifting the Overton window, Miller adopted the argument that the park would be good for business and land investments while generating income from tourists.

When voters are offered a choice between jobs and the environment, the stark income inequality in the United States will push jobs to the forefront most of the time. This is often a false choice, however. Green activists have better chances of success when they show more clearly that investments in new technologies can add more jobs in both the short and long terms. They would do well to learn from the 1960s battles to fund national parks—battles that demonstrated how reframing the parks cause as one that was good for business helped the environmentalists to win new allies.

Conclusion: The Tipping Point

The two distinct activist campaigns to establish the PRNS—and then to expand it and connect it by a continuous greenbelt to the Golden Gate headlands via the establishment of the GGNRA—altered the course of California environmental politics. These local battles proved to have national implications in at least seven respects:

1. The 1970 deal that quadrupled federal funds for Point Reyes land acquisition also reopened the LWCF for use by dozens of parks across the country.
2. The efforts to establish Cape Cod and Point Reyes led to the establishment of eleven more national seashores by 1975, while the original focus on public access to recreation at Point Reyes shifted dramatically from powerboat marinas and golf courses to the restoration of wilderness.
3. The original proposal for a shoreline park at Point Reyes as small as 28,000 acres grew to encompass dozens of sites and more than 150,000 acres around the San Francisco Bay.

4. Local grassroots groups associated with the Point Reyes battles grew into national organizations of exponentially greater capacity.
5. Conservation advocates working for the California parks helped fuel a national movement that produced a series of landmark environmental protection laws in both Washington and Sacramento.
6. The embrace of green politics by Democratic leaders in the late 1950s and 1960s helped flip the California congressional delegation to deep blue while costing Democrats favor with many rural voters throughout the Mountain West, from the Pacific Coast to the Mississippi River.
7. The culmination of environmental activism in these golden years was the 1978 omnibus "park-barrel" bill authored by San Francisco's Phil Burton, a gargantuan measure that expanded several California parks while funding NPS projects in more than 140 congressional districts across the country.

Local legend still maintains that grassroots activists secured Point Reyes simply by gathering petition signatures outside Bay Area grocery stores. The archival record shows that at key points, it was also grasstops tactics, efforts led by and targeting people working in Washington, that helped carry the day. The fact that these efforts were led by relative novices, Clem Miller and Katy Miller Johnson, only adds another human element to a story full of unexpected turns and enduring consequences.

Point Reyes Today and Tomorrow

The history of Point Reyes is told differently for different audiences. Local guidebooks invariably focus on Drake and the 1906 earthquake. Some versions glorify the clever lawyers, the Shafters, who seized the land. Other narratives vilify heirs of the Shafters and their tenants who managed the dairies. Those who would build homes for the soaring California population are caricatured in most versions of the Point Reyes origin story as heartless capitalists who sought to plunder the wilderness. NPS officials come in for sustained criticism even as they struggle to strike a balance between the interests of the ranchers and those of the wilderness hikers and tule elk champions. Some revisionist histories directly criticize the Save the Bay campaign, blaming the Berkeley activists who were intent on halting the dumping of garbage into the bay for the lack of affordable housing throughout much of the region.[28]

The reality on the ground is that, amidst sustained controversy that still makes local headlines, much of the Point Reyes Peninsula has been conserved and renewed as a thriving landscape while still reserving public lands for use by two dozen ranch leaseholders. The peninsula is again a bird sanctuary and home to elephant seals and tule elk. More than two million people visit the PRNS each year—and more than fifteen million people visit the companion GGNRA and Muir Woods on Mount Tamalpais—nearly eighteen million combined in 2020. In any fair accounting, the needs of these eighteen million citizens for engagement with a restored natural environment must be weighed against the interests of two dozen commercial ranches still operating on public parklands paid for, owned, and maintained by taxpayers. Yet how to strike a balance remains a challenge for policymakers. Many local environmental champions continue to believe that the presence of the ranches remains not just a commitment Congress and PRNS champions made in 1962 but also a choice that is still in the best interests of the agricultural community in West Marin. Each day, understaffed NPS rangers must mediate among these differing, righteous, and often litigious camps.

The people who originally championed more parks in the San Francisco Bay Area were explicit in their warnings about what would happen if the shorelines and hillsides were filled with freeways and housing tracts. It was young parents such as Clem Miller, Jack Kennedy, and Clair Engle who repeatedly invoked their obligation to future generations as a reason for action to conserve vanishing seashores. Their vision proved to be spot-on. The work of local citizens who labored to realize that vision also helped chart a path for generations of environmental activists in the United States.

Fire and water have reshaped these contested Marin County lands, even as the San Andreas Fault has remained ominously locked since 1906. In January 1982, a flash flood triggered by a Pacific storm that produced more than 10 inches of rainfall in less than twenty-four hours destroyed homes and roads, inundating the peninsula. West Marin towns were isolated for days. An illegal campfire on Mount Vision in October 1995 scorched more than 12,300 acres of woodlands and brush, destroyed forty-five homes adjacent to the national seashore boundary on Inverness Ridge, and threatened to wipe out the town of Inverness before it was contained.[29]

During a once-in-a-thousand-year drought in 2020, rare dry lightning strikes on August 17 ignited multiple fires near Sky Camp on Mount Wittenberg. Flames roared down the dry canyons and burned at the eastern end of Limantour Beach clear to the Pacific Ocean. The Bear Valley NPS headquarters and PRNS Archives were evacuated as more than 5,000 acres, one-fifth of the PRNS woodlands, burned. Fire lines were held at the Divide Meadow and at the Limantour Road, sparing the Clem Miller Environmental Education Center. Thousands of firefighters from across the western United States battled the blaze for six weeks before containment was finally achieved.

Within months of this conflagration on the Point Reyes Peninsula, new sprouts were visible, rising from roots beneath the dystopian landscape. The intense flames had cracked open seed cones, offering new life; it is clear that the uncontrolled burn had substantial ecological benefits. This capacity for healing is another silver lining amidst the dark future clouds represented by human-accelerated climate change. The challenges of preserving fragile public lands and addressing climate policies create an urgency familiar to generations of environmental leaders, who paraphrase an old baseball cliché: it may be the top of the ninth inning, and Planet Earth is taking its lumps, yet we can take some comfort in the fact that "nature bats last."

Today, you can walk for miles along the shoreline of Point Reyes and view a nearly pristine landscape. You are seeing the thriving open lands as the Coast Miwok appreciated them the day of first contact with Europeans in 1579, when Drake and his *Golden Hind* crew sailed in from the west, the first Englishmen to set foot on the North American continent. Through fire and flood, through the turmoil of American politics transformed, this unique preserve has, in fact, flourished. Political scientists and other public-minded citizens would do well to examine how this unlikely result was achieved.

In the final analysis, the Point Reyes case study offers cause for optimism. Here is a hopeful story where people of goodwill on all sides hammered out a series of compromises, agreements that protected extraordinarily beautiful lands and waters for future generations.

Timeline

1579	Englishman Drake harbors at Point Reyes
1769	Spaniard Portola travels overland to San Francisco Bay
1817	Catholic mission established at San Rafael
1820–1840	Coast Miwok population decimated
1830s	Mexican Republic offers land grants at Point Reyes
1848	Gold discovered in Sierra Nevada foothills
1850	California statehood ratified by US Congress
1850s	Shafter family lawyers secure titles to Point Reyes lands
1892	Sierra Club founded in San Francisco
1908	Theodore Roosevelt creates Muir Woods National Monument
1916	National Park Service (NPS) established
1935	NPS study suggests buying Point Reyes for $2.4 million
1937	Golden Gate Bridge opens Marin County to more autos
1941	World War II brings major military presence to Marin County
1950s	Cold War: US deploys nuclear missiles in Marin County
1956	NPS releases national study *Our Vanishing Seashore*
1955	Paradise Ranch Estates builds on Inverness Ridge
1956	Sweet Timber Lumber cuts at Inverness Ridge
1956	Road cut to new Limantour Beach subdivision
1958	NPS rushes study of Point Reyes National Seashore (PRNS)
1958	Congress earmarks $15,000 for PRNS economic study
1959	Rep. Miller and Sen. Engle jointly introduce PRNS proposal
1960	Drake's Bay Estates breaks ground at Limantour Beach
1960	Senate holds first PRNS hearing in Marin County
1961	Drake's Bay Pines subdivision incorporated
1961	House and Senate hearings on revised PRNS proposals
1961	President Kennedy signs Cape Cod National Seashore bill
1962	House and Senate pass $14 million PRNS authorization bill
1962	President Kennedy signs P.L. 87-657 creating PRNS
1962	Congressman Clem Miller dies in California plane crash
1963	President Kennedy is killed. Engle incapacitated by stroke.
1964	Wilderness Act and LWCF enacted
1965	Marin supervisors OK Marincello plans for 30,000 residents
1969	January: Santa Barbara oil spill draws nationwide coverage
1969	May: NPS proposes selling key parts of PRNS to developers

1969	November: President Nixon's Oval Office deal with Rep. Aspinall
1970	February: Pres. Nixon backs $320 million LWCF 1971 increase
1970	April: First Earth Day celebrated; 22 million participate nationwide
1970	April: President Nixon signs bill quadrupling funds for PRNS
1972	October: Department of the Interior completes/fully opens PRNS
1972	October: Nixon endorses GGNRA on visit to San Francisco
1972	November: California voters create Coastal Commission
1976	Congress creates 33,000-acre wilderness within PRNS
1981	Gulf of Farallones National Marine Sanctuary created by Congress
1989	Cordell Bank National Marine Sanctuary created by Congress
1989	US Army announces Presidio transfer to GGNRA
1995	Mount Vision fire rages, burns 12,300 acres at Point Reyes
1990s	GGNRA expands to thirty-seven San Francisco and Marin sites
2000s	MALT reserves 50,000-plus Marin acres for agricultural use only
2020	Mount Wittenberg fire burns 5,000 acres at PRNS
2022	Fiftieth Anniversary of PRNS completion

Key Participants

Grassroots Activists
Margaret Azevedo, Point Reyes National Seashore Foundation
Peter Behr, Save Our Seashore (earlier Marin County supervisor, later state senator)
David Brower, Sierra Club
Barbara Eastman, Point Reyes National Seashore Foundation
Esther Gulick, Save San Francisco Bay Association
Huey Johnson, The Nature Conservancy
Katharine Miller Johnson, Save Our Seashore
Catherine Kerr, Save San Francisco Bay Association
Caroline Livermore, Marin Conservation League
Bryan McCarthy, attorney for West Marin property owners
Sylvia McLaughlin, Save San Francisco Bay Association
Amy Meyer, Golden Gate National Recreation Area Foundation

Elected Officials
Representative Wayne Aspinall (D-CO)
Senator Alan Bible (D-NV)
Representative Phil Burton (D-San Francisco)
Representative Donald Clausen (R-Eureka)
Senator Alan Cranston (D-CA)
Representative William Kent (R-Kentfield)
Senator Thomas Kuchel (R-CA)
Representative Pete McCloskey (R-Palo Alto)
Representative Clement Miller (D-Corte Madera)
Senator George Murphy (R-CA)
Representative Nancy Pelosi (D-San Francisco)
Representative John Saylor (R-PA)

Federal Officials
George Collins, NPS San Francisco director of regional planning
William "Bill" Duddleson, office of Congressman Clem Miller
John Ehrlichman, White House domestic policy director
George Hartzog, NPS director

President Lyndon Johnson
President John Kennedy
Robert Mayo, Bureau of the Budget director
President Richard Nixon
Stuart Udall, secretary of the interior
John Whitaker, special assistant to President Nixon
Conrad Wirth, NPS director

Appendix: Key Documents Related to the Creation of PRNS

Document 1: 1962 Point Reyes Authorizing Bill as Enacted (excerpts)
PUBLIC LAW 87-657—SEPTEMBER 13, 1962
Public Law 87-657
September 13, 1962
An ACT
To establish the Point Reyes National Seashore in the State of California and for other purposes.

Be it enacted by the Senate and House of Representatives of the United States of America in the Congress assembled, That in order to save and preserve, for purposes of public recreation, benefit, and inspiration, a portion of the diminishing seashore of the United States that remains undeveloped, the Secretary of the Interior (hereinafter referred to as the "Secretary") is hereby authorized to take appropriate action in the public interest toward the establishment of the national seashore set forth in section 2 of this Act.

SEC. 2 (a) The area compromising that portion of the land and waters located on Point Reyes Peninsula, Marin County, California, which shall be known as the Point Reyes National Seashore, is described as follows by reference to that certain boundary map, designated NS-PR-7001, dated June 1, 1960, on file with the Director, National Park Service, Washington, District of Columbia.

. . .

SEC. 3 (a) Except as provided in section 4, the Secretary is authorized to acquire, and it is the intent of Congress that he shall acquire as rapidly as appropriated funds become available for this purpose or as such acquisition can be accomplished by donation or with donated funds or by transfer, exchange, or otherwise the lands, waters, and other property, and improvements thereon and any interest therein, within the areas described in section 2 of this Act or which lie within the boundaries of the seashore as established under section 5 of this Act (hereinafter referred to as "such area"). Any property, or interest therein, owned by a State or political subdivision thereof may be acquired only with the concurrence of such owner. Notwithstanding any other provision of law, any Federal property located within such area may, with the concurrence of the agency having custody thereof, be transferred without consideration to the administrative jurisdiction of the Secretary for use by him in carrying out the provisions of this Act. In exercising his authority to acquire property in accordance with the provisions of this subsection, the Secretary may enter into contracts requiring the expenditure, when appropriated, of funds authorized by section 8 of this Act, but the liability of the United States under any such contract shall be contingent on the appropriation of funds sufficient to fulfill the obligations thereby incurred.

(b) The Secretary is authorized to pay for any acquisitions which he makes by purchase under this Act their fair market value, as determined by the Secretary, who may in his discretion base his determination on an independent appraisal obtained by him.

(c) In exercising his authority to acquire property by exchange, the Secretary may accept title to any non-Federal property located within such area and convey to the grantor of such property any federally owned property under the jurisdiction of the Secretary within California and adjacent States, notwithstanding any other provision of law. The properties so exchanged shall be approximately equal in fair market value, provided that the Secretary may accept cash from or pay cash to the grantor in such an exchange in order to equalize the values of the properties exchanged.

SEC. 4 No parcel of more than five hundred acres within the zone of approximately twenty-six thousand acres depicted on map numbered NS-PR-7002, dated August 15, 1961, on file with the director, National Park Service, Washington, District of Columbia, exclusive of that land required to provide access for purposes of the national seashore, shall be acquired without the consent of the owner so long as it remains in its natural state, or is used exclusively for ranching and dairying purposes including housing directly incident thereto. The term "ranching and dairying purpose," as used herein means such ranching and dairying, primarily for the production of food, as is presently practiced in the area.

In acquiring access roads within the pastoral zone, the Secretary shall give due consideration to existing ranching and dairying uses and shall not unnecessarily interfere with or damage such use.

SEC. 5 (a) As soon as practicable after the date of enactment of this Act and following the acquisition by the Secretary of an acreage in the area described in section 2 of this Act, that is the opinion of the Secretary efficiently administrable to carry out the purposes of this Act, the Secretary shall establish Point Reyes National Seashore by the publication of notice thereof in the Federal Register.

(b) Such notice referred to in subsection (a) of this section shall contain a detailed description of the boundaries of the seashore which shall encompass an area as nearly as practicable identical to the area described in section 2 of this Act. The Secretary shall forthwith after the date of publication of such notice in the Federal Register (1) send a copy of such notice, together with a map showing such boundaries, by registered or certified mail to the Governor of the State and to the governing body of each of the political subdivisions involved; (2) cause a copy of such notice and map to be published in one or more newspapers which circulate in each of the localities; and (3) cause a certified copy of such notice, a copy of such map, and a copy of this Act to be recorded at the registry of deeds for the county involved.

Sec. 6 (a) Any owner or owners (hereinafter in this subsection referred to as "owner") of improved property on the date of its acquisition by the Secretary may, as a condition to such acquisition, retain the right of use and occupancy of the improved property for noncommercial residential purposes for a term of fifty years. The Secretary shall pay to the owner the fair market value of the property on the date of such acquisition less the fair market value on such date of the right retained by the owner.

(b) As used in this Act, the term "improved property" shall mean a private non-commercial dwelling, including the land on which it is situated whose construction was begun before September 1, 1959, and structures accessory thereto (hereinafter in this subsection referred to as "dwelling"), together with such amount and locus of the property adjoining and in the same ownership as such dwelling as the Secretary designates to be reasonably necessary for the enjoyment of such dwelling for the sole purpose of noncommercial residential use and occupancy. In making such designation the Secretary shall take into account the manner of noncommercial residential use and occupancy in which the dwelling and such adjoining property has usually been enjoyed by its owner or occupant.

Sec. 7 (a) Except as otherwise provided in this Act, the property acquired by the Secretary under this Act shall be administered by the Secretary, subject to the provisions of the Act entitled "An Act to establish a National Park Service, and for other purposes," approved August 25, 1916 (39 Stat, 535), as amended and supple-mented, and in accordance with other laws of general application relating to the national park system as defined by the Act of August 8, 1953 (67 Stat. 496), except that authority otherwise available to the Secretary for the conversation and man-agement of natural resources may be utilized to the extent he finds such authority will further the purposes of this Act.

(b) The Secretary may permit hunting and fishing on lands and waters under his jurisdiction within the seashore in such areas and under such regulations as he may prescribe during open seasons prescribed by applicable local, State, and Fed-eral law. The Secretary shall consult with officials of the State of California and any political subdivision thereof who have jurisdiction of hunting and fishing prior to the issuance of any such regulations, and the Secretary is authorized to enter into cooperative agreements with such officials regarding such hunting and fishing as he may deem desirable.

Sec. 8 There are authorized to be appropriated such sums as may be necessary to carry out the provisions of this Act, except that no more than $14,000,000 shall be appropriated for the acquisition of land and waters and improvements thereon, and interests therein, and incidental costs relating thereto, in accordance with the provisions of this Act.

Approved September 13, 1962.

Document 2: 1962 President Kennedy's PRNS Signing Statement

FOR IMMEDIATE RELEASE, SEPTEMBER 13, 1962
OFFICE OF THE WHITE HOUSE PRESS SECRETARY
THE WHITE HOUSE
REMARKS OF THE PRESIDENT
UPON THE SIGNING OF S. 476, AN
ACT TO ESTABLISH THE POINT REYES NATIONAL
SEASHORE IN THE STATE OF CALIFORNIA
IN THE PRESIDENT'S OFFICE

I am highly gratified by the action of the Congress in enacting legislation authorizing the establishment of the Point Reyes National Seashore in the State of California.

This is the second bill enacted by the 87th Congress authorizing a national seashore, the first being the Cape Cod National Seashore.

The Point Reyes National Seashore will preserve and make available to a great number of people the outstanding scenic and recreational characteristics of the area. This area is readily accessible to millions of our citizens, and its establishment as a National Seashore will pay vast dividends in the years to come.

The enactment of this legislation indicates an increased awareness of the importance of prompt action—and I emphasize that particularly with the population increases and these areas disappearing under that pressure—and the necessity for prompt action to preserve our nation's great natural beauty areas to insure their existence and enjoyment by the public in the decades and centuries to come. This is especially true about those areas close to the major centers of population.

We have a great many beautiful areas in this country but a good many of them are far away from the centers of population. Therefore programs such as this one and the Cape Cod National Seashore are great additions to the lives of a good many of our fellow citizens. This goal has been well laid out this year by the Outdoor Recreation and Resources Review Commission, and I hope we can stay at it.

I congratulate the members of both parties who participated in enacting this very advantageous piece of national legislation.

END

Document 3: 1969 Katy Miller Johnson Letter to House Leaders

Hon. HAROLD T. JOHNSON,
U.S. House of Representatives,
Washington, D.C.

Dear Bizz: I am terribly worried about Point Reyes National Seashore. Never has it been as threatened with so little time to protect it as it is today.

It is sad to think that nearly seven years after Clem rejoiced at the enactment of the original authorization, less than half of the land within the Seashore boundaries is actually owned by the government. The 2400-acre Lake Ranch, called the "crown jewel" of the Seashore, with two miles of ocean shoreline, is to be offered for subdivision this month. Grading has commenced. The owners cannot continue to pay the taxes.

And, at this exact point of crisis in the land acquisition program, the Seashore faces a wholly new threat posed by its guardian, the Interior Department.

Congressman Aspinall, Chairman of the full Interior Committee, and Congressman Taylor, Chairman of the Subcommittee on National Parks and Recreation recognized the urgency of the land acquisition crisis by scheduling the hearing on May 18th before the Subcommittee to consider bills to increase the authorization for the Park by $38 million dollars.

At the hearing, it was reassuring that the Members were clearly aware of the threat of imminent subdivision within the Seashore and gratifying that the same concern was unanimously expressed by other Members of Congress who testified, by Marin County landowners and officials, and by representatives of conservation organizations.

In contrast, the Interior Department proposal came as a great shock. First, the Department requested $10 million dollars less than House sponsors of both parties deemed necessary from figures originally emanating from the Department of Interior. This inadequate amount would be spent over five years, at a time of wildly escalating land values. Having made no attempt to make up this deficit, the Department then proposed that over nine thousand acres, one tenth of the National Seashore, (subject to condemnation from the original owners for creation of a public recreation area), be sold to new and different private owners to raise money. That money would not even be returned to Point Reyes, but would go instead into the Land and Water Conservation Fund.

The response of the Marin County witnesses was extremely heartening. Both county officials and landowners testified that they were opposed to any sell off. Mr. Douglas Maloney, County Counsel of Marin County, said the proposal would be considered simply a reduction in the site of the Park, to which the Board of Supervisors was on record as being opposed. Supervisor Louis Baar said he felt it would be poor judgment at this time to try to intermingle residential and commercial use with the park use. When asked if he would not welcome an increase in the county tax rolls, he replied that the Park would help the County tax base by increased revenues from tourism.

The San Francisco Chronicle reacted to this proposal with an explicit editorial: "TO RAISE MONEY, JUST SELL A PARK." The editorial began, "National Park Director George Hartzog was involved in a public act of despair . . ."

Clearly, behind this proposal is the desperate need for funds for the beleaguered Land and Water Conservation Fund and the Interior Department which Clem called the "stepchild" among the Executive Departments. Contrast the Interior Department budget for 1970 of $488 million as compared to that of the Department of Defense (military expenditures only) for $80.2 billion.

But whatever the pinch, the expressed Intent of Congress should not be violated, nor can one group of citizens be expressly favored by their Government over another group.

In 1962, when it created Point Reyes National Seashore, the Congress stated its purpose: "to save and preserve, for purposes of public recreation, benefit and inspiration, a portion of the diminishing seashore of the United States that *remains undeveloped.*" (Emphasis added)

During the luncheon recess, I saw in the Hearing Room, an elaborate drawing prepared by the Park Service, of one of two private commercial subdivisions contemplated at Point Reyes. In his testimony, Mr. Hartzog spoke of "low density" residential-commercial development This drawing depicted high density 1–6 and 1–10 acre zoning complete with a school, shopping center, motel, marina and country club with golf course (presumably open to residents only).

The Interior Department, in its prepared statement, claims it has the authority to create these new subdivisions within the Seashore, without asking leave of Congress, under the Land and Water Conservation Fund Act Amendments of 1968, PL 90–401. But Section 5 (a) of this Law specifically limits the authority of the Secretary to sell or lease property "subject to such terms and conditions as will assure the use of the property in a manner that is in the judgment of the Secretary, consistent with the purpose for which the area was authorized by Congress." (Emphasis added)

The Senate Interior Committee Report (#1071, 90th Congress, 2nd Session) on PL 90-401 explicitly states:

"While the Secretary is authorized to convey such freeholds or leaseholds in a manner which is, in his judgment, consistent with the purpose for which the area was authorized by the Congress, the Committee wishes to make clear *the legislative intent that new commercial development, such as residential subdivisions, within national parks, seashores, recreation areas, and the like, is not to be considered within the purposes for which such areas were, and will be, authorized by Congress.*" (Emphasis added)

In sum, Congress granted some discretion to the Department of the Interior, and the Department now declares its intention to do exactly what Congress expressly forbade. It proposes to deauthorize, by administrative action, one sixth of a National Seashore which Congress took pains to create.

Dearly as Clem loved Point Reyes, and would have been horrified at commercial subdivisions inside its boundaries, he would have felt far greater dismay at the possible establishment of a far reaching disastrous precedent affecting seashores and recreation areas all over the nation.

In addition to the harm to Point Reyes and other places not yet designated, the Department of Interior proposal can only discriminate between citizens whose lands are taken.

For example, Mr. Joseph Mendoza, a second-generation rancher at Point Reyes, testified at the hearing that he passed up the tax saving offered by the California Farm Conservation Act, and the consequent restriction on its use, with respect to the part of his land which would be in one of the two tracts the Park Service proposes to sell off for "low-density" residential and commercial development.

If the Park Service buys this parcel for the price it would command as farmland

and resells it for residential-commercial development, the Park Service would pocket the difference and Mr. Mendoza would fare the same as other landowners within the Park. If, on the other hand, the Park Service pays Mr. Mendoza the full value of his land for residential and commercial development. Mr. Mendoza would get premium prices for his land, unlike other landowners whose property was not selected for development, and the Park Service would get nothing. If Mr. Mendoza negotiates a higher price for this parcel, somewhere between its value for residential and commercial purposes and its value for ranching, to that extent Mr. Mendoza will be favored over other citizens whose land is not so selected by the Park Service and the Government will pocket the narrowed difference.

So, to the degree that the Government realizes a profit through its power of condemnation, the original owners of the land will be the innocent victims. On the other hand, to the extent that the original owners are actually compensated, other landowners are discriminated against. Once the Government goes into the business of reselling public land for development, it inevitably will be enmeshed in just this sort of discrimination.

The Congress should reject out of hand this unfortunate Interior Department proposal. It should reassert its authority over Point Reyes. It should institute a legislative taking to freeze land values, followed by appropriation of the full $88 million needed.

$88 million is a great deal of money but Point Reyes is beyond price. It is located less than two hours away from a metropolitan area of nearly five million people and there will be double that many by the end of the century. Half a million visitors came in 1968 alone. They were drawn there not by fancy facilities, nor by any specific famous attractions, but by a unique "Wild Peninsula" (the title of a new book for younger readers describing Point Reyes and its history, by Laura Nelson Baker). Many came from all over the United States and foreign countries as well as from the San Francisco Bay Area.

$88 million is not too large a sum when one projects the number of men, women and children who over many years to come will gratefully appreciate the foresight of the Congress in setting aside this beautiful land.

I would be grateful if you would forward this letter to Chairman Taylor with the request that it be included in the record of the Subcommittee hearings.

With best regards,

KATHARINE (MILLER) JOHNSON

Document 4: 1969 Save Our Seashore Campaign Plan (Excerpts)

CAMPAIGN OUTLINE

FOR

"SAVE OUR SEASHORE"

(S. O. S.)

S. O. S. Box 212k

714 "C" Street

San Rafael, Calif.

Objectives

1. To get Congress to raise the authorized ceiling for acquisition of 30,910 acres of privately owned property within the boundaries of the Point Reyes National Seashore from the present $19,135,000 (all spent or committed) to $57,500,000.

2. To get Congress to appropriate the $38,365,000 necessary to purchase this private property, which still remains in private ownership seven years after the Seashore was authorized.

3. To obtain the active support of President Richard Nixon and his administration to raise the authorized ceiling, as set forth above, and include in his forthcoming budget the $38,365,000 required to complete the National Point Reyes Seashore.

Policy

"SAVE OUR SEASHORE" is a non-partisan organization, and this campaign *must* be conducted on a STRICTLY NON-PARTISAN BASIS. Every member of the Executive Committee, any Subcommittee, or anyone else who works, speaks, or purports to speak for "Save Our Seashore" shall adhere to this basic policy at all times and in all places.

Urgency

Many of the private property owners can no longer afford the cumulative effect of property taxes and other carrying costs involved, having waited seven long years for the federal government to buy their lands, which, for the most part, produce very little income.

Both the Lake and Pierce Ranches (each 2500 acres in size) will be subdivided by their owners or sold for subdivision in the very near future, if Congress and the President do not act at once. These are regarded as two of the proposed Seashore's most beautiful, needed, and strategically located ranches. Others, equally unique but less publicized, are also soon to be broken up. In fact, one good-sized ranch has just been sold. Others are listed with local real estate brokers. Once subdivided, their value for park purposes will decline, and their cost to acquire will greatly increase.

Proposed Target for Our Campaign

(1.) To convince President Nixon that the Point Reyes National Seashore MUST be saved, and NOW, or it will be permanently lost, which is not the case with other high priority projects within the Department of the Interior.

(2.) To convince a majority of United States Representatives and Senators to the same effect.

Implementation

The key to success lies in the active cooperation of a great number and variety of existing organizations throughout the Bay Area, such as business and conservation groups, women's clubs, professional, service and youth organizations, improvement clubs, senior citizen's associations, Chambers of Commerce, and the like. This is a non-partisan issue, which enlists tremendous support from all ages and all points of view. People and organizations are eagerly waiting to be told what to do, and there is NO opposition we have heard about or encountered, either in the Bay Area or elsewhere in California.

The major thrust of this campaign is to elicit personal appeals, both public and private, by letters, petitions, and resolutions from all types of individuals, organizations, and elective bodies directed to President Nixon, key Congressional leaders and members of the Congressional Committees which must act favorably to get bills sent out of Committees to the House and Senate floors for a vote, with a "Do Pass" recommendation.

Timetable

Timetable for peaking the campaign is very short, no more than 90 days from September 2. 1969, when S.O.S. was first organized. The compelling reason is that the President's budget for the next fiscal year will be presented to Congress in early January, 1970, and while new additions can be grafted on to the budget after it is submitted to Congress, this is an extremely chancy possibility to rely on, in view of other competing needs, backed by powerful interests, many of which are admittedly entitled to high priority. We are honestly face-to-face with a "Now or Never" proposition. One of our strongest selling points is that "Parks are Forever," and the need for more of them is understood by almost every thinking individual. Their loss is irreversible. Quality land is scarce and rapidly becoming an anachronism.

Funds

"Save Our Seashore" is NOT a tax-deductible organization. We have no financial angel to bankroll this effort, nor are we depending on finding one It is a second effort to mobilize the "People Power," which so recently saved San Francisco Bay. To do the job and it CAN be done, VJB must find people who care enough to put a dollar or two in an envelope and send it along. We promise to force every dollar to "walk the second mile." We also promise to account for every dollar spent t the end of the campaign, with receipts for them too, available for public inspection

The Nitty-Gritty of the Campaign

The Petition Drive

A petition drive has already begun in Marin County, and will spread within the next two weeks to the other eight Bay Area counties, and then throughout the state and country. Our organization's goal is ONE MILLION SIGNATURES. Petitions are addressed to the President of the United States and ask him please to save this magnificent seashore for all generations of Americans, and state that only HE can do it, and it's NOW or NEVER. Petitions can properly be circulated and signed by anyone, regardless of age.

Children must be fully informed of ALL the facts before they are allowed either to sign or circulate a petition, and also must be of an age to understand what it's all about. However, it is an Article of Faith with the "Save Our Seashore" Executive Committee and Advisory Board that children have the most to gain, and the most to lose, depending on the outcome of those who believe in the Point Reyes National Seashore, and are willing to back up their belief with action, either independently or within the frame-work of the S. O. S.

All citizens must work to convince Congress and the President of the emergency facing the Seashore. Working together, we can cause this unsurpassed and yet unspoiled stretch of California's seacoast to be saved. Let us get it gift-wrapped and placed this very year under the Christmas Tree of every child in America.

SUGGESTED COMMITTEES

Organizations
Solicit local organizations to adopt resolutions, circulate petitions to members, send out fact sheets concerning the Point Reyes emergency in mailings to their members, and urge all members to get their children to circulate petitions in school and elsewhere. Also, and of utmost importance, get letters written to the President, Governor Ronald Reagan, and key legislators. If any organization can make a contribution to S. o. S., please ask them to do so. Among the key legislators are Senator Alan Bible of Nevada, Senator George Murphy of California, Congressman Wayne Aspinall of Colorado.

Publicity
Write press releases, set up T.U. and radio programs, arrange public relations events and particularly pay attention to the local newspapers, which can probably help the most, if they are given the help they need from you. All publicity of a policy nature MUST be cleared through S. O. S. in San Rafael, California, unless obviously in accord with policy already laid down in this outline.

Program
Arrange speakers for meetings and luncheons. Check with S. O. S. in San Rafael concerning availability of the newly revised Sierra Club 16 mm film, "Island in Time." It is in color, with sound, and very fine indeed. See if you can get it shown in your elementary schools for Nature Education, assuming we can make it available, which we cannot premise at present. It is strictly informational, of course, with absolutely no political undertones or overtones.

Schools
A working committee to involve the schools to the extent of "nature education," focused on Point Reyes, would be very valuable indeed, with poster contests, and painting for the lower grades of birds, flowers, beaches, seascapes, Sir Francis Drake's galleon, Miwok Indians, and so forth.

Finances

Prepare a budget for money needed for your own county's activities, appoint a finance committee of three to five persons, let them pick their own chairman, and set a realistic dollar goal, which need not be very much. Remind everyone that a dollar today is worth five dollars a week from now, for activity usually generates the dollars to finance it. To begin, however, is "The Name of the Game." Time is already about to run out for "The Island in Time."

Special Events

Draw up a calendar of all major events and locations where crowds will gather. Parks and other areas where people congregate mho know at first hand the crying need for more recreational land in the Bay Area are excellent locations in which to circulate petitions. At special events, arrange to have booths or card tables, staffed and, of course, sup plied with ample petitions and fact sheets, and other accurate literature and reprints about Point Reyes. We can help you with this. Just telephone!

. . .

Conclusion

These campaign plans have been prepared to help your County/Chairman. Under no circumstances are they meant to be regarded as more than one possible approach to organizing your county. They are a guide only, as the developers say about Master Plans. Each Chairman obviously has not only the right but the duty to follow his or her best judgment. What works in one county may well not work at all in another, and your chairman or committee will decide some of the above suggestions may be wrong, useless, unfeasible, or simply silly. If so, we promise not to be offended.

All basic points contained in this Campaign Outline were officially approved by the Executive Committee of "Save Our Seashore" at its open meeting of Thursday, September 11, 1969, at the Civic Center, San Rafael, California. The press was in attendance at this meeting and is formally notified in advance of all meetings of "Save Our Seashore."

Peter Behr
Chairman, S. O. S.

Document 5: Rep. Pete McCloskey Letter to John Ehrlichman, September 16, 1969

Congress of the United States
House of Representatives
Washington, D.C. 20515
September 16, 1969
Mr. John Ehrlichman
Counsel to the President
The White House
Washington, D. C.

Dear John:

Here's a starter. The only man who can save the Point Reyes National Seashore is the President. He is running out of time because the House Interior Committee is going to adjourn October 1, and the Bureau of the Budget Director, Robert Mayo, has made it clear that there are no funds available from BOB despite what has been properly characterized thus far as "weak White House support."

The money is available in the land and water conservation fund. All the President need do is order that it be released, ear marked for the national seashore projects, specifically, Point Reyes.

If you move this time, why not let a few of us know in advance so that we can properly give the President credit where it is due? It might also help to have the President announce that due to the efforts of George Murphy, Don Clausen and Bill Mailliard, he is taking this step to preserve a priceless national heritage.

Yr. Obt. Sevt.

Pete

Document 6: John Whitaker Memo to John Ehrlichman, November 13, 1969

November 13, 1969

MEMORANDUM FOR JOHN D. EHRLICHMAN

From: John C. Whitaker

Re: Purchase of Point Reyes California Peninsula Area, Northern San Francisco, as a National Park

BACKGROUND

1. Park Director Hartzog testifies today before the House Interior Committee in favor of *authorizing* an increase of $33.5 Million for the purchase of Point Reyes as a national park. His testimony will center largely around the rise in land values from the previous estimate of $28.3 Million, to the present estimate of $33.365 Million to purchase the area. When asked by the Committee if he favors a supplemental FY 1970 appropriation legislation, he will "waffle" and he is instructed to do so by me.

2. Perhaps as early as tomorrow, but certainly not more than two or three weeks from now, the Interior Appropriations Committee will introduce legislation to appropriate funds and make political hay out of it. All intelligence I can gather on it indicates that the Interior Appropriations Committee will pass an appropriation of $33.365 Million. In other words, the President will be "run over" by Congress and the Democrats will collect the credit.

3. I foresee no chance that ultimately the President will veto the entire appropriations package, but he could veto the authorization bill which will come to him as one item—but at great political expense.

4. After meeting with Carl Schwartz, Director of the Natural Resources Division, BOB; Carl McMurray, Advisory to Secretary Hickel, and Park Director Hartzog, Hartzog proposed the following plan:

RECOMMENDATION

If the above options to find any money are not fruitful, and I am pretty sure they will not be, then I recommend that we go ahead and put in legislation appropriations for supplemental FY 1970, although it may not have to be for the full $7.5 Million.

It may be that Hartzog can get started with less money than that, but at any rate we commit for a speedy purchase by the end of FY 1972 of the entire Point Reyes area. My rationale is that we are going to be run over by Congress on this one and we should therefore pick up the political credit and do it in the most dramatic way possible.

The following parks have requests in for acquisition for FY 1970, and the total cost for purchase of parks is indicated below:

Cape Cod, Massachusetts $17.401 Million
Point Reyes, California 33.5 Million
Padre Island, Texas 4.130 Million
Lake Mead, Arizona/Nevada 4.6 Million
$59.631 Million

a) Obviously, California has much more political clout when you look at the political situation in the above States.

b) It gives the President a chance to identify with California, but not at the expense of playing regional favoritism because he can point out that Point Reyes, more than any park, represents the prime example of major encroachment by suburban sprawl of any area in the country.

c) The political pressure on this one is extremely high. For example, Congressman Don Clausen now has 250,000 petitions for purchase of the park.

Prepare supplemental appropriations legislation for 1970 for $7.5 Million. This is the amount of money he usefully feels can be spent to purchase property in the Point Reyes area during this fiscal year. Hartzog could probably get by with $2 or $3 Million if authorized to negotiate with Sweet (the key land) for only a portion of his property and defer later negotiation until next year, but that would just make the tab stiffer in later years. His schedule for appropriations for purchase of the whole park will be:

FY 1970 $7.5 Million (may be only $2 or 3, Million)
FY 1971 $7.5 Million
FY 1972 $18.5 Million
$33.5 Million (approximately)

Hartzog, who is probably more aware than anyone about the escalating cost of land purchase, is convinced that he can purchase the park for $33.5 Million by the end of FY 1972.

5. Appropriations legislation should not include a clause for "legislative taking" since, obviously, we cannot have much of the $33.5 Million available in FY 1970. The purchase would have to be by way of the condemnation route through normal court procedures.

6. Other methods now being explored to find the necessary $7.5 Million in FY 1970 funds are as follows:

a) Carl McMurray is re-examining the possibility of reprograming funds in the Bureau of Outdoor Recreation in the Department of Interior.

b) Carl McMurray is making a delicate exploration of the possibility of making a deal with the Department of Agriculture whereby contract authority can be given from the National Park Service of Interior to the Forest Service of Agriculture in return for cash from the Department of Agriculture.

Carl Schwartz will not undertake this exploration with Agriculture until such time as an authorization bill on Point Reyes has been passed

c) Finally, on the Sweet property (a key portion of the park) developers have reportedly made the offer of $5 Million for purchase of this land for highrise apartments, right in the choice peninsula portion of the park.

Considering the above, I recommend that the President beat the Democrats to the punch and submit supplemental FY 1970 appropriation legislation—that he should do this in a dramatic way by inviting to the Cabinet Room the entire California Delegation (both Democrats and Republicans), together with Senators Jackson, Allott and Bible (Parks Sub Committee), Congressmen Aspinall, Saylor and Roy A. Taylor (Chairman of the House Park Subcommittee, Dem. N. C.) and Joe Skubitz (Rep. Kansas).

Just before a meeting with this large group, the President should meet privately for about ten minutes with Secretary Hickel, Senator Murphy and Don Clausen (the Point Reyes park is in his District) and then have the President announce his decision to the entire group, with an accompanying letter to Chairman Aspinall at the same time.

Assuming that no funds are forthcoming in FY 1970 from any of the above described options and further assuming that it's a real fact that we have gone through our $192.9 Billion budget level for FY 1970, then the money should come from some other program, e.g. cancel a space shot.

Document 7: John Whitaker Memo to President Nixon, November 18, 1969

November 18, 1969

MEMORANDUM FOR THE PRESIDENT

From: John C. Whitaker

Subject: Meeting with Senator George Murphy

and Congressman Don Clausen

Tuesday, November 18, 1969

3:25 to 3:40 P.M.

I. PURPOSE

To inform Murphy and Clausen of your decision to fund the purchase of the Point Reyes national seashore area.

II. BACKGROUND

The area covers 54,136 acres, of which only 22,16 acres have been purchased since 1962 for a cost of $19 Million. Because of the escalating land prices due to the proximity of this area to San Francisco, you have made the decision to go ahead and purchase the area over a three- year period under the following schedule:

FY '70 $7.5 Million
FY '71 7.5 Million
FY '72 18.5 Million
Total $33.65 Million

III. POINTS OF DISCUSSION

A. Ask Senator Murphy and Congressman Clausen to tell the press at the 4 o'clock Ziegler briefing of your intentions to go ahead and acquire the land; that the Administration will send a supplemental budget request for FY'70 to Congress (there is no reason why Murphy should mention the exact amount), contingent upon the enactment of authorizing legislation above the present funding level of $19 Million.

B. You may wish to caution Murphy that you do not wish to appear politically partisan in favor of California; that the justification for purchase of the park is the escalating land costs and proximity of this wonderful seashore area to San Francisco which is creating tremendous pressure for real estate development, including highrise apartments and suburban single family dwellings.

Document 8: John Whitaker Memo to Senator Murphy, November 18, 1969

THE WHITE HOUSE
WASHINGTON
November 18, 1969
MEMORANDUM FOR
Honorable George Murphy
Honorable Don Clausen
Subject: Point Reyes National Seashore Area

After your meeting with the President, you may wish to make the following points to the press:

1. That the Point Reyes national seashore area was originally authorized in 1962 but the funds have never really been appropriated to the full amount to purchase the area. To date, $19 Million have been appropriated to buy 22,816 acres, whereas the total park area is 54,136 acres, In other words, there are 31,320 acres left to purchase.

2. Even given the tightness of the FY'70 Budget, the President has told you that he wishes to go ahead with the purchase of this property as a national seashore area because the pressure to develop the area for highrise apartments and single-family suburban dwelling units is extremely high and the President feels this beautiful area must be preserved for present and future generations.

3. If you are asked by the press why the President has decided to go ahead with this park area and not with other national park areas, you may wish to indicate that Point Reyes is unique in the sense that there are higher pressures for real estate development and escalating land values here than in any place in the country. Therefore, the President has indicated action is required now.

4. You may wish to indicate that should the House Interior Committee enact authorizing legislation above the present funding level of $19 Million, the Administration will present a supplemental budget request for FY'70 and schedule funds for FY'71 and FY'72 to complete the purchase of the area.

John C. Whitaker

Deputy Assistant to the President

Notes

Introduction: Saving the "Island in Time"

1. The image of Point Reyes as an island preserved from another time was first popularized by *San Francisco Chronicle* reporter Harold Gilliam in a 1958 monthly *Sierra Club Bulletin* featuring Point Reyes.

2. Kenneth Brower, "Reflections on the 58th Anniversary of Point Reyes National Seashore, 2020," https://restoreptreyesseashore.org/reflections-on-the-58th-anniversary-of-point-reyes-national-seashore-by-ken-brower/.

3. PRNS was technically authorized in the 1962 legislation as a national *seashore*, not as a national *park*. It was later joined by a noncontiguous series of urban and rural parks, the Golden Gate National Recreation Area (GGNRA). For ease of expression herein, "PRNS," "the seashore" and "the park" are used interchangeably, as appropriate, to refer to the public lands protected at the Point Reyes Peninsula.

4. Miller died in October 1962, Kennedy in November 1963, and Engle in July 1964 after suffering a debilitating stroke several months earlier.

5. Legislators critical of the sharply escalating price tag for the California park, including Kansas Republican Joseph Skubitz, even suggested that the authorization act creating the national seashore might be rescinded by act of Congress.

6. Richard A. Walker, *The Country in the City: The Greening of the San Francisco Bay Area* (Seattle: University of Washington Press, 2007), 3–8.

7. John Hart, *San Francisco's Wilderness Next Door* (Novato, CA: Presidio Press, 1979), 17.

1. The Land and People of Point Reyes

1. Jack Mason quoting Stephen Richardson, *Point Reyes: The Solemn Land* (Inverness, CA: North Shore, 1970), 19.

2. Kevin Starr, *California: A History* (New York: Modern Library, 2005), xiii.

3. David Vogel, *California Greenin': How the Golden State Became an Environmental Leader* (Princeton, NJ: Princeton University Press, 2018), 4. See also Carolyn Merchant, *American Environmental History: An Introduction* (New York: Columbia University Press, 2007), 90.

4. Garci Rodríguez de Montalvo and Salvador Bernabeu Albert, *Las sergas de Esplandián* (Madrid, Spain: Aranjuez, 1510).

5. Gayle Baker, *Point Reyes: A Harbor Town History* (Santa Barbara, CA: Vaughan, 2004), 33.

6. Betty Goerke, *Chief Marin: Leader, Rebel, and Legend: A History of Marin County's Namesake and His People* (Berkeley, CA: Heyday, 2007), xv. The Coast Miwok lost their way of life, yet the tribe survived; today ancestors of the Coast Miwok in the community are working to bring their story forward in both PRNS and Marin County history.

7. Where Drake landed is a dispute that has generated numerous popular history articles. The evidence that Drake landed and repaired his ship at Point Reyes is both compelling and conclusive enough to lead local, state, and federal authorities to confirm Drakes Bay as the site of first contact. Most agree that the striking similarity of the soaring Point Reyes tawny cliffs to the (albeit whiter) cliffs of Dover adds weight, as especially does the fact that Fletcher reports that when Drake stayed in the cove for six early-summer weeks, the fogs did not lift for an hour. Bay Area residents for generations can attest that the so-called June Gloom fog burns off by noon most summer days only *inside* San Francisco Bay, where there are no white cliffs facing the open sea.

8. The complicated ruse revealed decades later was a prank gone wrong, one originally played on Professor Herbert Bolton by a local history club called E Clampus Vitus. The story is made accessible in the succinct account of journalist Katie Dowd, "This 'Treasure' Rewrote California History. It Was an Elaborate Hoax," *San Francisco Chronicle*, March 1, 2021.

9. Gary Kamiya, *Cool Grey City of Love* (New York: Bloomsbury, 2013), 43.

10. Richard H. Dana, Jr., *Two Years Before the Mast* (1911; repr., Orinda, CA: Seawolf Press, 2020), 216. Note Dana's account of a harrowing timber run to Marin's Angel Island, where he was bedeviled by driving rain and the infamous strong currents running between the island and the Tiburon Peninsula in Marin.

11. Mason, *Point Reyes*, 10.

12. Mason, 11.

13. Italian American and Japanese American farmers did have some success in pre–World War II years growing peas and artichokes in the area.

14. Mason, *Point Reyes*, 11.

15. Alan Taylor, *American Republics: A Continental History of the United States 1783–1859* (New York: W. W. Norton, 2021), 137.

16. Lincoln Fairley, *Mount Tamalpais: A History* (San Francisco: Scottwall Associates, 1987), 22.

17. Fights over disputed land claims were common over the first half century of California's statehood. Law firms ended up owning many choice parcels. Here, it was the San Francisco firm of Shafter, Shafter, Park, and Heydenfeldt. Joseph Hetherington shot Andrew Randall on July 24, 1856. Hetherington was hung without trial by members of San Francisco's Vigilance Committee, as noted in Mason, *Point Reyes*, 28.

18. Baker, *Point Reyes*, 31–35.

19. Dewey Livingston, *Discovering Historic Ranches at Point Reyes* (Point Reyes Station, CA: Point Reyes National Seashore Association, 2009), 46–47.

20. Fairley, *Mount Tamalpais*, 22.

21. Mason, *Point Reyes*, 40–48. By contrast, a regional NPS staff study conducted at the height of the Depression in 1935 indicated that the Point Reyes Peninsula lands could be bought for $2.4 million.

22. Mason, *Point Reyes*, 34.

23. Interview with Dewey Livingston, Inverness, California, July 1, 2022.

2. Point Reyes and the Origins of the California Conservation Movement

1. David Vogel, *California Greenin': How the Golden State Became an Environmental Leader* (Princeton, NJ: Princeton University Press, 2018), 4. See also Carolyn Merchant, *American Environmental History: An Introduction* (New York: Columbia University Press, 2007), 59.

2. Richard A. Walker, *The Country in the City: The Greening of the San Francisco Bay Area* (Seattle: University of Washington Press, 2007), 13.

3. Walker, 249.

4. Tom Killion and Gary Snyder, *Tamalpais Walking: Poetry, History, and Prints* (Berkeley, CA: Heyday, 2009) offer the most accessible narrative on how Mount Tamalpais inspired poets and moved politicians to act.

5. Vogel, *California Greenin'*, 59.

6. The rail line connecting Point Reyes to the San Francisco Bay and ferry landings was built by two thousand Chinese laborers. None of the Chinese workers were permitted to own land outside San Francisco's Chinatown.

7. Killion and Snyder, *Tamalpais Walking*, 61.

8. As quoted in Paul Sadin, *Managing a Land in Motion: An Administrative History of Point Reyes National Seashore* (Seattle, WA: Historical Research Associates, 2007), 50.

9. Theodore Roosevelt, letter to William Kent, February 5, 1908, National Park Service, www.nps.gov/muwo; see Historical Letters.

10. Killion and Snyder, *Tamalpais Walking*, 81.

11. John D. Leshy, *Our Common Ground: A History of America's Public Lands* (New Haven, CT: Yale University Press, 2021), 327.

12. Laura Alice Watt, *The Paradox of Preservation: Wilderness and Working Landscapes at Point Reyes National Seashore* (Oakland: University of California Press, 2016), 50.

13. Leshy, *Our Common Ground*, 130–137.

14. William Kent, *Reminiscences of an Outdoor Life* (San Francisco: A. M. Robertson, 1929). This work was published posthumously, as Kent did not live to see his hopes for a Mount Tamalpais National Park realized. One of William Kent's sons, Roger, would later become chairman of the California Democratic Party, indicative of how the environmental activists gravitated to the left politically. Roger and Alice Kent were instrumental in the successful scheme to block development of a hotel and casino in Bolinas Lagoon, at the south end of the Point Reyes National Seashore. See L. Martin Griffin, *Saving the Marin-Sonoma Coast: The Battles for Audubon Canyon Ranch, Point Reyes and California's Russian River* (Healdsburg, CA: Sweetwater, 1998), 104.

15. Killion and Snyder, *Tamalpais Walking*, 41.

16. Killion and Snyder, 79.

17. Killion and Snyder, 78–79.

18. Jack Kerouac's *The Dharma Bums* (New York: Viking Press, 1958) became a classic. Kerouac's references to Buddhist philosophy, culled from long talks between Snyder and Kerouac during hikes on Mount Tamalpais, were mainstreamed in the West, in part through such writings.

19. Carolyn Merchant, *The Columbia Guide to American Environmental History* (New York: Columbia University Press, 2020), 148. Leading Bay Area historians Richard Walker and John Hart have also worked to correct the historical record to reflect the role of women in leadership of environmental groups throughout the twentieth century.

20. Walker, *The Country in the City*, 89.

21. Carola DeRooy Davis, interview with author, August 6, 2021.

22. Sadin, *Managing a Land in Motion*, 53. See also Nancy Kelly and Kenji Yamamoto, *Rebels with a Cause* (New Day Films, 2012), and correspondence with John Hart, February 1, 2023.

23. Lincoln Fairley, *Mount Tamalpais: A History* (San Francisco: Scottwall Associates, 1987), 185.

24. Richard Rothstein, *The Color of Law: A Forgotten History of How Our Government Segregated America* (New York: W. W. Norton, 2017), 29.

25. Rothstein, chapter 1.

26. As late as 2020, the county population was less than 3 percent Black, and lawsuits were filed seeking better treatment for schools in Marin City by joining them with the far wealthier school district just across the 101 freeway in Sausalito.

27. John Soennichsen, *Miwoks to Missiles: A History of Angel Island* (Tiburon, CA: Angel Island Association, 2001), 159.

28. From Gary Yost's documentary film entitled *The Invisible Peak (Hidden in Plain Sight)*, 2014. One of the air force pilots flying these perilous Cold War missions out of Marin County in 1957–1958 was William Anders, who later joined NASA. Anders took one of the most famous photographs in history, the astronauts' *Apollo 8* picture of Earthrise from beyond the moon. See Robert Kurson, *Rocket Men: The Daring Odyssey of Apollo 8* (New York: Random House, 2018), 115–116. Note also that the key parts of the nuclear bomb dropped on Hiroshima also transited Marin's Hamilton Base in July 1945.

29. "U.S. Census Bureau: Marin County, California," accessed July 6, 2021, https://www.census.gov/quickfacts/marincountycalifornia/.

30. Samuel P. Hays, *Beauty, Health, and Permanence: Environmental Politics in the United States, 1955–1985* (New York: Cambridge University Press, 1987), 2–3.

31. The California population projections for the year 2000, made in 1950, proved remarkably accurate. These projections were used by both park proponents and opponents, the latter often pushing the development of urgently needed housing. Ironically, state of California mandates backed by the progressive Association

of Bay Area Governments at this writing are pressing Marin County to build *more* housing and increase density to ease acute affordable housing shortages.

32. *The Wonder Years* was reprised as the title for a nostalgic television show that ran weekly on the ABC network in the late 1980s and early 1990s. It ably captured the halcyon days of monochromatic bliss of California's suburban communities in the years after World War II and before a wider push for civil rights, Vietnam War protests, and the onset of culture wars.

33. Hays, *Beauty, Health, and Permanence*, 169.

34. "Planning in Marin Is Called Chaotic," *San Rafael Independent Journal*, May 23, 1963, 15. Disclosure: the Planning Commission chairman at the time was the author's father.

35. The history of the modern California environmental movement is recounted in Vogel's authoritative *California Greenin'*. Vogel details how many early conservation campaigns relied for success on a convergence of business interests and environmental concerns.

36. Hays, *Beauty, Health, and Permanence*, 44.

37. Vogel, *California Greenin'*, 11.

38. On the commercial interests buying Marin land to build housing, see Sadin, *Managing a Land in Motion*, chapter 3.

39. Watt, *The Paradox of Preservation*, 79.

40. Walker, *The Country in the City*, 84.

3. Mr. Miller Goes to Washington: The Fight in Congress for Point Reyes

1. Interview with Katharine Miller Johnson, quoted in *Saving Point Reyes National Seashore 1969–1970: An Oral History of Citizen Action in Conservation: Oral History Transcript* (Oakland: University of California Press, 1993), 1–101 (hereafter cited as UC).

2. UC, 8.

3. UC, 243, 253.

4. UC, 11.

5. National Park Service (NPS), "Study of a National Seashore Recreation Area, Point Reyes Peninsula, Calif.," 1935.

6. NPS.

7. John D. Leshy, *Our Common Ground: A History of America's Public Lands* (New Haven, CT: Yale University Press, 2021), 465.

8. Jackie M. M. Gonzales, "The National Park Service Goes to the Beach," *Forest History Today* (Spring 2017): 5.

9. NPS, *Mission 66 for the National Park System* (Washington, DC: Department of the Interior, 1956), 5.

10. Nancy Kelly and Kenji Yamamoto, *Rebels with a Cause* (New Day Films, 2012).

11. Senator Clair Engle and Representative Clem Miller, "The Proposed Point Reyes National Seashore," July 23, 1959, box 2, NSFR, BAN, 1. This joint statement introduced the partner bills S. 2428 and H.R. 8358 to Congress.

12. Engle statement from July 1959, quoted by Congressman Harold T. ("Bizz") Johnson, testimony before the National Parks and Recreation Subcommittee, House Interior Committee, May 13, 1969.

13. J. Michael McCloskey, *In the Thick of It: My Life in the Sierra Club* (Washington, DC: Island Press, 2005), 89.

14. Leshy, *Our Common Ground*, 130–134.

15. "Surprise Marin Action: Pt. Reyes Park Opposed," *San Francisco Chronicle*, September 17, 1958.

16. McCloskey, *In the Thick of It*, 65. McCloskey succeeded controversial David Brower in May 1969. He noted that the obligation of the Sierra Club to "do much of the work" required him "to master the full legislative process."

17. Laura Alice Watt, *The Paradox of Preservation: Wilderness and Working Landscapes at Point Reyes National Seashore* (Oakland: University of California Press, 2016), 77.

18. Senate Committee on Interior and Insular Affairs, *Point Reyes National Seashore Hearings on S. 248*, April 14, 1960.

19. Amy Meyer, *New Guardians for the Golden Gate* (Berkeley: University of California Press, 2008), 24–25.

20. *Point Reyes Light*, July 31, 1959, cited in Paul Sadin, *Managing a Land in Motion: An Administrative History of Point Reyes National Seashore* (Seattle, WA: Historical Research Associates, 2007), 82.

21. Duddleson Papers, box 4, PRNS Archives, NPS Bear Valley Headquarters, Point Reyes Station, CA (hereafter cited as Duddleson Papers.)

22. Duddleson Papers, box 4.

23. Sadin, *Managing a Land in Motion*, 57.

24. Point Reyes National Seashore Foundation box 3, PRNS Archives.

25. Clem Miller to Sierra Club, April 16, 1959, Papers of Congressman Clement W. Miller, Bancroft Library, Berkeley, CA, carton 4, Legislative Files (hereafter Miller Papers).

26. Aspinall favored greater use of public lands for mining, dams, and timber while deriding federal bureaucrats who stood in the way of resource extraction. The Sierra Club's David Brower assailed the Coloradan for frustrating environmental causes, actions that Brower claimed left "dream after dream [to be] dashed on the stoney continents of Wayne Aspinall," as quoted in Steven C. Schulte, *Wayne Aspinall and the Shaping of the American West* (Boulder, CO: University Press of Colorado, 2002), 246.

27. Sadin, *Managing a Land in Motion*, 77. The Senate bill number was S. 2460.

28. *Rebels with a Cause.*

29. Point Reyes National Seashore Foundation box 2, PRNS Archives.

30. Senate Committee on Interior and Insular Affairs.

31. Chapin A. Day, "Nature at Prettiest: Solons Impressed by Beauty of Pt. Reyes," *San Rafael Independent Journal* (April 14, 1960), 1.

32. Senate Committee on Interior and Insular Affairs.

33. As quoted in Gayle Baker, *Point Reyes: A Harbor Town History* (Santa Barbara, CA: Vaughan, 2004), 100.

34. Zena Mendoza-Cabral testimony, House Interior Committee, *Hearings on Proposed Point Reyes National Seashore* (Washington, DC: Government Printing Office, 1961).

35. Sadin interview of Duddleson, October 28, 2004, box 2, PRNS Archives.

36. Senate Committee on Interior and Insular Affairs.

37. Senate Committee on Interior and Insular Affairs.

38. Duddleson Papers, box 3.

39. Miller Papers, carton 4.

40. "Stewart L. Udall Oral History Interview II, June 19, 1969," conducted by Joe B. Franz, Lyndon B. Johnson Library Oral History Collection, www.lbjlib .utexas.edu/johnson/archives.hom/oralhistory.hom/Udall.asp, 16.

41. Kennedy had come to the White House with the reputation of a lackluster legislator. His Senate career had been noted by his contemporaries more for his absenteeism and his national ambition than for his ability to shape legislation. Many liberals regarded Kennedy with suspicion and favored Adlai Stevenson, the cerebral Illinois governor. Kennedy had missed the Senate vote to censure Joseph McCarthy—for whom his younger brother Robert F. Kennedy had worked for several years on the Senate's Permanent Subcommittee on Investigations. See Frederick Logevall, *JFK: Coming of Age in the American Century 1917–1956* (New York: Random House, 2020) and Elizabeth Drew, *Richard M. Nixon* (New York: Holt, 2007) in the American Presidents Series.

42. Daniel Lombardo, *Cape Cod National Seashore: The First 50 Years* (Charleston, SC: Arcadia, 2010), 7.

43. John F. Kennedy. "Remarks of the President upon the Signing of S. 476, an Act to Establish the Point Reyes National Seashore in the State of California in the President's Office," transcript of speech delivered in the Oval Office of the White House, Washington, DC, September 13, 1962, https://www.jfklibrary.org /asset-viewer/archives/JFKPOF/040/JFKPOF-040-003.

44. Bill Duddleson to Bill Grader, December 13, 1961, Miller Papers, carton 4, Point Reyes files.

45. Miller to Marin Board of Supervisors, January 12, 1962, Miller Papers, carton 4.

46. Miller to Aspinall and Subcommittee Chairman J. T. Rutherford, January 18, 1962, Miller Papers, carton 4.

47. At the inauguration of the association, the three women pitched a group of two dozen men leading other Bay Area environmental groups involved in preserving the Sierra Nevada parks and California's remaining redwoods. They initially gained little support from the men. As Harold Gilliam recalled from the meeting, the only initial backing given by the established conservation groups to the Save San Francisco Bay Association was the sharing of a few mailing lists. Victoria Bogdan-Tejeda, "SF Bay Area: What Might Have Been," 2014. http://www .whatmighthavebeen.org.

48. John Reber, "San Francisco Bay Project," San Francisco: CA, 1946. As part of a feasibility study for this plan, the US Army Corps of Engineers later

built a massive model to track the strong tidal flows in the Bay Area. Today, the model is warehoused on prime real estate once used by the Sausalito shipyards in World War II and hosts local school groups and science classes. Historian John Hart notes that Save the Bay activists exploited a cautionary map produced by the US Army Corps of Engineers as a tool to argue against any more bay fill. Correspondence with John Hart, February 1, 2023.

49. Editorial, *San Francisco Chronicle*, March 22, 1961.

50. David Vogel, *California Greenin': How the Golden State Became an Environmental Leader* (Princeton, NJ: Princeton University Press, 2018), 98.

51. Sadin, *Managing a Land in Motion*, 59.

52. UC, 173.

53. Miller Papers, carton 4, and Sadin interview of Duddleson.

54. Sadin interview of Duddleson, 5.

55. Carolyn Merchant, *American Environmental History: An Introduction* (New York: Columbia University Press, 2007), 100.

56. Merchant, 218.

57. Megan Kate Nelson, *Saving Yellowstone: Exploration and Preservation in Reconstruction America* (New York: Scribner's, 2022), 16.

58. Kenneth Brower, "Reflections on the 58th Anniversary of Point Reyes National Seashore, 2020," https://restoreptreyesseashore.org. Brower's son recalled the frenetic rush to finish the book in 1962 in an advocacy piece he penned a half century later.

59. "Drakes Bay Subdivision Is Rejected," *San Rafael Independent Journal*, February 24, 1962, 1.

60. Miller to Gustafson, April 16, 1962, Miller Papers, carton 4, Legislative Files.

61. Cong. Rec. 108 (April 14, 1962).

62. House Interior Committee, Report 1628, April 19, 1962.

63. Miller papers, carton 36, Newsletters File.

64. Miller, October 1962 newsletter, courtesy of Jack Mason Museum of West Marin History, Inverness, CA.

65. Senate Committee on Interior and Insular Affairs, Report 807, August 29, 1961, 6.

66. "The Meaning of the Occasion," prepared remarks (with edits in Duddleson's hand) as delivered May 2, 1987, Duddleson Papers, box 3.

67. Cong. Rec. H14414 (July 23, 1962).

68. Stewart L. Udall, recorded interview by W. W. Moss, May 20, 1970, John F. Kennedy Library Oral History Program, 105.

69. Cong. Rec. H13445 (July 23, 1962).

70. UC, 236–272.

71. Watt, *The Paradox of Preservation*, 81–82.

72. "Remarks of the President upon the Signing of S. 476."

73. Miller Papers, carton 35, 1962 Campaign Materials.

74. On Miller's death, see Wallace Turner, "Congressman Clem Miller, 45, Dies

in California Plane Crash: Democrat Was Campaigning in Craft—Leaves Wife and 5 Daughters," *New York Times*, October 9, 1962.

75. "STORM DISASTER: Mud, Floods Hit Bay Area, Huge Losses, Death Toll Numbers 46 along Coast," *Oakland Tribune*, October 14, 1962. The Columbus Day storm raged for four days, dumping more than 10 inches of rain in a normally dry month and flooding West Marin towns.

76. See Jack Mason, *Point Reyes: The Solemn Land* (Inverness, CA: North Shore, 1970), 171, on White House plans for a presidential visit to Point Reyes in November 1963.

77. Watt, *The Paradox of Preservation*, 81.

78. Huey D. Johnson, *Something of the Marvelous: Lessons Learned from Nature and My Sixty Years as an Environmentalist* (Wheat Ridge, CO: Fulcrum Group, 2020), 104.

79. *Sacramento Bee*, August 7, 1969.

80. Samuel P. Hays, *Beauty, Health, and Permanence: Environmental Politics in the United States, 1955–1985* (New York: Cambridge University Press, 1987), 164.

81. Meyer, *New Guardians for the Golden Gate*, 31.

82. Marin Planning Commission Chairman Felix Warburg led the unsuccessful commission dissent. He was then a landscape architect working on the Sonoma-Mendocino headlands on the Sea Ranch project as part of a team led by Lawrence Halprin.

83. See plans in Anne T. Kent California Room, Marin County Library.

4. The Battle That Had to Be Won Twice

1. John D. Leshy, *Our Common Ground: A History of America's Public Lands* (New Haven, CT: Yale University Press, 2021), 465–469.

2. Gregg Coodley and David Sarasohn, *The Green Years 1964–1976: When Democrats and Republicans United to Repair the Earth* (Lawrence: University Press of Kansas, 2021), 84.

3. David Vogel, *California Greenin': How the Golden State Became an Environmental Leader* (Princeton, NJ: Princeton University Press, 2018), 79. In the 1978 parks bill, California Democrat Phillip Burton included the watershed upslope from Redwood Creek that environmentalists had tried but failed to include in park boundaries a decade earlier. Burton's 1978 moves nearly doubled the size of this park at considerable taxpayer expense. Leshy, *Our Common Ground*, 543–545.

4. Nixon and Ehrlichman visited the site in a widely covered photo op on the beach at Santa Barbara on March 21, 1969.

5. See detailed mock-ups and artist rendering of fully realized Marincello development and plans for Marin freeways to Point Reyes at whatmighthavebeen .org and Nancy Kelly and Kenji Yamamoto, *Rebels with a Cause* (New Day Films, 2012). See also Huey D. Johnson, *Something of the Marvelous: Lessons Learned from Nature and My Sixty Years as an Environmentalist* (Wheat Ridge, CO: Fulcrum Group, 2020), 97–103.

6. H. Erskine, "The Polls: Pollution and Industry," *Public Opinion Quarterly* 36 (Summer 1972): 263–280.

7. Malvina Reynolds, "Little Boxes," recorded by Pete Seeger, "Little Boxes"/"Mail Myself to You," Columbia, 1963; Jesse Colin Young, "Ridgetop," on *Song for Juli*, Warner Bros, 1973.

8. Duddleson's interview with Ehrlichman, *Saving Point Reyes National Seashore 1969–70: An Oral History of Citizen Action in Conservation: Oral History Transcript* (Oakland: University of California Press, 1993), 355–362 (hereafter cited as UC).

9. UC, vi.

10. Peter Behr oral history interview with Anne Lage, UC, 66–73.

11. Message to Congress, Presidential Documents, February 10, 1970, Richard Nixon Presidential Library and Museum, Yorba Linda, CA.

12. Samuel P. Hays, *Beauty, Health, and Permanence: Environmental Politics in the United States, 1955–1985* (New York: Cambridge University Press, 1987), 58.

13. John C. Whitaker, *Striking a Balance: Environment and Natural Resources Policy in the Nixon-Ford Years* (Washington, DC: American Enterprise Institute, 1976), 158.

14. J. Brooks Flippen, *Nixon and the Environment* (Albuquerque: University of New Mexico Press, 2012), 25.

15. The oral history interviews of key citizen activists and White House officials involved in the 1969–1970 push for funding in the Bancroft Library, Berkeley, CA, have recently been supplemented by the opening of the Save Our Seashore (SOS) campaign files recovered from the descendants of Clem and Katy Miller (Katharine Miller Johnson Papers, hereafter cited as KMJ papers. These papers remain in family hands pending donation to the Point Reyes Archives; documents reviewed in San Francisco, July 2022). These files contain SOS minutes, strategy documents, and crucial packets of press clippings and legislative history documents used in frequent mass mailings. Miller's Washington aides and field staff in Marin still then communicated mostly by US mail; their mailed memos offer a written record summarizing key events of the day in candid language; they helpfully fill out the picture of what advocates were seeing in real time.

16. UC, 355–362.

17. To authorize the appropriation of the additional funds necessary for the acquisition of land at the Point Reyes National Seashore in California, Public Law 91-223, *U.S. Statutes at Large*, 87 (1970).

18. Nixon had won the Electoral College in the 1968 election by a 301–191–46 margin. Former Democrat George Wallace received 14 percent of the popular vote, running as a populist/white supremacist and carrying four states in the heart of the Deep South. Humphrey won 42.7 percent to Nixon's 43.4 percent.

19. UC, 285–384.

20. Laura Alice Watt, *The Paradox of Preservation: Wilderness and Working Landscapes at Point Reyes National Seashore* (Oakland: University of California Press, 2016), 84.

21. UC, 21, 25.

22. Stewart Udall letter to Save Our Seashore, October 6, 1969, KMJ papers.

23. UC, 352.

24. Katy Miller Johnson's second husband, Stuart H. Johnson, Jr., played a major role in advising her in the 1969 Save Our Seashore campaign. She credited him with being the first to suggest that they target Murphy's reelection effort as the best way to get President Nixon's attention. She recalled vigorous debates with both Johnson and Duddleson over how tough a line to take and frequently reminded them that she was the one signing the letters, so her preferred wording prevailed.

25. UC, 104.

26. Katy Miller Johnson to the Honorable Harold T. Johnson, May 26, 1969, KMJ papers.

27. UC, 321.

28. See Meir Ringe, "Richard Nixon and the Rise of Environmentalism," *Distillations: Science History Institute*, June 2, 2017.

29. As quoted in Ringe.

30. Flippen, *Nixon and the Environment*, 142.

31. There were intramural fights within the executive branch about this issue, detailed by McCloskey, Ehrlichman, and Duddleson. The problem stemmed from Bureau of the Budget director Robert Mayo missing cues that the man in the Oval Office was the final decider on budget requests.

32. UC, 77, 79.

33. UC, xvii–iii.

34. UC, xx.

35. UC, 349.

36. Leo Rennert, "President Signs Pt. Reyes Bill, Snubs Demos," *Sacramento Bee*, April 3, 1970.

5. Who Saved Point Reyes?

1. The PRNS today manages 16,000 contiguous acres of hiking trails and ranchlands in the Olema Valley on behalf of the GGNRA, creating an actual PRNS footprint under NPS management of more than 87,000 acres.

2. Senate Committee on Interior and Insular Affairs, *Point Reyes National Seashore Hearings on S. 1530 and H.R. 3786,* February 26, 1970, 60.

3. John Hart, *San Francisco's Wilderness Next Door* (San Rafael, CA: Presidio, 1979), 49.

4. *Saving Point Reyes National Seashore 1969–1970: An Oral History of Citizen Action in Conservation: Oral History Transcript* (Oakland: University of California Press, 1993), 31 (hereafter cited as UC).

5. Nancy Kelly and Kenji Yamamoto, *Rebels with a Cause* (New Day Films, 2012).

6. Duddleson Papers, box 20, PRNS Archives, NPS Bear Valley Headquarters, Point Reyes Station, CA (hereafter cited as Duddleson Papers).

7. Katharine Miller Johnson Papers, reviewed in San Francisco, July 2022.

8. UC, 332, 350.

9. UC, 348.

10. Senate Committee on Interior and Insular Affairs, *Point Reyes National Seashore Hearings*, 37.

11. Senate Committee on Interior and Insular Affairs, , 43.

12. UC, 355.

13. UC, 355.

14. UC, 340.

15. James E. Bylin, "Conservation Gains Political Weight," *Wall Street Journal*, November 20, 1969. Researcher William Duddleson reported that the copy of the article Nixon had marked up and sent to Ehrlichman warned that "conservation will be a major issue in upcoming elections" while highlighting the impact of environmental activism and its election impact. Nixon instructed his top staff in writing to follow up "to preempt the issue." UC, xxii; see also John C. Whitaker Subject Files, box 91, White House Central Files, "Point Reyes, CA," Richard Nixon Presidential Library and Museum, Yorba Linda, CA (hereafter cited as Whitaker Files).

16. Marquis Childs, "Sub-dividers Are Threatening Last Areas of Unspoiled Land," *Washington Post*, October 22, 1969; Phillip Hager, "Pressure Mounting to Preserve Point Reyes National Seashore—Legislators and Conservationists Join in Campaigning to Get Nixon's Help in Saving Spectacular Scenic Landmark," *Los Angeles Times*, October 27, 1969; "To Save Seashore, Nixon Should Act," *Salt Lake City Deseret News*, November 10, 1969.

17. UC, 378–379.

18. UC, 43.

19. UC, 149.

20. UC, 149.

21. John Ehrlichman, *Witness to Power: The Nixon Years* (New York: Simon & Schuster, 1982), 102n.

22. Whitaker Files.

23. Bill Duddleson interview as quoted in Paul Sadin, *Managing a Land in Motion: An Administrative History of Point Reyes National Seashore* (Seattle, WA: Historical Research Associates, 2007), 23–24.

24. UC, 149; and *Rebels with a Cause*.

25. The comprehensive reform measure, the Nuclear Nonproliferation Act of 1978, is an example. The public law draft first produced by chief House sponsor Jonathan B. Bingham in March 1977 ran nearly one hundred pages. Yet most of its titles contained proposals previously drafted by other House and Senate legislators who had been unable to overcome industry and executive branch opposition to stricter nuclear export standards. Some provisions used language lifted verbatim from the failed proposals of previous sessions of Congress. Many of the measures included proposals that had long languished in arms control policy think tanks.

26. Frank Gannon, "No More Calls Please—We Have a Winner," *Richard Nixon Foundation* (blog), November 6, 2008, https://www.nixonfoundation.org/2008/11/no-more-calls-please-we-have-a-winner/.

27. UC, 376.

28. UC, 376.

29. UC, 376.

30. Cong. Rec. 108, October 9, 1962, H22850.

31. UC, 18–19.

32. Senate Committee on Interior and Insular Affairs, 69.

33. UC, i.

34. "Senator Clair Engle of California Dies," *New York Times*, July 31, 1964, A1.

35. John Lawrence, interview with the author, August 10, 2021.

36. Gregg Coodley and David Sarasohn, *The Green Years 1964–1976: When Democrats and Republicans United to Repair the Earth* (Lawrence: University Press of Kansas, 2021), 1.

6. What Happened Next: Point Reyes and Environmental Politics

1. Amy Meyer, *New Guardians for the Golden Gate* (Berkeley: University of California Press, 2008), 35.

2. Meyer, 34.

3. Don Nicoll, "Duddleson, William J. and Denise F. oral history interview," Edmund S. Muskie Oral History Collection (Lewiston, ME: Bates College, 2000), 124, https://scarab.bates.edu/muskie_oh/124.

4. Gregg Coodley and David Sarasohn, *The Green Years 1964–1976: When Democrats and Republicans United to Repair the Earth* (Lawrence: University Press of Kansas, 2021), 8.

5. Coodley and Sarasohn, 8.

6. Coodley and Sarasohn, 10.

7. Interview with Pete McCloskey, quoted in *Saving Point Reyes National Seashore 1969–1970: An Oral History of Citizen Action in Conservation: Oral History Transcript* (Oakland: University of California Press, 1993), 298 (hereafter cited as UC).

8. UC, 299.

9. J. Brooks Flippen, *Nixon and the Environment* (Albuquerque: University of New Mexico Press, 2012), 27.

10. UC, 333.

11. Interview with John C. Whitaker, University of Colorado Center of the American West, November 19, 2003, https://drive.google.com/file/d/1FMBMPv CevU0aKBtbtrmFSdyaFt5cw1CJ/view.

12. Nancy Kelly and Kenji Yamamoto, *Rebels with a Cause* (New Day Films, 2012).

13. Burton famously complained to Ansel Adams after they had stepped out of a San Francisco board meeting to walk the sidewalk for a cigarette break that it was the longest walk he had ever taken—or wanted to take. See John Jacobs's biography of Burton, *A Rage for Justice: The Passion and Politics of Phil Burton* (Berkeley: University of California Press, 1995).

14. Donald J. Hellman, "The Path of the Presidio Trust Legislation," *Golden*

Gate University Law Review 28, no. 3 (1988): 324. Note that certain shoreline portions at the western end of the Presidio were in the GGNRA plans from the outset.

15. Kevin Starr, *California: A History* (New York: Random House, 2005), 241.

16. Jacqueline Alyse Mirandola Mullen, *Coastal Parks for a Metropolitan Nation: How Postwar Politics and Urban Growth Shaped America's Shores* (PhD diss., State University of New York, Albany, 2015), 108.

17. Interview with Dewey Livingston, Inverness, CA, July 1, 2022.

18. UC, 33.

19. Jonathan B. Jarvis and T. Destry Jarvis, *National Parks Forever: Fifty Years of Fighting and a Case for Independence* (Chicago: University of Chicago Press, 2022), 11.

20. Jarvis and Jarvis.

21. An excellent account of this dynamic is in the authoritative *Class of '74: Congress after Watergate and the Fruits of Partisanship* (Baltimore, MD: Johns Hopkins University Press, 2018) by University of California historian John Lawrence, who served as Interior Committee staff director under Chairman George Miller (D-CA) and then as chief of staff to Speaker Nancy Pelosi.

22. Tim Turner, *David Brower: The Making of the Environmental Movement* (Berkeley: University of California Press, 2016), 184.

23. UC, xvii.

24. Kelly and Yamamoto, *Rebels with a Cause*.

25. Turner. In his Foreword, author Bill McKibben argues that Brower, together with John Muir was "the most important conservationist in twentieth century America . . . because he figured out how to do the hardest thing for any movement leader: capture the zeitgeist and thus allow a new set of political possibilities . . . he understood intuitively that Muir's homely ecological insight about everything in nature being hitched to everything else applied also to politics."

26. Turner, *David Brower*, 117.

27. Coodley and Sarasohn, *The Green Years 1964–1976*, 13.

28. NRDC, *Consolidated Financial Statements and Supplemental Schedules Together with Report of Independent Certified Public Accountants* (New York: Natural Resources Defense Council, 2020).

29. Coodley and Sarasohn, *The Green Years 1964–1976*, 253.

30. Meir Rinde, "Richard Nixon and the Rise of American Environmentalism," *Distillations: Science History Institute*, June 2, 2017.

31. H. R. Haldeman, personal notes, February 19, 1971, Richard Nixon Library and Museum, as quoted in Flippen, *Nixon and the Environment*, 135.

32. Flippen, 213.

33. Carl Bernstein and Bob Woodward, *The Final Days* (New York: Simon and Schuster, 1976).

34. UC, 347–384.

35. UC, 109.

36. Carolyn Merchant, *American Environmental History: An Introduction* (New York: Columbia University Press, 2007), 199.

37. Samuel P. Hays, *Beauty, Health, and Permanence: Environmental Politics in the United States, 1955–1985* (New York: Cambridge University Press, 1987), 59–60.

38. Coodley and Sarasohn, *The Green Years 1964–1976*, 239.

39. Jacobs, *A Rage for Justice*, 351–353. Burton told the Wilderness Society's director William "Bill" Turnage that "the only thing that really lasts forever is parks. *That's* my accomplishment." Burton's protégé, Representative George Miller (D-CA), confirmed that "[Burton] looked at parks not as adding acres here or there but as a political statement." Jacobs, 353.

40. Coodley and Sarasohn, *The Green Years 1964–1976*, 235.

41. John Hart, *Legacy: Portraits of 50 Bay Area Environmental Elders* (Berkeley: University of California Press, 2006), 50, 149.

42. Laura Alice Watt, *The Paradox of Preservation: Wilderness and Working Landscapes at Point Reyes National Seashore* (Oakland: University of California Press, 2016), 87.

43. Merchant, *American Environmental History*, 230.

44. See multiple folders on the GGNRA website, www.ggnra.gov.

45. As quoted in Clare Miller Watsky, "Little Old Ladies in Tennis Shoes: Heroes of the Conservation Movement in the San Francisco Bay Area, 1930s–1970s," Point Reyes National Seashore Association newsletter, August 2020.

46. Johnson letter to *Marin Independent Journal*, August 12, 1970, Katharine Miller Johnson Papers, reviewed in San Francisco, July 2022. John Hart notes that despite the ubiquitous references by policy advocates and cartographers to the estuary where most believe Drake repaired the *Golden Hind*, Drakes Estero is really a bay, inlet, or marshland, not an estuary, as there is very limited freshwater flow.

47. Watt, *The Paradox of Preservation*, 96, and Kelly and Yamamoto, *Rebels with a Cause.*

48. Memorandum of Ralph G. Mihan, field solicitor, to PRNS superintendent, February 26, 2004, quoted in Summer Brennan, *The Oyster War: The True Story of a Small Farm, Big Politics, and the Future of Wilderness in America* (Berkeley, CA: Counterpoint, 2015).

49. Watt, *The Paradox of Preservation*, 2.

50. Mullen, *Coastal Parks for a Metropolitan Nation*, 126.

51. See Watt, *The Paradox of Preservation*, 1, on the 2012 ruling.

52. Susan Ives, "Pt. Reyes Elk Plan Cannot Be Preordained to Status Quo," *Marin Independent Journal*, June 23, 2022.

53. William Cronon, ed., *Uncommon Ground: Rethinking the Human Place in Nature* (New York: W. W. Norton, 1995), 25, 76.

54. Watt, *The Paradox of Preservation*, xii.

55. Watt, 44.

56. Watt, 95.

57. Watt, 99.

58. Kelly and Yamamoto, *Rebels with a Cause.* See also Watt, 96.

59. Watt, 215.

60. Merchant, *American Environmental History*, 200–201.

61. David Vogel, *California Greenin': How the Golden State Became an Environmental Leader* (Princeton, NJ: Princeton University Press, 2018), 4, 11.

62. Ned Resnikoff, "California Can Solve Its Homelessness Crisis," *New York Times*, July 26, 2021.

63. Jessica Lage, "Know the Hands that Feed You: Gentrification and the Labor Migration in West Marin," *BOOM*, May 16, 2022, 1.

64. Ezra Klein, "The Gavin Newsom Recall Is a Farce," *New York Times*, July 9, 2021.

65. Miriam Pawal, "California Wakes Up from Its Dream," *New York Times*, July 11, 2021.

66. Paul Sadin, *Managing a Land in Motion: An Administrative History of Point Reyes National Seashore* (Seattle, WA: Historical Research Associates, 2007), 141.

67. Sadin, 141.

68. Mullen, *Coastal Parks for a Metropolitan Nation*, 104.

69. Daniel Selmi, *Dawn at Mineral King Valley: The Sierra Club, the Disney Company, and the Rise of Environmental Law* (Chicago: University of Chicago Press, 2022), 259.

70. Will Houston, "Point Reyes water quality tests find high bacteria levels," *Marin Independent Journal*, September 5, 2022.

71. Center for Biological Diversity, "Rigorous New Study Finds Significant Water Pollution from Cattle Ranching at Point Reyes National Seashore," press release, September 1, 2022, https://biologicaldiversity.org/w/news/press-releases/rigorous-new-study-finds-significant-water-pollution-from-cattle-ranching-at-point-reyes-national-seashore-2022-09-01/.

7. Lessons Learned: Point Reyes and Future Policy Challenges

1. Richard Walker, *The Country in the City: The Greening of the San Francisco Bay Area* (Seattle: University of Washington Press, 2007), 8.

2. John Hart also comments on the relative absence of villains and the broader economic forces at work. See John Hart, *An Island in Time: Fifty Years at Point Reyes National Seashore* (Fairfield, NJ: Lighthouse, 2012). This slim volume is a highly visual love letter to the land of the peninsula, thoughtfully covering much of the natural and human history.

3. On Zena Mendoza Cabral's March 1961 testimony, see Gayle Baker, *Point Reyes: A Harbor Town History* (Santa Barbara: Vaughan, 2004), 96, and Laura Alice Watt, *The Paradox of Preservation: Wilderness and Working Landscapes at Point Reyes National Seashore* (Oakland: University of California Press, 2016), 129.

4. House Committee on Interior and Insular Affairs, Subcommittee on National Parks and Recreation, *Point Reyes National Seashore Hearing on H.R. 3786 and Related Bills*, May 13, 1969.

5. See Baker, *Point Reyes*, 108.

6. Gregg Coodley and David Sarasohn, *The Green Years 1964–1976: When Democrats and Republicans United to Repair the Earth* (Lawrence: University Press of Kansas, 2021), 255.

7. Their Save San Francisco Bay Association became the model for a Marin County–based group eager to preserve the Sausalito shoreline and later for the 1969 Save Our Seashore drive to petition for the Point Reyes National Seashore.

8. John D. Leshy, *Our Common Ground: A History of America's Public Lands* (New Haven, CT: Yale University Press, 2021), 579.

9. The Drake name remains ubiquitous, appearing on area bays, beaches, and roads. Little controversy remains as to where Drake repaired his ship in 1579. The definitive conclusion in 2012 of scholars including the Drake Navigators Guild led by Edward Von der Porten created a National Historical Landmark designation at the mouth of Drakes Estero. In 2016, a plaque was placed on Limantour Beach marking the Drakes Bay Historical and Archaeological District to incorporate recognition of the first contact between Coast Miwok villages and Drake along the southern-facing white cliffs at Point Reyes. Controversy *has* grown about the character of the Englishman who served as an officer, and later captained a ship, involved in the slave trade. The San Anselmo high school long known as Drake was renamed Archie Williams High in May 2021 to honor a longtime Marin teacher and 1936 Olympic champion who helped train the Tuskegee airmen. See Keri Brenner, "Drake Panel Taps Archie Williams for New High School Name," *Marin Independent Journal*, May 7, 2021, 1.

10. Braden Cartwright, "Seashore Closes Drakes Beach for Parking Lot Overhaul," *Point Reyes Light*, April 14, 2021, https://www.ptreyeslight.com/article /seashore-closes-drakes-beach-parking-lot-overhaul.

11. Robert F. Bruner and Gerald F. Warburg, "Governing NGOs: A Challenge in Four Acts," *Stanford Social Innovation Review*, July 26, 2018.

12. John Hart, *Legacy: Portraits of 50 Bay Area Environmental Elders* (Berkeley: University of California Press, 2006), 20–21.

13. Prepared testimony of Katharine Miller Johnson, Duddleson Papers, box 1, PRNS Archives, NPS Bear Valley Headquarters, Point Reyes Station, CA.

14. *Saving Point Reyes National Seashore 1969–70: An Oral History of Citizen Action in Conservation: Oral History Transcript* (Oakland: University of California Press, 1993), 81 (hereafter cited as UC).

15. Hart, *Legacy*, 19.

16. Hart, 19.

17. Amy Meyer, interview with Golden Gate National Parks Conservancy *Gateways* (Spring 2022): 3.

18. Remarks before the California Wildlife Federation, July 1961, Papers of Congressman Clement W. Miller, carton 5, Bancroft Library, Berkeley, CA (hereafter cited as Miller Papers).

19. Miller Papers, carton 5.

20. See "The Overton Window," *Mackinac Center for Public Policy*, 2019, https://www.mackinac.org/OvertonWindow.

21. Walker, *The Country in the City*, 16.

22. Kyle Paoletta, "Give the People What They Clearly Need: More National Parks," *New York Times*, August 29, 2021.

23. Arthur M. Schlesinger, Jr., *The Cycles of American History* (Boston: Houghton Mifflin, 1986).

24. A similar phenomenon is evident in foreign policymaking. The United States moves perceptibly between isolationist and interventionist phases, a natural reaction of generational change. George H. W. Bush and John F. Kennedy were hostile to isolationists in part because they had lived through the policies of their parents' eras. As World War II veterans, both men had firsthand experience of what isolationist policies had wrought. Kennedy's father was ambassador to England but late to abandon his advocacy of appeasement. His son Jack wrote an undergraduate thesis, later published as *Why England Slept*, that indicted his father's generation for being too slow to react to Hitler, Mussolini, and the threat of fascism.

25. When the New York Giants moved to San Francisco in 1958, their star player, the legendary Black outfielder Willie Mays, was unable to buy a house in several Bay Area neighborhoods still then governed by racist covenants.

26. One local who worked in the Nicasio dairies and later as a lineman in Point Reyes Station for the new Pacific Gas and Electric Company was a teenaged baseball player named Vernon "Lefty" Gomez. The affable pitcher was of Irish, Portuguese, and Mexican descent. The San Francisco Seals, who had strong ties at the time with the New York Yankees, bought the Gomez contract and soon sent him to New York. Gomez was a star of the dominant Yankee teams of the 1930s destined for enshrinement in baseball's Hall of Fame and was pals with other sons of Bay Area fishermen, including the fabled DiMaggio brothers, Tony Lazzeri, Frank Crosetti, and Charlie Silvera.

27. Ken Bouley, "Restore the McClure Ranch," *Point Reyes Light*, May 26, 2021.

28. Edward Glaeser and David Cutler, "The American Housing Market Is Stifling Mobility," *Wall Street Journal*, September 7, 2021, C3.

29. Baker, *Point Reyes*, 106–107.

Bibliography

This case study is enriched by the archival work conducted by several scholars who were pursuing different aspects of this story. Historians owe them an enormous debt of gratitude. This study has synthesized a large amount of information—often data that was gathered by researchers who were focused on subjects other than the *politics* of preserving Point Reyes—in the attempt to create an accurate narrative based in part upon their original research.

Bill Duddleson is first among this group of archival researchers. It was the late Bill Duddleson, Congressman Clem Miller's legislative assistant from 1959 through 1962, who first uncovered in 1990 the paper trail of Point Reyes documents from the Nixon White House. These documents confirmed the crucial endgame role played by Congressman Pete McCloskey and Nixon adviser John Ehrlichman. Duddleson's files are now in the Point Reyes National Seashore Archives stored in the red barn at the Bear Valley Visitor Center, Point Reyes Station, California. His family has been generous with their insights; his initial research left a path to guide those reexamining the political history behind the creation of the Point Reyes National Seashore (PRNS).

Also standing out as a researcher is Ann Lage, who led the University of California's oral history project on Point Reyes. Lage created the extraordinary set of oral histories that the University of California Berkeley compiled in the early 1990s, with major input from Duddleson. These provide hundreds of pages of rich interview transcripts covering most of the key participants in the fight to create and fund the national seashore at Point Reyes.

A third key source is the work of historian Paul Sadin. While his initial study of PRNS management was conducted under contract for the National Park Service (NPS), Sadin turns an unsparing eye towards both the successes and failures of park management. He offers insights that are essential to guide the future work of NPS administrators. An outstanding guide through all these materials is Carola DeRooy Davis. Davis is an author and dedicated archivist who for two decades assembled a first-class trove of documents at Point Reyes while assisting numerous other parks in the NPS system to preserve their records for historians.

This work benefits greatly from the scholarship extant in the field of environmental policy history. The comprehensive work of Carolyn Merchant identifies the broad course of American environmental history; Merchant gives us both a definitive chronology of environmental politics and a thorough bibliography of scholarship in this relatively young field. Similarly, Samuel Hays gives us an environmental history focused on the twentieth century and comprehensive in its coverage. John Leshy effectively chronicles the political history of America's public lands in *Our Common Ground*. Richard Walker takes a unique approach in his study of local environmental politics throughout the San Francisco Bay Area, demonstrating how green politics came to be synonymous with the region. David Vogel's compelling work looks at how the state of California created the regulatory infrastructure essential to the advancement of a green agenda. A helpful chronicle of the golden era for environmental policy is the University Press of Kansas's Environment and Society series, including Gregg Coodley and David Sarasohn's excellent study *The Green Years, 1964–1976: When Democrats and Republicans United to Repair the Earth*. These works were built upon by American historian Doug Brinkley in a brilliant work that emerged just as *Saving Point Reyes* was going to press. Brinkley's *Silent Spring Revolution: Rachel Carson, John F. Kennedy, Lyndon Johnson, Richard Nixon, and the Great Environmental Awakening* does an exceptional job of placing these events in the context of the Kennedy, Johnson, and Nixon years, focusing both on the political leaders and on the grassroots activists.

This strong body of research has spawned a parallel narrative about the compelling beauty and ecological diversity of Point Reyes. Marin County historians, artists, poets, and activists have written passionately about parts of these land use battles. Historian John Hart thoughtfully chronicles the legacy of Point Reyes, the region's environmental leaders, and the GGNRA. Dewey Livingston and Carola DeRooy Davis ably capture and interpret the cultural history of West Marin towns and ranches. Amy Meyer, a citizen-activist with a nuanced appreciation of history, tells the story of Point Reyes's partner, the GGNRA, with great optimism and detail. Similar books and great films, like *Rebels with a Cause*, celebrate the land, while issuing new calls to action, but few offer much analysis of alternative political perspectives.

Often unnoted in these studies is an important fact: many of the key activists responsible for saving Point Reyes, protecting California redwoods, preserving the San Francisco Bay, blocking another freeway through the bay's center that would have decapitated Angel Island, and leading the local campaign to create the GGNRA had one thing in common: they were all women. Their names include Margaret Azevedo, Barbara Eastman, Esther Gulick, Kay Kerr, Caroline Livermore, Sylvia McLaughlin, Amy Meyer, and one of the heroes of this story, Katharine Miller Johnson.

The optimistic literature about the Bay Area environmental movement has more recently been challenged by other perspectives. The most thought-provoking counter to the conventional wisdom that "the environmentalists won—isn't that marvelous?" is the analysis by Laura Alice Watt. Watt presses some inconvenient truths, challenging readers to weigh the assumptions made by national seashore advocates, especially the notion that the greening of regional politics has been free of cost.

The archival materials contain clues rich in meaning. Often hiding in plain sight, the documents are now supplemented by detailed oral histories, first-person accounts of participants. These animate an extensive paper trail now available to the public, including the recently recovered files of Save Our Seashore leader Katy Miller Johnson. Taken together, these records offer clarity on what happened.

Following are key sources used in researching this study.

Books

Baker, Gayle. *Point Reyes: A Harbor Town History*. Santa Barbara, CA: Vaughan, 2004.

Saving Point Reyes National Seashore 1969–1970: An Oral History of Citizen Action in Conservation: Oral History Transcript. Oakland: University of California Press, 1993.

Blythe, Cain, and Paul Jepson. *Rewilding: The Radical New Science of Ecological Recovery*. Cambridge, MA: MIT Press, 2022.

Brennan, Summer. *The Oyster War: The True Story of a Small Farm, Big Politics, and the Future of Wilderness in America*. Berkeley, CA: Counterpoint, 2015.

Brinkley, Douglas. *Silent Spring Revolution: Rachel Carson, John F. Kennedy, Lyndon Johnson, Richard Nixon, and the Great Environmental Awakening*. New York: HarperCollins, 2022.

Cannon, Lou. *President Reagan: The Role of a Lifetime*. New York: Simon & Schuster, 1991.

Carson, Rachel. *Silent Spring*. Boston: Houghton Mifflin, 1962.

Cohen, Michael. *History of the Sierra Club, 1892–1970*. San Francisco: Sierra Club, 1988.

Coodley, Gregg, and David Sarasohn. *The Green Years 1964–1976: When Democrats and Republicans United to Repair the Earth*. Lawrence: University Press of Kansas, 2021.

Crawford, Brian K. *Shipwrecks of Marin*. San Anselmo, CA: Crawford, 2022.

Cronon, William, ed. *Uncommon Ground: Rethinking the Human Place in Nature*. New York: W. W. Norton, 1995.

DeRooy, Carola, and Dewey Livingston. *Point Reyes Peninsula*. Charleston, SC: Arcadia, 2008.

Dunaway, Finis. *Natural Visions: The Power of Images in American Environmental Reform*. Chicago: University of Chicago Press, 2005.

Ehrlichman, John. *Witness to Power: The Nixon Years*. New York: Simon & Schuster, 1982.

Fairley, Lincoln. *Mount Tamalpais: A History*. San Francisco: Scottwall, 1987.

Fanning, Branwell. *Marin County*. Charleston, SC: Arcadia, 2007.

Faragher, John Mack. *California: An American History*. New Haven, CT: Yale University Press, 2022.

Fiege, Mark. *The Republic of Nature: An Environmental History of the United States*. Seattle: University of Washington Press, 2012.

Fletcher, Francis. *The World Encompassed by Sir Francis Drake*. London: Bourne, 1628.

Fletcher, Scott. *Moments in Marin History: Familiar Tales and Untold Stories.* Charleston, SC: Arcadia, 2022.

Flippen, J. Brooks. *Nixon and the Environment.* Albuquerque: University of New Mexico Press, 2012.

Fox, Stephen. *John Muir and His Legacy: The American Conservation Movement.* Boston: Little, Brown, 1981.

Gilliam, Harold. *An Island in Time.* New York: Scribner's, 1962.

———. *Between the Devil and the Deep Blue Bay: Struggle to Save San Francisco Bay.* San Francisco: Chronicle, 1969.

Gilliam, Harold, and Ann Lawrence. *Marin Headlands: Portals in Time.* San Francisco: Golden Gate National Park Association, 1993.

Goerke, Betty. *Chief Marin: Leader, Rebel, and Legend: A History of Marin County's Namesake and His People.* Berkeley, CA: Heyday, 2007.

Griffin, Martin. *Saving the Marin-Sonoma Coast: The Battles for Audubon Canyon Ranch, Point Reyes, and California's Russian River.* Healdsburg, CA: Sweetwater, 1998.

Hart, John. *San Francisco's Wilderness Next Door.* San Rafael, CA: Presidio, 1979.

———. *Farming on the Edge: Saving Family Farms in Marin County, California.* Oakland: University of California Press, 1991.

———. *An Island in Time: 50 Years at Point Reyes National Seashore.* Mill Valley, CA: Lighthouse, 2012.

Hart, John, and Nancy Kittle. *Legacy: Portraits of 50 Bay Area Environmental Leaders.* Oakland: University of California Press, 2006.

Hays, Samuel. *Beauty, Health, and Permanence: Environmental Politics in the United States, 1955–1985.* New York: Cambridge University Press, 1987.

Helvarg, David. *The Golden Shore: California's Love Affair with the Sea.* New York: St. Martin's, 2013.

Jacobs, John. *A Rage for Justice: The Passion and Politics of Phillip Burton.* Berkeley: University of California Press, 1995.

Jarvis, Jonathan B., and T. Destry Jarvis. *National Parks Forever: Fifty Years of Fighting and a Case for Independence.* Chicago: University of Chicago Press, 2022.

Johnson, Huey. *Something of the Marvelous: Lessons Learned from Nature and My Sixty Years as an Environmentalist.* Wheat Ridge, CO: Fulcrum Group, 2020.

Kent, William. *Reminiscences of Outdoor Life.* New York: Robertson, 1929.

Killion, Tom, and Gary Snyder. *Tamalpais Walking: Poetry, History, and Prints.* Berkeley, CA: Heyday, 2010

Kirkpatrick, Sale. *The Green Revolution: The American Environmental Movement, 1962–1992.* New York: Hill and Wang, 1993.

Lage, Jessica. *Point Reyes: The Complete Guide to the National Seashore and Surrounding Area.* Berkeley, CA: Wilderness, 2006.

Lawrence, John. *The Class of '74: Congress after Watergate and the Roots of Partisanship.* Baltimore, MD: Johns Hopkins University Press, 2018.

———. *The Arc of Power: Inside Nancy Pelosi's Speakership, 2005–2010.* Lawrence: University Press of Kansas, 2022.

Leshy, John. *Our Common Ground: A History of America's Public Lands.* New Haven, CT: Yale University Press, 2021.

Lifset, Robert D. *Power on the Hudson: Storm King Mountain and the Emergence of Modern American Environmentalism.* Pittsburgh, PA: University of Pittsburgh Press, 2017.

Livingston, D. S. (Dewey). *Ranching on the Point Reyes Peninsula: A History of the Dairy and Beef Ranches within Point Reyes National Seashore 1834–1992.* San Francisco: National Park Service, 1993.

———. *Discovering the Historic Ranches at Point Reyes.* Inverness, CA: Point Reyes National Seashore Association, 2009.

Lombardo, Daniel. *Cape Cod National Seashore: The First 50 Years.* Charleston, SC: Arcadia, 2010.

Madley, Benjamin. *American Genocide: The United States and the California Indian Catastrophe.* New Haven, CT: Yale University Press, 2016.

Margolin, Malcolm. *The Ohlone Way: Indian Life in the San Francisco–Monterey Bay Area.* Berkeley, CA: Heyday, 1978.

Mason, Jack. *Point Reyes: The Solemn Land.* Inverness, CA: North Shore Books, 1970.

———. *The Making of Marin.* Inverness, CA: North Shore Books, 1975.

May, Walter, and Richard Neustadt. *Thinking in Time: The Uses of History for Decisionmakers.* New York: Freedom, 1988.

McCloskey, J. Michael. *In the Thick of It: My Life in the Sierra Club.* Washington, DC: Island Press, 2005.

McGinniss, Joe. *The Selling of the President 1968.* New York: Trident, 1969.

McPhee, John. *Assembling California.* New York: Farrar, Straus & Giroux, 1993.

Meyer, Amy. *New Guardians for the Golden Gate.* Berkeley: University of California Press, 2006.

Merchant, Carolyn. *American Environmental History: An Introduction.* New York: Columbia University Press, 2007.

Miller, Clem. *Member of the House: Letters of a Congressman.* New York: Scribner's, 1962.

Mullen, Jacqueline Alyse Mirandola. *Coastal Parks for a Metropolitan Nation: How Postwar Politics and Urban Growth Shape America's Shores.* PhD diss., State University of New York, Albany, 2015.

Munro-Fraser, J. P. *History of Marin County.* San Francisco: Alley, Bowen, 1880.

Nash, Roderick Frazier. *Wilderness and the American Mind.* New Haven, CT: Yale University Press, 1967.

National Park Service. *Mission 66 for the National Park System.* Washington, DC: Department of the Interior, 1956.

Nelson, Megan Kate. *Saving Yellowstone: Exploration and Preservation in Reconstruction America.* New York: Scribner's, 2022.

Perlstein, Rick. *Nixonland: The Rise of a President and the Fracturing of America.* New York: Scribner's, 2008.

Rome, Adam. *The Bulldozer in the Countryside: Suburban Sprawl and the Rise of American Environmentalism.* New York: Cambridge University Press, 2001.

Rothstein, Richard. *The Color of Law: A Forgotten History of How Our Government Segregated America.* New York: W. W. Norton, 2017.

Runte, Alfred. *National Parks: The American Experience,* 5th ed. Lanham, MD: Rowman & Littlefield, 2022.

Sadin, Paul. *Managing a Land in Motion: An Administrative History of Point Reyes National Seashore.* Seattle: Historical Research Associates, 2007.

Selmi, Daniel. *Dawn at Mineral King Valley: The Sierra Club, the Disney Company, and the Rise of Environmental Law.* Chicago: University of Chicago Press, 2022.

Schlesinger, Arthur M. *The Cycles of American History.* Boston: Houghton Mifflin, 1986.

Smith, Thomas. *Green Republican: John Saylor and the Preservation of America's Wilderness.* Pittsburgh, PA: University of Pittsburgh Press, 2006.

Soennichsen, John. *Miwoks to Missiles: A History of Angel Island.* Tiburon, CA: Angel Island Association, 2001.

Stoll, Mark. *Inherit the Holy Mountain: Religion and the Rise of American Environmentalism.* New York: Oxford University Press, 2015.

Stover, Douglas. *Cape Hatteras National Seashore.* Charleston, SC: Arcadia, 2015.

Switzer, Jacqueline Vaughn. *Green Backlash: The History and Politics of Environmental Opposition in the United States.* Boulder, CO: Lynne Rienner Publishers, 1997.

Thalman, Sylvia Barker. *The Coast Miwok Indians of the Point Reyes Area.* Washington, DC: National Park Service, 2001

Thomas, Evan. *Being Nixon: A Man Divided.* New York: Random House, 2016.

Toogood, Anna Coxe. *Civil History of Golden Gate National Recreation Area and Point Reyes National Seashore.* Denver, CO: National Park Service, 1980.

Turner, Frederick Jackson. *The Frontier in American History.* New York: Holt, 1921.

Vogel, David. *California Greenin': How the Golden State Became an Environmental Leader.* Princeton, NJ: Princeton University Press, 2018.

Walker, Richard. *The Country in the City: The Greening of the San Francisco Bay Area.* Seattle: University of Washington Press, 2007.

Warburg, Felix Max. *So Far, So Good: A Memoir.* San Francisco, CA: privately published, 2004.

Warburg, Gerald Felix. *Dispatches from the Eastern Front: A Political Education from the Nixon Years to the Age of Obama.* Baltimore, MD: Bancroft, 2014.

Watt, Laura Alice. *The Paradox of Preservation: Wilderness and Working Landscapes at Point Reyes National Seashore.* Oakland: University of California Press, 2016.

Whitaker, John C. *Striking a Balance: Environment and Natural Resources Policy in the Nixon-Ford Years.* Washington, DC: American Enterprise Institute, 1976.

Wirth, Conrad. *Parks, Politics and People.* Norman: University of Oklahoma Press, 1980.

Zelizer, Julian. *The Fierce Urgency of Now: Lyndon Johnson, Congress, and the Battle for the Great Society.* New York: Penguin, 2015.

Zelizer, Julian, and Kevin Kruse. *Fault Lines: A History of the United States since 1974.* New York: W. W. Norton, 2019.

Articles and Archival Materials

"Acreage Cutback: Marin Board Won't Budge on Pt. Reyes." *San Rafael Independent Journal*, March 20, 1961.

Bennet, Gordon. "Between Extremes: Understanding Congressional Intent at Point Reyes." *Point Reyes Light*, October 5, 2022.

Bosso, Christopher. "Rethinking the Concept of Membership in Nature Advocacy Organizations." *Policy Studies Journal* 31, no. 3 (2003): 397–411.

Bouley, Ken. "Point Reyes Something-or-Other." *Counterpunch*, March 21, 2021.

Brower, Kenneth. "Reflections on the 58th Anniversary of Point Reyes National Seashore, 2020." https://restoreptreyesseashore.org.

Bruner, Robert, and Gerald Warburg. "Governing NGOs: A Challenge in Four Acts." *Stanford Social Innovation Review* (June 2018).

Bylin, James. "Conservation Gains Political Weight." *Wall Street Journal*, November 20, 1969.

Byrne, Peter. "Apocalypse Cow: The Future of Life at Point Reyes National Park [*sic*]." *Pacific Sun*, December 9, 2020.

———. "The Befouling of Point Reyes National Seashore." *Pacific Sun*, November 16, 2022.

Cart, Julie. "National Park Service Seeks to Ease Tensions with Point Reyes Farmers." *Los Angeles Times*, May 26, 2014.

Childs, Marquis. "Sub-dividers Are Threatening Last Areas of Unspoiled Land." *Washington Post*, October 22, 1969.

"Cranston, Tunney Would Close Seashore to Cars." *Sacramento Bee*, September 23, 1971.

Dalby, A. F. "'Dead Duck' Gets a New Lease on Life." *New York Times*, July 12, 1970.

Davies, Lawrence. "Naturalists Get a Political Arm." *New York Times*, September 17, 1969.

Day, Chapin A. "Nature at Prettiest: Solons Impressed by Beauty of Pt. Reyes." *San Rafael Independent Journal*, April 14, 1960, 1.

Dolezel, Janine, and Bruce Warren. "Saving San Francisco Bay: A Case Study in Environmental Legislation." *Stanford Law Review* 23, no. 2 (January 1971): 349–366.

Dowd, Katie. "This 'Treasure' Rewrote California History. It Was an Elaborate Hoax." *San Francisco Chronicle*, March 1, 2021.

Duddleson, William. "The Miracle of Point Reyes." *Living Wilderness* 35, no. 14 (1971): 15–24.

Gilliam, Harold. "The Big Windy Battle of the Point Reyes Peninsula." *San Francisco Chronicle*, September 27, 1959.

Gonzales, Jackie M. M. "The National Park Service Goes to the Beach." *Forest History Today* (Spring 2017).

Gulick, Esther, Catherine Kerr, and Sylvia McLaughlin. "Saving San Francisco Bay." Horace M. Albright Lectureship in Conservation. Berkeley: College of Natural Resources, no. 28, April 14, 1988, 1–10.

Hager, Phillip. "Pressure Mounting to Preserve Point Reyes National Seashore—Legislators and Conservationists Join in Campaigning to Get Nixon's Help in Saving Spectacular Scenic Landmark." *Los Angeles Times*, October 27, 1969.

Hart, John. "Saved by Grit and Grace." *Bay Nature,* July 2003.

———. "Protecting Bay Area Open Space: A Quarter of a Victory." *SPUR*, September 2006.

———. "Finding an Oyster Accord." *Marin Independent Journal*, May 31, 2013.

———. "New Plan for Point Reyes." *Bay Nature*, 2020.

Hill, Gladwin. "Point Reyes in California a Patchwork Park in Trouble." *New York Times*, August 5, 1969, 31.

———. "Environment May Eclipse Vietnam as College Issue." *New York Times*, November 30, 1969, 1.

House Interior and Insular Affairs Committee. *Point Reyes National Seashore Hearings*, 1962, House Report No. 1628.

House Subcommittee on National Parks. *Hearings on H.R. 2775*, August 11, 1961.

"Issue of the Year: The Environment." *Time* magazine, January 4, 1971.

Ives, Susan. "Pt. Reyes Elk Plan Cannot Be Preordained to Status Quo." *Marin Independent Journal*, June 23, 2022.

Johnson, Katharine Miller. Correspondence Files, Miller for Congress 1956, Save Our Seashores 1969, Marin Conservation League 1970, Miller family. These papers remain in family hands pending donation to the Point Reyes Archives; documents reviewed in San Francisco, July 2022.

Kupfer, David, "Phyllis Faber: A Remembrance," *Point Reyes Light*, January 5, 2023.

Lage, Jessica. "'Know the Hands That Feed You': Gentrification and the Labor Migration in West Marin." *BOOM*, May 16, 2022.

Lunny, Kevin. "Point Reyes Ranching Family Makes a Commitment to Preservation." *Marin Independent Journal*, July 21, 2020.

Meral, Jerry, "Marin Voice: 50 years later, the story of Point Reyes legislation inspires environmental activism," *Marin Independent Journal*, October 31, 2020.

"More Money for Pt. Reyes." *San Francisco Chronicle*, November 15, 1969, 3.

National Park Service. "Point Reyes Peninsula, CA: Study of a National Seashore Recreation Area." NPS, 1935.

———. *A Report on Our Vanishing Shoreline*. Washington, DC: US Government Printing Office, 1955.

———. "Land Use Survey for the Proposed Point Reyes National Seashore." NPS, 1961.

Neff, Kirsten Jones. "The Trailblazing Women Who Shaped Marin." *Marin Magazine,* May 2000.

Paoletta, Kyle. "Give the People What They Clearly Need: More National Parks." *New York Times*, August 29, 2021.

Perlman, David. "Great Seashore Park in Marin Urged for U.S." *San Francisco Chronicle*, June 29, 1958.

"Planning in Marin Is Called Chaotic." *San Rafael Independent Journal*, May 23, 1963, 15.

"Point Reyes Park Alternative Asked." *San Rafael Independent Journal,* April 10, 1961, 1.

"Point Reyes Plan for Elk Needs a Look." *Marin Independent Journal,* April 11, 2022, 12.

"Reagan Plea to Nixon on Pt. Reyes." *San Francisco Chronicle,* November 15, 1969, 3.

Rennert, Leo. "President Signs Pt. Reyes Bill, Snubs Demos." *Sacramento Bee,* April 3, 1970.

Resnikoff, Ned. "California Can Solve Its Homelessness Crisis." *New York Times,* July 26, 2021.

Richardson, Stephen. "The Days of the Dons: Reminisces of California's Oldest Native Son." *San Francisco Bulletin,* April 20–June 8, 1918.

Rinde, Meir. "Richard Nixon and the Rise of Environmentalism." *Distillations: Science History Institute,* June 2, 2017.

Sahagún, Louis. "Tule Elk Get Rude Reception from Dairy Farmers and Ranchers." *Los Angeles Times,* December 29, 2014.

"Save Pt. Reyes." *San Francisco Chronicle,* September 14, 1969, 1.

Semple, Robert B., Jr. "Nixon Executive Style Combines Desires for Order and Solitude." *New York Times,* January 12, 1970.

———. "The Man Who Edits Ideas for Nixon." *New York Times,* April 12, 1970.

———. "Vexed Nixon Prods Congress on Ecology." *New York Times,* September 6, 1972.

Senate Committee on Interior and Insular Affairs. *Point Reyes National Seashore Hearings on S. 2428, Hearings on S. 248.* April 14, 1960.

———. *Point Reyes National Seashore Hearings on S. 476.* March 31, 1961.

———. *Point Reyes National Seashore Hearings on S. 1530 and H.R. 3786.* February 26, 1970.

Slatkin, Beth. "All Our Gains Are Temporary." *Bay Nature,* October 15, 2012.

Thurber, Scott. "Pt. Reyes Jewel Menaced: Ranch May Be Subdivided." *San Francisco Chronicle,* May 23, 1969, 2E.

"To Save Seashore, Nixon Should Act." *Salt Lake City Deseret News,* November 10, 1969.

Watsky, Clare Miller. "Little Old Ladies in Tennis Shoes: Heroes of the Conservation Movement in the San Francisco Bay Area, 1930s–1970s." Point Reyes National Seashore Association, August 2020.

Wirth, Conrad L. "Summary Report of the Director of Emergency Conservation Work on the Operations of Emergency Conservation Work." Washington DC: National Park Service, 1935.

Documentary Films

An Island in Time, Laurel Reynolds/Mindy Willis, Sierra Club, 1960.

The Invisible Peak (hidden in plain sight), Gary Yost, 2014.

Rebels with a Cause, New Day, Nancy Kelly and Kenji Yamamoto, 2012.

What Might Have Been, whatmighthavebeen.org, 2014.

Oral Histories and Interviews

Margaret Azevedo
Peter Behr
George L. Collins
Josh Collins
Chance Cutrano
Carola DeRooy Davis
Barbara Booth Eastman
John Ehrlichman
John Hart
Katy Miller Johnson
Ann Lage
John Lawrence
Dewey Livingston
Bryan McCarthy
Pete McCloskey
Sylvia McLaughlin
Abby Miller
Deborah Moskovitz
Boyd Stewart
Stuart Udall
Clare Miller Watsky
John Whitaker

Index

Aspinall, Wayne
  in Congress, 55, 57, 59, 62–64, 67–68,
    70–72, 77, 84–85, 98, 118
  and Nixon, 99–101, 107, 109–110,
    112–114, 116
  passing the Point Reyes bill, 118–119, 125,
    129, 132–133, 156
  legacy of, 170–171, 173, 176–177
Avery, Bill, 73

Bay Area Rapid Transit (BART), 153, 180
Bay Conservation and Development
    Commission (BCDC), 80–81, 114,
    152, 176
Behr, Peter
  campaign for California State Senate,
    108–109
  legacy of, 137, 155, 166
  on the Marin County Board of
    Supervisors, 53, 62, 65, 86, 94, 99
  passing the Point Reyes bill, 110, 112–114,
    116, 118–119, 127, 131, 135
Bible, Alan, 69, 71, 87, 110, 116, 118–119,
    156, 170
Bonelli, Benjamin, 143
Boxer, Barbara, 5, 132, 166
Brower, David, 31, 68–70, 77, 84, 125, 132,
    133, 135
Brown, Pat, 45, 55, 81, 138
Burton, Phillip, 127, 139–140, 165, 169,
    177, 184
Bush, George H. W., 140, 177
Bush, George W., 166

Cabral, Zena Mendoza, 63, 164
California Coastal Commission, 141,
    145–146, 150, 152, 159, 176

California Environmental Quality Act
    (CEQA), 46, 153–154
Cape Cod National Seashore
  Kennedy's advocacy for, 63–64, 70, 73,
    102, 119, 162, 169, 176
  as a precedent for future national
    seashores, 115, 140, 149, 183
Carson, Rachel, 68
Carter, Jimmy, 138, 140
Center for Biological Diversity, 159
Civilian Conservation Corps (CCC), 35,
    37, 69
Clausen, Don, 86, 97, 99, 109
Clean Water Act, 6, 126
Coast Miwok, 6, 14, 19–23, 30, 153, 159,
    181, 186
Cold War, 27, 41, 82
Collins, George, 51–54
  lobbying for Point Reyes, 119
  at NPS, 59, 73–74, 108, 144, 148, 155, 158
Cordell Bank National Marine Sanctuary, 165
Cranston, Alan
  in Congress, 85, 86, 102, 110–111, 119,
    124, 127, 135
  legacy of, 138, 140, 169
Cronon, William, 147

DDT, 68, 126
Democratic Study Group (DSG), 97, 118
Dirty Dozen, 125, 133, 135, 177
Drakes Bay Oyster Company, 142–143, 149
Drakes Beach, 10, 38, 58
Drakes Estero, 13, 19, 21, 47
  map of, 11, 28
  regarding Point Reyes National
    Seashore, 65, 96, 142–144, 146,
    148–149, 155, 159

Duddleson, Bill
  on Clem Miller, 55, 72
  on Peter Behr, 62
  and Point Reyes National Seashore,
    96–97, 119, 123–125, 155, 169
  on Richard Nixon, 92, 94, 111, 113–114,
    117, 137
  on Wayne Aspinall, 62

Earth Day 1970, 5, 93, 120–121, 123–125,
    133, 162, 177
Ehrlichman, John, 4, 90, 94
  as counselor to Nixon, 94–95, 97–100,
    109–114, 116–117, 119, 123, 125, 134,
    166, 170, 176
  legacy of, 137
Emmanuel, Rahm, 176
Endangered Species Act, 6, 125, 134, 140
Engle, Clair, 1, 55, 108, 114
  in Congress, 55–56, 65, 70–71, 77, 156,
    168, 173, 175
  legacy of, 79, 119, 162, 185
Environmental Protection Agency (EPA),
    136, 138

Feinstein, Dianne, 5, 132, 142, 166
Finch, Robert, 113
Ford, Gerald, 106, 138, 140, 177
Free Speech Movement, 85
Friends of the Earth, 3, 133, 135
Frouge, Thomas, 82, 88–89

Gilliam, Harold, 10, 20, 67, 69–70, 112, 171
Gnoss, William, 65
Golden Gate National Recreation Area
    (GGNRA)
  map of, 167
  and Point Reyes, 3, 41, 89, 106, 139, 141,
    154, 161, 163, 166, 170–171, 183
  present day, 176, 185
  and the role of public–private
    partnerships, 9
  visit by Nixon, 117, 120–122, 127, 174
Goldwater, Barry, 53, 84, 86, 95, 137
Grader, Bill, 58–59, 62, 67
Gulick, Esther, 66, 128
Gustafson, Joel, 59, 62, 70, 119

Haldeman, H. R., 90, 137
Harris, Kamala, 5, 134
Hart, John, 7, 38, 77, 108, 144, 170–171
Hartzog, George, 92, 95–97, 102, 130,
    148, 150
Hayes, Denis, 124–125, 133
Hertz, Douglas S., 47, 62
Humphrey, Hubert, 77, 84

Johnson, Harold "Bizz," 97–98, 119
Johnson, Huey, 80, 89, 127, 133–134, 146, 169
Johnson, Katharine "Katy" Southerland
    Miller, 49–52, 81, 94
  legacy of, 129, 142, 155, 161, 169, 171, 184
  and Save Our Seashores, 96–98, 101–
    102, 108–109, 112–114, 116, 118–119,
    123, 127
Johnson, Lyndon Baines "LBJ"
  as president, 77, 84–85, 132–133, 157,
    177–178
  as vice president, 35, 64
  and Wayne Aspinall, 59, 133
Johnson, Stuart, 96–97

Kehoe, James, 58, 75, 159, 181
Kennedy, John F.
  assassination of, 79, 84
  in Congress, 116–117
  parks efforts of, 1, 35, 63–64, 69,
    70, 76–77, 97–98, 119, 166, 169,
    176–177, 185
  presidential election of 1960, 53, 63,
    83, 125, 162
Kent, William, 33–36, 39, 41, 56, 169,
    175, 179
Kerr, Kay, 66, 128
Knight, Emerson, 54, 108, 148, 158, 175
Kuchel, Thomas, 71, 80, 85, 156

Lage, Jessica, 153
Land and Water Conservation Act, 6
Land and Water Conservation Fund
    (LWCF), 79, 155
  consequences of, 183
  and Lyndon Johnson, 85, 187
  and Point Reyes, 98, 100–103, 109,
    129–131, 155, 171

League of Conservation Voters (LCV), 3, 133, 135, 174
Livermore, Caroline, 38, 58, 65, 67–68, 154, 174
Livingston, Dewey, 25–27, 128
Lowenthal, David, 147
Luntz, Frank, 166

Marin (San Rafael) Independent Journal, 43, 58, 62
Marin Agricultural Land Trust (MALT), 154–155
Marin Art and Garden Club, 38, 66
Marincello, 81–82, 88–89, 120, 136, 164
Marin Conservation League, 38, 58, 108–109
Marin County Board of Supervisors, 57, 62, 82, 107, 128, 132, 138, 150, 159, 170
Marin County Planning Commission, 82
Marine Mammal Protection Act, 6, 134, 140
Marin Municipal Water District (MMWD), 35
McCarthy, Bryan, 57–58, 62, 73, 102, 147, 158
McCloskey, Michael, 57
McCloskey, Pete
  1972 presidential campaign, 95
  in Congress, 4, 53, 94, 97–99, 110, 113–114, 116–117, 119, 123–126, 131, 142, 166
  legacy of, 134–137, 170, 177
McLaughlin, Sylvia, 66, 128
Mendoza, Joe, 38, 58, 107
Meyer, Amy, 123, 127, 141, 169, 171
Mihan, Ralph, 158
Miller, Clement ("Clem") Woodnutt
  in Congress, 1, 72, 78, 86, 92, 108, 116, 132, 137, 142, 155
  election of 1958, 53
  death and legacy of, 94, 97, 98, 100, 102, 119, 157, 161–162, 169, 172, 184–186
  pre-Congress career, 49–50, 52
Mineral King, 68, 86–88, 105, 112, 136, 142, 158, 174
Mission 66, 54, 77
Mountain States Legal Foundation, 138
Muir, John, 32, 34, 179
Murphy, George, 86–87, 94, 99–100, 102, 109, 111, 113, 118, 135, 176
Muskie, Edmund, 90, 125, 130, 136, 176

National Environmental Policy Act (NEPA), 6, 46, 136
National Labor Relations Board, 50, 52
Natural Resources Defense Council (NRDC), 3, 136
Nixon, Richard
  environmental policies and legacy, 92–102, 106, 108–109, 133–134, 136–137, 166, 170–171
  and Point Reyes funding, 114, 117, 119–131, 133–134, 140, 155, 162, 166, 174, 176–178
  as president, 4, 53, 59, 83–84, 87–88, 90
  as vice president, 53, 59, 63, 116, 162
northern coastal prairie, 57, 141, 147–148

Obama, Barack, 142, 175–176
Orange County, 94, 128, 177
Overton window, 172–173, 175–177, 183

Pelosi, Nancy, 5, 120, 127, 134, 139–140, 141, 166, 169
Point Reyes Land and Development Company, 62
Point Reyes National Seashore Foundation, 38, 59–60, 62, 67–69, 77, 139, 174
Portolá, Gaspar de, 21–22

Reagan, Ronald
  as governor of California, 45, 81, 86, 95, 107, 112, 150–151, 153
  as president, environmental policies, 131, 133, 138, 140, 151, 177–178
Redwood National Park, 56, 86–87, 105, 112, 139, 174
Resource Renewal Institute (RRI), 145–146, 149, 159

San Francisco Bay Conservation and Development Commission (BCDC), 80–81, 114, 152, 176
Santa Barbara oil spill, 87–88, 93, 106, 117, 162, 169
Serra, Father Junípero, 6, 153
Sierra Club, 58, 127
  and 1969 Point Reyes lobbying, 155–156
  and *An Island in Time*, 1, 68–70, 77

Sierra Club (*continued*)
  and David Brower, 84, 132–133,
    135–136, 144
  and membership, 136, 151
  and Mineral King, 86–87, 158
  and NPS, 35, 57
  and San Francisco origins, 3, 32, 174,
    179, 187

Turtle Island Restoration Network, 159

Udall, Stuart, 55, 59, 63–64, 68–70, 73–74,
  76–77, 81, 84, 97, 119, 138, 150
US Army Corps of Engineers, 42, 44,
  65–66

Vizcaíno, Don Sebastián, 21
Vogel, David, 32, 46, 88, 151–152, 170

Walker, Richard, 3, 32, 161
Watergate, 94, 132, 134, 137
Watt, Laura Alice, 57, 143, 148–151, 181
West Marin Property Owners Association,
  57–58
Whitaker, John, 93–94, 100, 109, 111,
  113–114, 123–125, 150, 176
Wilderness Act, 6, 84–85, 100, 108, 132–133,
  143, 157
  debate on, 133
  and NPS, 157
  passage of, 84–85
Wirth, Conrad
  and Everglades precedent, 74
  as NPS Director, 64, 69, 76–77, 116,
    119, 150
  as NPS staffer, 54, 108, 148, 158, 169, 175
  Point Reyes testimony of, 61, 64

About the Author

Gerald Warburg has served as professor of public policy and assistant dean at the Frank Batten School of Leadership and Public Policy at the University of Virginia in Charlottesville, where he teaches seminars in the master of public policy program on legislative strategy and best practices for NGO leaders. A faculty affiliate of Batten's Center for Effective Lawmaking, he previously served as a legislative assistant to Jonathan Bingham of New York and Alan Cranston of California, members of the US House and Senate leadership. He has taught courses at the University of Pennsylvania's Annenberg School of Communications, Georgetown University's Walsh School of Foreign Service, and for his alma maters of Hampshire College and Stanford University. He is the author of numerous works about public policymaking, including *Conflict and Consensus: The Struggle between Congress and the President over Foreign Policymaking* and *Dispatches from the Eastern Front: A Political Education from the Nixon Years to the Age of Obama*. He was born just north of San Francisco at Marin General Hospital in Greenbrae, graduated from Redwood High School in Larkspur, and has lived in several Marin County towns near the Point Reyes National Seashore in California.